WINFIELD

W · W · NORTON & COMPANY
NEW YORK · LONDON

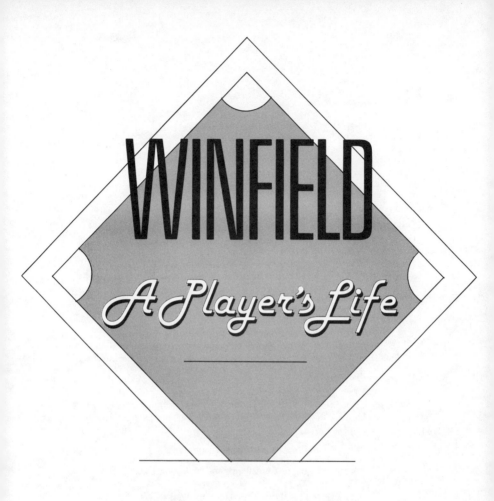

WINFIELD

A Player's Life

DAVE WINFIELD

WITH

TOM PARKER

The text of this book is composed in Janson Alternate, with display type set in
Siqnum and Harlow. Composition and manufacturing by The Haddon Craftsmen,
Inc. Book design by Antonina Krass.

First Edition

Library of Congress Cataloging-in-Publication Data
Winfield, Dave, 1951–
  Winfield: a player's life/Dave Winfield with Tom Parker.
    p. cm.
  1. Winfield, Dave, 1951– . 2. Baseball players—United States—
Biography. 3. New York Yankees (Baseball team) I. Parker, Tom,
1943– . II. Title.
GV865.W57A3 1988
796.357′092′4—dc19
[B]   87–35313

ISBN 0-393-02467-9

W. W. Norton & Company, Inc., 500 Fifth Avenue, New York, N. Y. 10110
W. W. Norton & Company Ltd., 37 Great Russell Street, London WC1B 3NU
1 2 3 4 5 6 7 8 9 0

I dedicate this book to my mother, who gave me the necessities to make it in life, and whose positive attitude makes her the ultimate team player.

WINFIELD

MARCH 1988

It's spring again, the time when, in major-league training camps in Arizona and Florida, a young man's fancy turns to freshly mowed fields, a well-worn glove, a yard or so of seasoned ashwood, and a white, cowhide-covered ball with neat red stitching spinning at ninety-plus miles per hour. I'm still one of those young men, though at thirty-six I'm among the older young men out there. And while I get older every year, the younger players get younger, as new blood gets pumped through the system—college draft picks, hot-shots from the minors, spring training phenoms, and infant prodigies from Lord-knows-where. Guys who think they'll play forever.

I've always known it's not possible. The body is still strong, I work out through the winter, the mind is clear, I'm hungry to play every day. But a ballplayer's life is full of uncertainty—injuries, trades, ownership trouble, injuries again—and every guy out there, young or younger, has to wonder if he'll play well, contribute to the team, last through the season. Dozens of games, hundreds of at-bats, and thousands of pitches; some you'll hit, others that'll hit you. On the eve of a new season I ask myself, How much longer will I keep at it? Meet my manager's, my teammates', and, most important, my own standards of high-quality play?

And how much longer can I keep at it as a Yankee, the team I joined eight years ago—the most sought-after free agent in the golden age of baseball free agency—after signing a record-breaking contract that made me the $23 Million Man, as some reporters put it? It's a ten-year contract, and the upcoming 1988 season is the last that's guaranteed. Come 1989, it'll be up to my boss, George Steinbrenner, if I continue to play for him, or if he'll exercise his half-price option to buy out my last two years. Even then, it'll cost him a cool $1 million-plus per season to have me hang up my pinstripes and leave town for another team. Still, stranger things have happened.

Eight years in New York—the city I share a love/hate relationship with—eight years as a Yankee, counting this one. It feels like I've been playing here for a lifetime. But it's only half the distance I've traveled as a pro, starting with eight years as a San Diego Padre, in a stadium as big as an airport, on an expansion team almost as green as I was. Sixteen years since I left the University of Minnesota, the only athlete ever picked in the pro football and basketball drafts, as well as by major league baseball.

After a while, though, it stops feeling like years or seasons, and you think about it instead as one long ball game that lasts a career. And you can't tell where you stand until you make your last catch, take your last at-bat. Still, some folks say that the results on Winfield are already in; they'll tell you right now that I'm not a winner. And it's true that during my tenure with the Padres and the Yankees, neither has won a World Series. It's true that the team that gets more press than any other hasn't gone all the way since I've been aboard—though we've come close, winning the American League pennant in '81, placing second in the division in '85 and '86, and leading the division through most of '87.

But awards and Series wins are only part of the story, one that's also about a ballplayer who's made a long-term, well-balanced contribution to my team. To tell it, I take comfort in numbers, my lifetime stats: 300+ home runs, 2,000+ hits, 11 consecutive All-Star games, a slugging percentage of nearly .500, five consecutive years of over 100 runs batted in. Numbers that most guys playing major-league ball never come close to achieving. Plus, a strong defensive contribution, aggressive offensive play, and a knack for getting on base that's enabled me to score runs in droves.

For my efforts I've been praised and bad-mouthed from San Diego to New York, called everything from a "superstar" to "Mr. May," the label George Steinbrenner used to claim I didn't finish strong like "Mr. October," Reggie Jackson. The numbers show it isn't true, but even if it were, it doesn't take a genius to figure out a top-flight team needs both. And there's an old saying, "It's not what they call you, it's what you answer to." Because in my gut, winning is what I'm about, whether it shows up on the MVP ballot, on the scoreboard, in the box score, or in the papers.

But how long *can* I keep at it? How many more chances will I have to accomplish what I haven't, most important of all take my team to the Series, make the catch, hit the game winner that wraps it up? Some may want it as much as I do. No one wants it more.

I don't have the excuse for writing a book that most ballplayers have when they take a shot at the bookstands rather than the grandstands. You know how it is, a guy's team wins big, and if he's played a big enough part in it, he tells his version of the championship season.

I wish I had *that* story to tell, and I'm still playing to make it possible. But I've already played a long game with stretches as interesting as the road to the Series—things I've done, things I've failed to do, places I've been, ballplayers I've known. Things I'd like to tell you about, not to boast, but to show what *can* be accomplished, both as an athlete and as a citizen of the world. It's a story of a kid from a broken home, a convicted felon, and a dean's list student; a ballplayer who left college credits short of a degree and was made an honorary Doctor of Laws by Syracuse University; a ballplayer who went to court against one of the heaviest hitters in America and won, and whose Foundation has helped hundreds of thousands of kids; who's been on the cover of the *New York Times Magazine* and on "Lifestyles of the Rich and Famous"; who's made millions as a ballplayer and intends to earn even more as a businessman; and who went on safari, then traveled to Senegal to see the very last place his ancestors stood before they were shipped off to a new and dangerous world.

It's all in the game . . .

PREGAME HYPE: "WINFIELD, MATTINGLY IN TITLE FIGHT"

They say that hitting a baseball is the hardest single feat in professional sports. Why else would the best in the game succeed an average of only three times for every ten attempts? Well, in 1984 my Yankee teammate Don Mattingly and I were beating those odds for most of the season, and doing better at it than anyone in the league. We'd raised our success rates to nearly three and a half hits for every ten at-bats and one of us would go on to win the American League batting title.

Going down to the last few games I was still a few percentage points up on Donnie—a quiet, serious guy, a hard worker, a terrific hitter who, at twenty-four, was nine years younger than I. He was having a hell of a year.

So was I. On the field with Mattingly and the rest of the team, and off the field with the Yankees' principal owner, my boss, the "man"—the very man I had to sue two years in a row—George Steinbrenner.

George was really sore. He had hired Roy Cohn as his attorney. The very same Roy Cohn who was Senator Joe McCarthy's man in the fifties, and who less than two years after rendering his services to George would be grilled by Mike Wallace on "60 Minutes," barred from practicing law in the state of New York, and just a few months after that, dead of AIDS.

One mid-season afternoon in 1984 we were sitting in Cohn's Upper East Side townhouse-office, my lawyer, my agent, and I, and across from us this odd, peculiarly New York Mutt-and-Jeff team. Cohn had dark, sunken eyes, a pasty, drawn face, and was wearing, get this, a smoking jacket and little scuff slippers. And floating around behind him like a moon, checking up on him every few seconds, was this *guy* . . .

Steinbrenner, at least, was dressed for the occasion and so was I—the "occasion" being that he owed my nonprofit operating foundation hundreds of thousands of dollars—a foundation which, in one form or another, had been providing health education, passes to ball games and cultural events, and scholarship assistance for disadvantaged youngsters ever since I first started playing professional ball at the age of twenty-one. Even then, I knew there was more to life than baseball. And more to community service than giving a kid a bat, a ball, and a glove and saying, "Go play by yourself, don't bother me." I wanted to do something more substantial.

But the real issue that day in Cohn's apartment wasn't whether George wanted me to help kids or not. Nor was it even money. The real issue was embarrassment. Like me, George hates to lose or be embarrassed, and despite the fact that he owed every penny the Foundation was suing for—as spelled out in a personal contract that George, himself, had typed and signed—despite the fact that he must have known he had no more chance of winning the lawsuit in 1984 than he had in 1982, George was intent on embarrassing me.

Perhaps it was because there was still talk from time to time that he'd been snookered when he signed my original contract. Or because the healthy chunk of money he paid me had bought him a pennant but as yet no World Championship. Or because he just plain didn't care for me, or detested my agent, which he did. No matter. Sitting there across from him, watching that self-satisfied look on his chubby face as gaunt lawyer Cohn scribbled away madly on a legal pad as big as his chest, I was more convinced than ever that George would have to lose this round. Later for this, I thought.

I'd actually said those very words to him earlier that season, at spring training in Fort Lauderdale, where George arrived with his usual entourage—a gaggle of reporters following him around like so many ducklings waddling behind the mother duck. And as usual, his appearance cast a pall over the entire operation. It's funny, as a player you can always tell when George is in town. It's like knowing when it's raining. Anyway, the word is Steinbrenner wants to settle things; he has a "plan." Anticipating that I'm not going to like it, I devise one of my own. This way if he says anything other than "Okay, I'll give you your money on this date and this date and this date," if he *asks* me for anything, I'll have some things ready to ask him. The best defense is a good offense.

Following an exhibition game, he invites me to "discuss things." We jump into his white Eldorado and drive to a restaurant called Bennigan's. Over sandwiches and soft drinks, he runs down a list of concessions I'm supposed to make before he'll pay a penny. I stop him and tell him that, no matter what, the bottom line is that he'll have to pay the Foundation its money. This gives him pause; it sounds like embarrassment in the making. I suggest a way he can save face. I tell him if he's concerned that by giving the Foundation the money people might think I "beat" him, he could show that we weren't really adversaries by making me the 1984 team captain. Frankly, if he went for it I thought I'd be a good captain. But the real underlying strategy was I figured that George would dislike the idea of naming me captain so much that paying the money he owed wouldn't sound so bad.

George opted to do neither. No money, no captaincy. Lunch cost $12.95, he still owed hundreds of thousands. So three months later we were in Roy Cohn's apartment for a game of hardball. Litigation, arbitration, irritation. The business of baseball. Over the course of the season there'd be plenty of meetings like it, apparently convened just to harass me. Once, for example, on a big game day they had me downtown for three hours during which virtually nothing got accomplished—George's way, I figured, to show me he was still boss, something I never contested. An hour later I'd be out of my suit and in my pinstripes, taking the field at Yankee Stadium, trying to concentrate on winning a batting title—while Donnie had probably been at home catching some Z's, maybe working out; not being interrogated by the likes of Roy Cohn, Esq., in any event. The fans don't know anything about it, they've just come to see baseball.

Completing the 1984 cast of major characters was the Yankees' Manager of the Year, the "Yogs," Yogi Berra. Like his predecessor of decades earlier, Casey Stengel, Yogi had a unique way with words. On the rubber chicken circuit they claim that when he arrived for his first spring training as a manager, for example, the equipment man asked him what size hat he wore. Yogi said, "Hell, I don't know. I ain't in shape yet." Or later that spring, right before our first exhibition game, when Yogi was a little hesitant filling in the lineup on the scorecard and one of the players asked, "Hey, Yogi, have you made up your mind yet?" Yogi replied, "Not that I know of."

But Yogi's success as a player and his credible year with us as a manager—and maybe even more significant, his real success as a businessman—soon made me realize that Yogi was nobody's fool. Sure, there was some luck involved. He was on a great team during a great era for the Yankees. And he was one of those fortunate guys who happened to invest in soft drinks and handball courts at just the right time. But add it all up and you've got a lot more than luck. In fact, Yogi was an extremely talented athlete, though physically the exact opposite of what you'd expect in a great ballplayer. And he was a shrewd investor. He was also a nice guy, a fair guy, and a good man, which is why just about everybody was angry and kicking trash cans when the word came down early next spring in Chicago that he had been fired.

Still, for most of the 1984 season Yogi was talking to me but not about me. Nor would any of the coaches go on record about me, though in private they might give me a hug or comment on my contribution to the club. And you'd have to scour the pages of *Yankee Magazine* to even know I was on the team, much less leading the American League in hitting. I'd become the Yankees' Invisible Man.

Then, one day late in the season, Yogi pulled me into his office to tell me that the "Yankees" had managed to get a story into a "national magazine." A week later *Sports Illustrated* had a story on the stands with a photo of Mattingly and me together, all smiles. It had been taken a few weeks before in California, and the story with it painted Mattingly as a real team player and me as being only out for myself. Listening to Yogi and not knowing what the story said, I decided to let it pass and concentrate on playing baseball. But then Yogi told me that if I said anything, *anything* to the press about it, I'd be suspended. I was being asked, in other words, to participate in this conspiracy of silence. So, game tired, I began, sounding beaten down and low key, "Okay, Yogi, I'm tired and I'm beat . . ." Then when I had Yogi breathing easy, I cranked it up a few decibels and shouted, "But I'm going to go for Steinbrenner's mother-f___ing neck!" "Oh, no, no, no!" Yogi said, with a real serious, concerned look. I didn't mean it literally, of course, and I almost cracked a smile, but I just wanted to try it out on Yogi, though I knew he wasn't any too happy to be the one to have to pass the edict on. It was just one of many times that season when my gut would be in turmoil from all the disinformation about my play or my attitude.

Late in the season, when things were finally settled, I asked Jerry Azar, a local TV sportscaster, why he'd never mentioned anything about the court case or the settlement on the air. After all, I told him, I'd always given him stories when he needed them, been a real cooperative ballplayer. Jerry grinned sheepishly and said, "Hey, Winnie, the man's going to be around a lot longer than you are—gotta go with the flow, you know." And the man and I were clearly flowing in different directions.

It all made for tense times for me as well as for everyone on the team, and our play often reflected it. Worst of all was when George showed up in the clubhouse to tell us how hurt and embarrassed he was by our poor performance, and gave notice that if we didn't take care of our business we wouldn't receive the first-class treatment we were used to. He'd usually conclude these heart-to-hearts by exhorting us all to go out there and "just have fun!"

The fact is, no matter what you read about "the boys of summer," professional baseball is rarely fun—though I suppose those of us pulling down million-dollar salaries shouldn't expect it to be. Money notwithstanding, I think some spirit of the game should prevail, but for the most part it doesn't. Instead, for younger guys it's always a matter of trying to make the team, and then trying to stay. And for older guys it's "Am I still good enough or will I be traded?"

Sure, every now and again, back in early '86, for example, I'd be warming up on the first-base line mugging back over my shoulder at Ken Griffey, who'd be cracking up. Great fun! But only for those few moments and only on the field, the only place where we're left alone, where we're in our own little world.

The second you get to the dugout, though, the only teams that are having fun are the teams that are winning, and the only players that are having fun are those having a good year—feasting on pitching or blowing down hitters and garnering all the adulation that goes with it. There's certainly some fun to be had in that. But if you're not hitting, or not throwing well, or are injured, or worst of all, have your own ownership dogging you all the time, you better look for fun someplace else.

As a business, though, baseball is booming, beginning in spring training where, just like in the season to follow, the name of the game is parking, concessions, seats, and TV revenues. Having to pay the salaries they do, I understand the owners' need to capitalize on their "investment" from the get-go, but I feel that the pressure they put on the players the second they arrive at spring training—pressure to be in shape before they get there, pressure to start playing games and winning, right off—can be counterproductive to putting together a strong team for the season.

Down in Florida, for example, the Yankees used to play the Mets in an early exhibition game, a televised contest with as much pressure from management as a regular-season game. In fact, I've seen guys on the Yankees banished to Siberia for pitching a bad game to the Mets—in *March!* And win *or* lose, the man is always there hyping, screaming, and threatening.

I'll always remember the day it started to pour right before a scheduled television game. The field was soaked. Suddenly, two helicopters appeared on the horizon, coming at us like something out of *Apocalypse Now*, not with napalm, but on a special management-ordered field-drying mission. Directing them from the ground was our own commander-in-chief, who later demonstrated his solidarity with the blue-collar grounds crew by raking along with them, stopping only to reposition the copters. Other times when it rains they forgo the helicopters and we play on a wet field, the sentiment being, "We can replace the man, but not the gate.

A thriving business, baseball has also become more of a science than ever. And I'm not talking just about the science of hitting and base running and fielding. I'm talking about baseball and the computer revolution. Nowadays, scouting reports look like Ph.D. theses, and owners and managers have got their Winchester hard disks crammed with percentages and averages—who's hitting left-handers, who's hitting right-handers, who's hitting everyone, and who's just plain stopped hitting altogether. They can tell you what you've hit in day games on Thursdays in odd-numbered years on the west side of the Mississippi. And when it comes time for arbitration, you'd better believe both teams and players arrive with their computer printouts, not just hastily scribbled notes—with the winner being the side with the most convincing presentation.

At its heart, however, if baseball is a science, it's not a very exact one, as some of what happened on the field during 1984 demonstrated. Donnie and I were both getting our share of bad breaks and questionable calls, and as a veteran of twelve seasons I should have been better prepared to deal with it. But it's hard to forget that game in Baltimore where I trickle a ball past the pitcher toward second. The second baseman barehands it, throws to first, but I'm already across the bag, safe by at least a step. As I come back to the bag, though, there's Yogi running onto the field. I've been called out. I can't believe it.

Then, a few days later, on a one-two count, I'm watching a curveball, outside, *way* outside. I don't even consider taking a cut at it. The ump calls strike three. "Strike three???" I throw down my helmet, turn to him. But he's already gone, the side's retired, he's pulling off his mask and ambling away. Next day he takes me aside to explain the call; he tells me he pressed the wrong button.

And there's certainly no science to figuring the fans who, along with George or despite him, were pulling for Mattingly. I got my first real sense of it on the radio in late July. We were in Seattle, and while I'd had the league lead in hitting for months, Donnie had been gradually moving up on me. That day I went two-for-three and had to leave the game with an injured leg. I was in the clubhouse getting treatment and listening to the feed from the Yankee broadcast booth when Donnie got his third hit of the game and passed me for the first time. "He got it!" the voice of the Yankees cried out. "He caught him!" sounding like he was echoing the sentiments of baseball fans everywhere, a real sense of relief. And from then on I could hear and feel it. There was nothing I could do about it but keep on playing, keep on hitting. But it hurt. Not the cheers and the praise for Mattingly, which were all deserved—he was tearing up ballpark after ballpark. What hurt were the boos I'd get when I stepped up to bat at home, in Yankee Stadium.

Willie Randolph, our second baseman and the man with the longest tenure of any playing Yankee, told me when I joined the team that you can be a "good" Yankee and a well-respected one—both, in the case of Willie—but as a black man, you're never going to be a "true" Yankee. He said that there's something subtle and unspoken working to keep it that way. The older and more tradition bound the team, I think, the longer it played without black athletes, the truer that may be.

Whatever it is, the Yankees don't have a monopoly on it,

as former Dodger executive Al Campanis demonstrated in his now-famous 1987 "Nightline" interview where he let slip his view that blacks lack the "necessities" for managing a team or working in the front office. Also, that blacks can't swim because they aren't buoyant. While Campanis's remarks were hardly representative of all management, of course, he nevertheless showed how entrenched in old stereotypes a lot of baseball people are—though I'll admit the business about buoyancy was a new one on me. Even though I don't swim that well myself, I look good at the beach.

Then again, acceptance for anyone as a Yankee—black *or* white—comes hard. Wearing these pinstripes you're always being compared to someone in the past, and no matter what you're doing, you're never as good as somebody else once was. Precious few players with the Yankees are given credit or recognition. As for respect, it seems you've either got to be retired, dead, or Reggie Jackson, who, before he was sanctified by George, had been ridden out of New York by him as a pariah, an aging slugger with severe optical problems.

It's Reggie, in fact, who provides me with one of the few opportunities to release some of the tension of that season. We're out in California playing the Angels, Reggie's team after he left the Yankees. The Angels have targeted Bobby Meacham, our shortstop, a good-natured guy who'd been hitting well against them. So when Meacham takes his first at-bat the Angel's pitcher, Ron Romanick, throws one right at his head. *Bop!* Meacham goes down. Then later in the game Bobby Grich slides into second and crashes right into Meacham, who's covering on the play. Meacham goes down again, this time with a cut on his lip. He's bleeding but he manages to say to Grich, "Why'd you do that?" To which Grich says, "Hey, f__ you. It's a game."

Next at-bat, just in case Meacham isn't getting the picture,

Romanick throws too close to his head a second time, and this time I'm flying out of the dugout, I don't even think I touch the steps. Suddenly, there are fifteen guys on the mound and I grab Romanick in one hand and Grich in the other to knock their heads together like you see in the movies. But then the umpires break it up, and it's over. For that day.

Our first at-bat the next day they knock another one of our guys down and you can just feel the tension beginning to build. On the field everyone stays cool. In the dugout the command is given to retaliate. The side's retired, we take the field. On the mound for us is left-hander Ray Fontenot, who's been giving it up, so I figure I'd better play deep in case he lays one right over the plate and Juan Beniquez, their lead-off batter, sends it sailing over my head. Next thing I know *zoom!* Fontenot powers one right at Beniquez, who pirouettes to avoid a fractured kneecap. No reaction for a moment, then suddenly Beniquez drops his bat and charges the mound. Fontenot stands his ground. First he throws his glove at Beniquez, then he throws a tackle at him. Then the stuff really hits the fan. Everybody's there. Mattingly jumps in. Willie jumps in. Meacham's there. They're throwing haymakers. And I'm still on the way in from deep, deep right field. It's taking me forever. Somewhere around second I cross paths with Brian Downing, toss him out of the way. Then, *boom! tumble! boom!* I'm in there throwing people. Suddenly, three or four guys grab me and I'm down on my knees with Downing coming right at me for revenge, and I'm thinking, "This sucker is going to kick me right in the face." Just then Donnie heads him off and miraculously I'm up on my feet again, with more people in my sights. Suddenly, someone grabs me from behind and pins my arms to my sides with a bear hug. This mother is strong, I think. I look at the guy's wrists locked around my middle. They're gigantic. This is no little dinky infielder. This mother is Reggie!

"Take it easy, Winnie," he whispers in my ear. He knows what I've been through with the man, having gone through some of it himself.

"Let me at him!" I yell back, fighting his hold on me.

"You really want him?" he says. "Really?"

"Yeah. I'm going to kick his ass."

"Really?"

"Yeah." And suddenly he relaxes his grip, and I'm gone, in the middle of the pile again having a great old time, a real battle royal. My last two at-bats, I'm too exhausted to swing and take six called strikes, but I feel good, great, better than I've felt in weeks.

Finally, it's the last day of the season and I'm less than one percentage point up on Mattingly. With the same number of at-bats and the same number of hits, I win the title. One less hit than Donnie, and he gets it. We're playing Detroit in Yankee Stadium and right before the game Sparky Anderson, the Tigers' manager, asks for one of my bats. I'm sure he asks Mattingly for one, too. So I give him a bat. Why not? The way I'd been pitched to over the last month, I wasn't even sure I'd get to use it.

A few minutes later I'm standing next to Ken Griffey and Don Baylor. I think they wanted us both to do well out there—as a whole, the team was great, not leaning overtly in either direction—but maybe were pulling a little more for me, the guy they'd known longer. Just before my last at-bat, Baylor comes up and says with a smile, "The way I see it, you're damned if you do and damned if you don't. They'll be on your ass either way."

And though I don't want to admit it, it's true. For me, the real title fight of 1984 isn't between Don Mattingly and me. It's between George Steinbrenner—his writers, his cronies, his bevy of lawyers—and me. And all I can do is hit the ball if I can, play the game the best I know how. So I scan the stadium, take a few more cuts in the on-deck circle, then step up to the plate.

1

Early Innings

THE GAME

Every professional baseball player has a glove story. Mine is that when I was five going on six—living in St. Paul, Minnesota, with my ma and my seven-year-old brother, Steve—I asked for a baseball glove for my birthday. I didn't know anything about baseball yet, but I knew I was right-handed, so I asked for a right-handed glove. October 3, my birthday, I pull the glove out from a mess of wrapping paper and put it on, surprised to find that it fits my left hand, not my right. So here I am sitting at the kitchen table with my first glove, certain a mistake has been made, while my ma looks on expectantly, the way mothers do when they think they've given you just what you asked for.

Nowadays, my glove is my most important piece of baseball gear. I have three, actually. One is ten years old, one eight, one relatively new. My favorite, the ten-year-old, looks like it's been through a couple of wars. Guys on the team are always making fun of how raggedy it is, but I've finally broken it in just the way I want it—flexible, like an omelet, a glove that can snag anything.

It's the kind of glove that makes memorable catches. Once we were playing the Orioles in New York when Doug DeCinces hits a boomer that looks like it's gone. I coast back, the sun in my eyes, plant my foot in a notch in the wall, then, fully extended, reach into the stands and make the catch. I can still remember the play unfolding before me like it was in slow motion. A glimpse of the home fans in the stands reaching out, waiting for the ball to arrive, then my own backhand reach over the top of the wall to snatch it from them, knowing that if I can get my raggedy old glove on the ball, I'll hold on to it.

Another time, Billy Martin brings his Oakland A's into Yankee Stadium for the opening game in the American League Championship series. In the second inning Tony Armas really puts the wood to one, a certain line-drive home run. Soon as I hear the contact, I race to the wall, time my leap perfectly, and grab it out of the stands. Billy calls it "one of the greatest plays I'd seen in years." I'd like to think it helped break their spirit that day—along with three-run homers by Lou Piniella and Graig Nettles. We took the game and swept the series. After nine years of professional baseball, and my first on the Yankees, I was finally on a pennant winner.

Steve and I were not yet baseball crazy the October I got my first glove, but that next spring, Tom Hardy, an older cousin Steve and I looked up to, began playing organized ball, so we figured that baseball was probably a good thing for us to do, too. It wasn't long before we discovered how much fun it was and how good we were at it. Hitting, running, sliding, scoring, catching, and throwing runners out, what could be better?

Fortunately, there were plenty of adults in the community who took our fun seriously and worked with us. Like Mac Burch, our next-door neighbor and first Little League coach, a short, muscular guy with a mustache, who liked kids and knew quite a bit about the game. And our PeeWee League coach, Bob Carter, a guy with a huge belly we nicknamed "Big 6" because he was six feet tall and six feet wide. He didn't know much about baseball, but he was a great guy, a warm, generous man, and you just really wanted to play for him, really wanted to give him a win.

Once Steve and I became baseball players, we started to follow the pros. Like all kids I had my heroes—Bob Gibson, Willie Mays, Hank Aaron—guys I could see only on television because Minnesota had no major-league team. But more than one single player I was aware of a team—the New York Yankees. It seemed they were always winning, were always in the World Series. Rather than root for them, though, I'd root for the underdog, and imagine myself as the star of the team that came out of nowhere to beat the high and mighty Yankees. Nowadays, I feel a lot different about the Yankees. I'm hungry for a season that would take us back to those glory days, a high and mighty season that would carry us all the way through October.

When I was nine the Twins came to Minnesota and I forgot about all the others and turned my allegiance to them—Bob Allison, Rich Rollins, Earl Battey, Tony Oliva, Harmon Killebrew. Finally, we—all the kids in the neighborhood—had players we could actually *watch* all season long on local TV or on a rare trip to the left-field bleachers. I once saw Carl Yastrzemski flip the local fans the bird. I was amazed that professionals could be so outrageous.

It wasn't long before we kids could imitate every player in the American League—the way they swung a bat, the way they styled on the base paths after hitting a home run, the way they talked, even the way they straightened their cup (at the time I didn't know what a cup was) when they thought no one was watching. I never tried to imitate Yaz, though. If I had, Ma would have sent me out back for a switch so she could whip me across the river to Minneapolis and back.

My first position was third base, but I really liked the action at shortstop and had the best arm on the team, and soon split my time between short and third. Steve was a pitcher and the star in those early days. By the time he was eleven he had a wicked curveball just about no one could hit. He also had great control—too much for his own good, maybe, because he never had to develop the arm strength that would have enabled him to make it in the pros.

I suppose there was some jealousy between us as brothers, but not as teammates. People often liked Steve more, and because he was older he'd get more opportunities, more attention, and sometimes I'd just be overlooked. Also, Steve was extremely coordinated, a good athlete, whereas I had to work much harder for the same effect. But for the most part we were both so good at the game as kids, we weren't really looking to outdo each other. We figured we'd outdo the world together. Always the night before a game we'd talk about it—how Steve would shut 'em out. How I'd suck up balls in the infield. How he'd steal a base, how I'd hit him home.

Best of all were game days. Ma's mother, Grandma Jessie, who lived one street over, would have washed our uniforms and laid them out for us. Steve and I would get ready at the same time, same room, dress real slow, like we were matadors or something, then walk down the street to the playground in our tennis shoes and our uniforms that fit so well, looked so good, were as blue as the sky.

And we'd just about always win. Whatever teams Steve and I were on together—Little League, PeeWees, Midgets, Junior, American Legion—we'd end up champions. Come summer, all around St. Paul, kids and adults, too, knew who we were.

Even when we lost, the adults made sure we had fun. Parents then seemed a lot more easygoing about winning than parents nowadays—you know, "Son, I want you to go out there and beat that other team, because I know that kid's old man and I gotta look better than he does!" The George Steinbrenner school of coaching.

LESSONS

Just down the street from our house—in a neighborhood of one- and two-family homes along tree-lined avenues—was the Oxford Playground, a scrubby, flat field, the ugly stepsister of the St. Paul Parks Department. We used to play kid games like tag there in the summer, and in the winter we'd hose the field down with water, then when it froze, we'd use it as a skating rink. There was even a little shed—a warming house—where you could put on your skates.

The spring I was seven the folks in the neighborhood decided what the playground really needed was a baseball field, and set out to build one. All of us helped out. I remember holding the tape as we marked off the pitcher's mound, taking a spade to what would be the infield, using its point to scrape away all the crabgrass, then resting awhile, watching as it took shape. It was a few years before it matured into a true baseball field, but it's still there; kids play all the time on the field I helped build.

I learned a lot on that field, first from Big 6 and then from Mac Burch, but the real heavy-duty lessons came when Bill Peterson, a young white man fresh out of the University of Minnesota, took the job of supervisor at the playground—a job no one else in St. Paul's all-white Parks Department wanted. But Bill had grown up nearby, had played ball at Central High with guys from our neighborhood, and felt as comfortable with us as with anyone. We're still great friends.

Bill was a solid, hairy guy—the type that's got hair curling out over his T-shirt collar—not six feet tall, but a blocky 230 pounds. He was an ex-marine, an ex-football, hockey, and baseball star at Central, and a former catcher on the University of Minnesota baseball team. His first experience working with kids at the playground was when some of his old Central teammates drafted him as a volunteer coach for a hockey team made up of their kid brothers and nephews. Bill and his buddies scrounged what they could in the way of equipment, and when they couldn't find any shin guards, they used rolled-up magazines instead. Suddenly there was this ragtag team of black kids, many of whom had never skated before, passing and shooting and goal tending on a makeshift rink. First year out they won the St. Paul championship, the only all-black team ever to do so. Heck, it may have been the only all-black hockey team *ever,* period.

If that didn't win us over, there was that hot summer night the first year Bill supervised the playground when a street gang decided they were going to take over our turf. All of us were scared, more than ready to run on home. Not Bill. He picked up a bat and banged it on the ground a couple of times, face-to-face with a dozen of the baddest dudes I'd ever seen. "There's not going to be any bulls___ on my playground," he told them. What followed was the usual muttering, the "motherf___ing this" and the "motherf___ing that," but then they just drifted away and we had ourselves a genuine hero.

He didn't take any nonsense from us either. He organized playground teams on his own time, and drafted the best to play for the Attucks-Brooks American Legion Post baseball squad. He knew the fundamentals and if we wanted to play on his team, we'd have to learn them. No one-handed catches in the infield, for example. You blocked the ball and caught it with two hands or took infield practice without a glove. And me, sometimes I'd just love to field a ball nonchalantly, snag it one-handed at short, whip it over to first, make the great, gorgeous play so people would ooh and ahh. But whether I made the out or not Bill would be all over me. Then come winter, to make sure we'd stay in baseball shape, he'd take us to a nearby gym where we'd take infield practice using kids' mittens instead of baseball gloves.

Bill's infield drills had players and balls flying all over the place, and the only way they would work was if everyone in the infield was in perfect synch. After a while we could just about do those drills with our eyes closed. When we worked a drill just right, we called it the Attucks-Brooks Automatic. Then when we actually executed the play during a game and people were going crazy, we'd just shrug it off and say, "Aw, that's automatic."

For his outfielders Bill had a drill he called "overplaying the fly ball" that put fielders into the habit of getting rid of the ball quickly after the catch. Rather than catch the ball where we stood, he'd have us back up four or five steps, then run into the catch, take one quick step and fire, letting our forward momentum carry us into the throw—a better fielding technique than most pros use who make the catch and *then* have to take two or three steps before they've got the momentum to fire a bullet.

On offense Bill stressed extra hustle on the bases and head-first slides—always demanded super-aggressive ball. He'd pitch batting practice full speed from 45 feet instead of 60 feet away, constantly yelling, "Attack! Attack the ball! Tomahawk it!" To teach us to keep our eye on the ball when we bunted, we'd practice using the bat like a pool cue, bunting with the fat end, rather than along its length. It was the only hitting drill Bill slowed his pitches for.

Bill was really an all-around coach. He made us study the rule book. He had us running and working out with weights before that kind of conditioning was fashionable. The only thing I wish Bill had taught me that he didn't was how to switch-hit. It would be yet another way I could contribute to the team, another weapon in my arsenal. Take a guy like Ted Simmons or Eddie Murray, who can hit better from either side than most players can from one. It's that type of versatility coupled with base running and defensive skills that makes for the truly complete ballplayer.

I often think back on those practices when someone calls me a "natural athlete." It happened a few months back. Some guy came up to me in the clubhouse after I'd made a moderately difficult catch look easy. "Of course, you're such a great natural athlete," he said, complimenting me on the catch and dismissing me at the same time. Had Bill Peterson heard it, he would have laughed his head off. Sure, I had a lot of ability back then, but for years I couldn't get it to work for me. I was the most uncoordinated kid in the world, banging my knuckles on tables as I walked by, knocking over lamps, two left feet on the dance floor. I wasn't the fastest kid. I wasn't the best player. It wasn't until my junior year in high school, in fact, that I had grown into myself fully, and had the coordination to pull off difficult plays with any consistency. To get there I had to work hard on every drill, on conditioning, lifting weights, running, flexibility. High school dances were useful, too, as a matter of fact. They helped supply the rhythm that nature hadn't.

It's interesting, growing up I had a number of friends who were better ballplayers than I was—maybe because they were older, they'd been playing longer, or just had more natural ability—but one by one I watched them leave high school, get a car, a job, a girlfriend, drink, smoke, get high, give up on the game, on their own abilities. Thinking back, I sometimes wonder what made me stick to it back then when a young kid like myself could have been easily seduced by a few bucks, some wheels, a girl.

Aside from the fundamentals, Bill was also a stickler for attitude. He was big on team chatter. Folks would often comment on our team spirit; at tournaments we'd make the other guys look like they were asleep.

Bill would never harp on mistakes if we had tried our best, but if we played a sloppy game, or acted like we didn't care, he'd be all over us. Once we lost a game like that and afterward Bill called a special practice. Soon it started to rain—more than rain, a thunderstorm. With lightning zigging across the sky, we figured he'd let us go home, but he didn't. The rain drenched us, ruined our uniforms. Our spikes, our gloves, our spats were gummed with mud. He even made us practice sliding in the mud. And if we screwed up, we had to take laps. Our own little boot camp.

The most important thing I learned from Bill, though, happened when I misplayed a ball I had all the time in the world to catch. In the dugout he asked me, "What happened?" I knew I should have made the play, but I started to tell him about the ball taking a bad hop or losing it in the shadows, or something like that. He cut me off. "I don't want to hear it," he said. When I persisted, he cut me off again. Finally he told me, "That's not an explanation, that's an excuse. What happened is you made a mistake. Don't make any excuses for it."

FAMILY

I was born David Mark Winfield on October 3, 1951, the second son of Frank Charles and Arline Vivian Allison Winfield, in St. Paul, Minnesota.

My father was born 150 miles to the north, in Duluth, a small city where he was one of only a few hundred blacks. His father, my grandfather, ran a shoe-shine parlor—shining shoes and blocking hats—and my grandmother was a housewife and an early civil rights activist. By the time he

was twenty-one my father had served in World War II—
dodged buzz-bombs in Liverpool, England, guarded Ger-
man POWs in a stockade in France—and returned to
Duluth, a man of some experience. Bored with small-city
life, in the late forties he moved to St. Paul where he hired
on with the Great Northern Railroad, riding the Empire
Builder as a Pullman porter from St. Paul to Chicago, from
Chicago to Seattle, and from Seattle back to St. Paul again,
five days on, five days off. It was on one of those days off
he met Arline Allison. They were married in 1949.

My mother came from more exotic stock. She was the
granddaughter of Andrew Hunt, son of a slave shipped to
America from Guinea, on the west coast of Africa. While
living in the South, Hunt met and married a woman who
was part black, part Indian and they had twelve children.
Following a cross-country odyssey that lasted two decades,
they finally settled in St. Paul at the turn of the century. The
Hunts stayed on until 1926, then moved to Indiana, leaving
behind in St. Paul a bunch of their older children, including
my grandmother, Jessie Hunt. Grandma Jessie married Everett Allison in 1919. They had eight children including my
mother.

There isn't a whole lot I can recall about the time my
mother and father were together, what with his five-days-
on, five-days-off schedule, and their complete breakup by
the time I was three. But I do remember hearing voices
raised in the front room a few times while Steve and I were
in bed, knowing it was some kind of argument, wondering
what would happen next. There were never any fisticuffs,
never anything like that. And there were good times, too.
But much of the time they spent together they were at each
other. Nothing a three-year-old could understand, though
later, growing up with my mother, I would hear her version
of it, which was that my father wasn't very interested in

fatherhood or responsibility, and after he left he often didn't come through with the child support the court had ordered.

Now, I realize, it wasn't as simple as that, and on those rare occasions I see my father he'll sometimes offer his version, about how energetic he was, how he was always looking for ways to make money, about the plans he had for us, about the time he wanted to invest in some old houses, fix them up and sell them, but my mother nixed the deal. In any event, they just didn't see eye-to-eye, as he puts it. And then he was gone.

But I can't complain. I had a good childhood, living with my ma and Steve on Carroll Street, only a block away from Grandma Jessie, and only a few blocks away from the rest of Ma's family—aunts, uncles, and cousins. Having so many of them nearby was great for Steve and me, and I'm sure it was a real solace to Ma, making my father's departure a little easier for her to take, although Ma almost never seemed down, never seemed to be without hope or optimism.

Coming home from school, Steve and I would stop at Grandma Jessie's for a snack and a little TV—soap operas, usually—before running out to play for a couple of hours or so with our cousins until Ma would get home from work. She'd almost always cook us dinner, then afterward maybe go to a PTA meeting or send us off to Cub Scouts.

If some important decision had to be made about school or the house or money, she'd call a family conference, and the three of us would sit on the couch and we'd talk. She wanted our opinions, she told us, and though I'm sure she could have made whatever decisions there were to make without us, I feel it was valuable that she thought to consult us, to make us feel that we had some say in our lives.

Sundays there'd be church and Sunday school, and as hard as it would be to get up on those Minnesota winter mornings, Ma'd always be up early, early, early, dressed and rousting us out of bed. I remember my feet hitting the cold floor, and wondering whether they'd freeze solid before I could get my socks and shoes on. We attended the African Methodist Episcopal St. James Church where the services were long—an hour and a half or more, too long for this kid to learn to love religion—but the singing was spirited and good, and early on I developed a belief in God that I've never come to doubt, though I rarely go to church anymore. Just as likely I'll show up at a synagogue for a friend's kid's Bar Mitzvah, or at a Buddhist or Hindu temple in my travels.

There were a few men in Ma's life, but she never remarried. I remember a guy from Indiana named Hudley and a guy from Cleveland named Clevey, but as for marriage she always told us that if she ever ran into a "rich Texas oil millionaire" she might give it some thought, but "I'm not lettin' just old anybody come up here and put their feet on top of my table."

There was always a lot of joking and storytelling going on in the Winfield household, and I've tried to hold on to the free-and-easy sense of humor I developed as a kid. Still, humor is like dancing. Sometimes you dance like crazy, other times you don't want to dance at all. Also, as I got older I realized that people no longer knew me like my family did, and sometimes they just didn't know whether I was joking or not. You know, they'd stare at me and think, Look at that big mother; he probably doesn't have a funny bone in his body. I doubt, for example, that George Steinbrenner thinks of me as particularly amusing.

More important than joking back then—and now—was the pleasure I'd take in telling stories and the language I'd use to make them interesting. It was a skill I developed with Ma. Many nights we'd sit together in the living room and talk, telling each other stories, playing games with language.

Every now and again she'd come home with a tough new word—"ostensibly," for example—and drop it on me. "How about that one?" she'd say. And if I didn't already know the meaning she'd either tell me or I'd look it up. Then, the next chance I had I'd drop one on her, back and forth like that. A playful thing that made me aware of how much the English language could convey.

More than anything Ma and I *did,* I learned from the example she set, learned the value of education, family, work, and a positive attitude. I know it sounds corny but I feel that more than any one thing, it's my attitude that has made my life work, that's enabled me to achieve the success I've had. It's also something I look for in other people, the ballplayers I play with, the people I spend time with outside the game. I don't have much tolerance for constant complainers. It's contagious, it's demoralizing, it's something I really don't want to be around. Sure, everybody bitches and moans sometimes, but to do it all the time will do you in. Take Rollie Fingers, for example, a good ballplayer who would always worry, worry, worry; complain, complain, complain. It got you down. Everybody said, "Shut up, Rollie, *please.*" The team would beg him to stop.

I try, instead, to take my cues from guys like the Tommy Johns, the Willie Stargells, the Pete Roses, the Willie McCoveys. You pitch a bad game, you blow a play, you strike out—it happens. It can't be avoided. So when it happens you just set your helmet down and walk off the field, all dignity. I can't say I do it that way every time, but I'm working on it.

MONEY

There wasn't a lot of money around while I was growing up. Ma worked full time in the St. Paul School District's audiovisual department, and there were my father's occasional support checks. It was slim pickings for a family of three and things were always very, very tight. Still, there was so much love and affection from my mother's relatives, I never thought of us as poor, I never felt deprived. As for Ma, she was always doing for us. As a treat, every once in a while she'd borrow one of those heavy classroom projectors from work and lug it home on the bus to show us an educational film. We might have been poor, but we were never neglected.

Only a couple of times do I remember seeing Ma cry. Once she came home from work in tears. She told us her supervisor had criticized her. I took it at face value then, but now I'm sure it was a lot more than that—having to raise two rambunctious boys, not making enough money, times being rough. And transportation was terrible—no car, leaving for work in the dark, getting home in the dark, a fifty-degree-below wind chill, walking back and forth to the bus stop with a stick to ward off stray dogs, a woman all alone. Seeing her cry back then, I vowed that when I grew up I'd make sure she'd never cry again.

Family finances being what they were probably explains why I was so impressed when shortly after the Twins arrived in Minnesota they signed a black Cuban rookie named Zoilo Versalles—nickname, "Zorro"—for $5,000. It was in all the papers, on the radio, the TV. I said to Steve, "That's big money for just playing baseball." He agreed. And that *was* big money in those days, especially for a *black* Zorro. So we decided that's what we wanted to be—professional ballplayers—though I'm certain we were the only ones who truly believed it could happen. I remember telling a friend once about my career plans and he said, "Yeah, you don't know what you're talking about," then he slapped me on the side of the head to knock some sense into me. "Now, what do you *really* want to be?"

COLOR

Though St. Paul was mostly white, I grew up in a neighborhood that was mostly black. It wasn't a ghetto, or a "bad" neighborhood. Sure, there may have been a couple of blocks—areas a mile or so from our house designated "redo," or that now have a freeway running through them—where you might see a few pimps, or somebody with drugs, or disreputable types hanging out drinking wine from brown-bagged bottles, but for the most part that kind of stuff was the exception rather than the rule. Also, St. Paul wasn't like some cities where if you were young and black and tough you'd have to join a gang. It was a pretty wholesome place. And the fifties were a pretty wholesome time for me to be growing up, running under the streetlights on a summer evening, stealing apples off my neighbor's tree, putting firecrackers on neighbors' doorsteps on the Fourth of July, just like on "Leave It to Beaver."

Still, being black I was sometimes made to feel separate, uncomfortable. I remember sitting in school in the sixth grade and being embarrassed when white kids in my geography class giggled when the teacher talked about Africa— "The Dark Continent!" Visions of witch doctors and voodoo. And what did that mean about me?

In history class, on the other hand, there was never any mention of black people or their accomplishments; no one ever proffered a black person as a role model. It made me feel that history was just that, *his* story, a white man's story, not mine, in any event.

I remember, too, being afraid I wouldn't know how to act the first time I was invited to a friend's house in all-white Highland Park, wondering whether neighbors would gossip as they peeked through their windows at me, or how soon someone in my friend's family would ask, "How come this colored boy is in our house?"

Same thing with the city swimming pools. When I was real young, black people simply weren't allowed to swim there. A few years later, though, it was suddenly okay, so I'd go swim, but I'd still wonder, What's the deal? How are people going to act? Are there still crazy people out there that have it in for your butt the second they see you dip your little, black toes into their pool? I just didn't know.

But that was background stuff, on the fringes of a childhood that was never bothered much by the color issue. My mid-teens, 1965–1968, were a different story, not so much because of anything that happened to me, but because of what was happening in the country—civil rights marches, race riots, the Vietnam War, black studies departments, the assassination of Martin Luther King, Jr. I remember they let us out of school when the news broke about King. Kids were crying. Not as many as when JFK was killed, but a whole lot of them. Me, anyhow, seventeen years old and more upset than I can remember having been for a long time. Most of all I was frustrated and angry.

Three or four years before I'd taken the hard line around the Allison dinner table: "I'm not going to just sit there and get a club up the side of my head." But gradually, listening to Martin Luther King and my ma, aunts, and uncles, I came to think, Yeah, maybe the man's got an answer that makes more sense. Then they shot him down. Sure, it made me cry, made me think, This is what society is all about. Here's a man who wanted to make it better for everyone and they killed him anyhow.

More than a bunch of black militants, his assassination created a bunch of black cynics, which I think may turn out to be a whole lot more dangerous and subversive to the system. After he was gone, too, I remember seeing black leadership founder and asking myself, Now, whom do I look up to? Whom do I respect? For a while the answer was simply no one.

Another part of those years was an entire culture having to make the transition from being "Negro" or "colored" to being "black." It was easy enough for young guys like myself to make the change, but it was a lot harder for our parents. They'd often still say "colored girl," or "light-skinned" or "dark-skinned girl." To adopt a single word, "black," to encompass the whole culture was a huge leap for them to take. Some, like Ma, gradually made the transition and became stronger for it. Others were left behind.

FEARS

Twice my life was almost over before it really began. The first time I was nine years old. I'm on my way to school with a bunch of other kids, about to cross Selby Avenue into the schoolyard. We're all messing around, showing off. When the crossing guard puts up the flag, I just shoot out into the crosswalk. Suddenly, I get a whiff of danger. A huge truck, one of those giant refrigerated delivery jobs, is barreling down on me. I turn, but this enormous bumper smashes into my shoulder. I spin around, fall, somehow end up sitting on the street, just as the truck stops, but not before its left front wheel rolls over my left leg. My jeans are torn, I can actually see tread marks on them. My leg feels like someone is stabbing it from the inside and twisting the knife.

Next thing I know I'm in an ambulance and the medics are cutting my jeans and jockey shorts off, and I'm thinking of all the times my mother told me to make sure I had on clean underwear. You never *can* tell when you're going to be in an accident. But I never believed it would happen to me, not in a million years. Finally, I'm in the hospital, strapped down on a gurney in a corridor waiting for a doctor, and the only thing covering my lower half is a sheet of opaque white waxed paper—the type doctors always have you sit on to protect their lime green examining tables. Every time someone opens a door anywhere in the whole corridor—anywhere in the whole hospital, it seems—this sheet flutters up around me, and I find myself thinking not about my leg, but about what I can do to keep this piece of paper from blowing off and exposing my private parts.

Not long after that my mother shows up, they wrap the leg in bandages—not even a cast—and send me home. I missed nine days of school, and after that it was okay. It's never bothered me again. Except, even today, whenever I cross the street I always look both ways. And I always make sure I've got on clean underwear.

The other time I almost cashed out was about a year later when I fell down and a tiny stone lodged in the palm of my hand. A small, little, nothing stone. A couple of days later my arm hurts and I ask my mother if I can see a doctor, but she says no, I shouldn't worry about it, I'll feel fine soon enough. I guess she figures compared to a refrigerator truck, a stone isn't even worth talking about. A couple of days after that, though, a reddish-purple streak is running all the way from my palm up my left arm. This time I do go to the doctor, who gives me some pills and tells me I'm very lucky I've seen him when I did; another few days and I would have been gone. "Gone? Really?" I ask. "Gone," he repeats solemnly, and for a moment I let the idea of "gone" sink in, not liking it one bit.

My first real exposure to death was a couple of years later when Warren Durdowski, a friend of mine all through elementary school, died of leukemia—just disappeared into a hospital one day and never came back. Somebody truly gone, *poof!* It didn't really scare me, but I simply couldn't make any sense of it.

What *did* scare me was the water, a fear I developed one summer at a neighborhood camp, swimming in a nearby lake that kids from all over the city were bussed to. On the surface, the lake looked peaceful and pretty, but it took me only a couple of seconds in the water to realize that, below the surface, things were going on. There were mud and weeds and, worst of all, leeches. Every few minutes some kid would come screaming and yelling out of the water with one of them on his leg or something, and then we'd all watch it sizzle and die as a counselor sprinkled salt on it. One leech was all it took for me to be doing my watching strictly from the shore.

You'd think you'd forget stuff like that, but years later when I was fourteen, I remember playing baseball in Cold Springs, Minnesota, staying at a lakeside cabin owned by Bill Peterson's father. One day after a game we're standing on the dock in front of the cabin, still dressed in our uniforms after crushing the competition, fooling around, when suddenly someone comes up with the bright idea "Let's throw Winnie in!" I run for the shore, but they get me anyhow, toss me in, and all I'm thinking about as I hit the water is what's underneath—mud, weeds, leeches—and I'm truly frantic, swim for my life just to get the heck out of there. It takes a couple of seconds, seemingly an eternity, before I realize it's only a few feet deep and I can walk to shore, and I do. But the fear is real.

Another time, when I was younger, I went swimming at the Highland Park pool—no mud, no weeds, no leeches. Only Bob and Howard Ellis, who pulled me out to the deep end and then held me underwater until I coughed and sputtered, crazy with the fear of choking and dying. They must have done it a half-dozen times, laughing each time they let me up. There are people like that, people you can hate.

Finally, though, I've won out over that fear, deciding a few years ago to confront it head-on. I took scuba diving lessons, first in a pool and then in the ocean, until I gradually felt more comfortable in the water. And now to test myself I'll go out in a boat and say to the person I'm with, "Hey, it's only thirty feet deep . . . let's go!" It was simply something in me I had to beat, that fear. Though, to be frank, I still prefer paddling around a pool to leaping into lakes and oceans. And I sure wouldn't mind another chance at Bob and Howard Ellis.

THE ROAD

Travel has always been one of baseball's big attractions for me. Ma couldn't afford a car and we'd only get to ride in one of the Allison relatives' cars on "special" occasions, like a visit to the doctor. Not what you'd call a pleasure trip. It wasn't until we got into Little League that Steve and I got to venture farther than we could walk. Both Mac Burch and Big 6 had huge, wonderful sedans that the whole team would pile into for away games. We'd ride all over St. Paul it seemed, eyes glued to the windows. And as star players, Steve and I sometimes had dibs on the front seat for the best view.

Later on, when we played on Bill Peterson's teams, the more we won, the farther we'd travel. Across the river to Minneapolis, which seemed like an enormous journey that first time, for a Twin Cities tournament. To other towns in Minnesota for American Legion games and tournaments. And then on weekend trips to his father's cabin in the country where I first experienced the outdoors—boating, fishing, camping out. It was a genuine thrill seeing my first animal that wasn't a house pet, great meeting new people in new places.

We got even more of an opportunity to travel after my father moved to Seattle where, by the time I was in high school, he was working as a skycap for Western Airlines. This entitled him to a number of free passes for his family anywhere that Western flew. At first, Steve and I would use our passes to visit him and his new wife, Uldine, an okay lady who never gave us any grief. They lived in a nice, comfortable house, lived a nice comfortable life. Whenever we'd visit, first thing he'd do would be to drag us along to one of his friends' houses, every time a different friend. "These are my sons," he would say. It went downhill from there, and I always left Seattle feeling a little empty, a little sad.

Steve wasn't as disappointed by these visits as I was and kept on going, but I decided to sample some other destinations. Despite the fact I was only sixteen and had no particular place to go, I figured, what the heck, I might as well go *somewhere*. So I'd take day trips, leave in the morning, fly, let's say to L.A., take the bus downtown, buy a cheap lunch, window shop, check out the people, and fly back.

One time in downtown L.A. I saw these terrific shoes—

two-tone patent leather with a sort of spat effect—and I bought them, wore them that night to a party in St. Paul. I remember dancing in them feeling like, Hey, everybody check out these shoes! when some guy dancing next to me says, "Say, man, what'd you do today?" And never breaking stride—I'm dancing with utter concentration, styling with these great shoes—I say, "I went to L.A."

"Yeah?" Dance, dance.

"Yeah." Dance, dance.

"Well, f__ you!"

It was okay, though. I was wearing the best shoes in all of Minnesota and the day was already history.

Trouble is, with feet the size of mine I still have to travel to buy shoes. Once, when I was in Dayton, Ohio, for the Mideast Regional Basketball Tournament I found a nice pair. Got another pair once in New York City. Then, finally, a few years back in Atlanta I found the store that my size thirteens had been searching for for years. I've bought dozens of pairs there since. Sent the owners lots of new customers. I'm one of their best friends, they tell me.

One day, though, my day-tripping backfired on me. I'd taken a Sunday trip to San Francisco, seen the sights, had an espresso in North Beach, watched the fog roll in through the Golden Gate, then around dusk grabbed a bus for the airport for a seven o'clock flight. The bus seemed to be taking its time, and every few minutes or so I'd check my watch to see if I'd be late. "Don't worry," some dude sitting next to me finally said, "there's no rush. The airport's closed."

"Closed?" You close restaurants, you close schools, you close streets, but not airports. Not in April. Not during baseball season. Not when I've got a game the next afternoon. "Closed?"

"Fog." He gestured out the window to the freeway where

I could barely make out the shape of a nearby car, its head-lights feebly trying to bore a hole in the murk. It looked like we were driving through a swamp.

"Nothing going to Minneapolis tonight . . . nothing going *anywhere* tonight . . ." was the word at the airport, where I spent the night trying to stretch across four contoured plastic seats, wondering what I'd say to my mother, my teachers, my coach. Finally, around ten in the morning, the fog cleared, leaving me with a three-and-a-half-hour flight, a two-hour time difference, and a one-hour ride from the airport to contend with. Needless to say, by the time I got there, school was over, the game was over, we'd lost. And everyone was all over me.

It was something like the nightmare that most ballplayers have, that they'll oversleep, miss a game. The closest I've ever come to that happening in the nearly 3,000 regular-season and exhibition games I've played as a pro was during spring training when I was with the Padres. We were at a motel in Phoenix. It wasn't even dark when we checked in, but I was exhausted, so I just pulled the shades way down and sacked out. Next thing I knew, the phone rang, my wake-up call, so I grabbed it—the room's still pitch black—and said in that super-alert voice people use to prove they've been up for hours just waiting for the call, "Yes, I'm up." That's what I told them. But it was a lie. I just hung up, rolled over, and wasn't honestly up until a few hours later when I cracked one of the shades to see the parking lot deserted.

"Damn!" It was almost noon. But the game wasn't until one, so I still had a chance. I called a cab that broke every traffic law on the Arizona books, and we pulled into the lot, my uniform draped over my arm, at 12:55. "No problem, Winnie," an assistant coach told me, "we were going to rest you today, anyway."

SUCCESS

Sure, I wanted to win baseball games so I could extend my horizons beyond St. Paul. But mostly I wanted to win because winning was fun. Beating the other team, playing so well that they didn't stand a chance was exciting. It was also a terrific ego boost and a powerful motivator. Steve and I earned reputations as good baseball players in the neighborhood at first, and then in a bigger way in high school as we won city and state tournaments and were named to All-City and All-State teams. With it came the attention, the admiration, the notoriety that spurred me on to become an even better player, that fueled my dream of playing pro ball. By the time I was seventeen I was on top of the world—a lofty perch from which I found it difficult sometimes to be humble.

The summer before my senior year, for example, the Attucks-Brooks team traveled to St. Cloud for the American Legion state tournament. We were staying in a local hotel, scheduled to play the local favorites the next day. By this time I had myself pegged as a real hotshot; not only was I playing vacuum-cleaner shortstop and whacking the hide off the ball, I'd also started blowing batters away as a pitcher. So when I ran into a guy from the team we'd be playing, I asked him, "Have you ever heard of Dave Winfield?" The guy shook his head, no. "Well, by tomorrow," I said, "you will. Believe me, you will." He walked away, unimpressed. Next day, though, we kicked their butts, and I was a major contributor to the damage, leaving town as the tournament MVP.

No doubt about it, as a teenager I could be free, cocky, egotistical, loud, and just a bit overbearing. You sure couldn't have convinced me of it then, but I had a lot to learn.

Around about then, the tables were turning for Steve and me. Always the younger, smaller brother, I had overtaken him, and was suddenly taller and bulkier. And though he still was a terrific pitcher—with an array of curveballs including a Juan Marichal special, some good off-speed stuff, and a crafty pickoff move to first that was actually a balk the umps never caught—he'd injured his arm a few years back, weakening it. While he could largely make up for his lack of strength with guile, by the time he was a junior he was no longer an automatic star, just about the time I'd begun to be. But I don't think I ever lorded it over him. I hope not, anyway.

Still, one day when I'm sixteen, Steve and I and a friends of ours, Hilton Hicks, are fooling around at our house. A while later Ma comes home and tells me to do something and I give her a smart-aleck answer and the next thing I know Steve throws a plastic rat-tail comb at me from across the room and it pokes me in the head—right in the head—and I'm pissed. And he knows it. Suddenly, we come at each other in the middle of the living room, first just grabbing, then hooking. Ma sees what's happening, or what's about to happen, and gets right in the middle of it, this little five-foot-two-and-three-quarter-inch lady standing between her two six-foot-plus sons. But it's already accelerated beyond stopping and one of us just shoves her away and we go at it again, crashing from room to room. And the more we do, the more confident I feel I can win this fight, until I've got Steve in our bedroom, on his back over the edge of his bed, staring him right in the face, my adrenaline pumping. But now I just don't know what to do. I don't want to punch him in his face or anything. I just want to win. I want him to know it, admit it. Yet I can't figure out how to make it happen. So I tell him through clenched teeth how I'm really going to whip his butt, I really am, really. And to convince him of my superior power, I do the only thing that comes to mind; I start ripping the buttons off his sweater, one by one. Right about that time Hilton and Ma break us up. Turns out it's Hilton's sweater, so there was a genuine incentive. And that was about the only time that Steve and I fought, really fought.

The spring of my senior year in high school I was drafted by the Baltimore Orioles, to be sent to the minors for some "seasoning." I was also offered a half scholarship by the University of Minnesota in nearby Minneapolis to play ball there. A lot of my friends thought the choice was obvious. One or two years in the minors and I could be in the big leagues. A half scholarship to the "U" meant living at home for four years, having to go to all those classes, and just scraping by. But the way I saw it, it was a matter of deciding whether to ride a bus for peanuts in some redneck town with a double-A farm club, or seizing the opportunity for an education and remaining a local hero.

PEOPLE

JD

There are two stories about how I met my best friend in college and partner in crime, JD. Mine and his. Mine is, one day in the late summer, just before I'm to start classes, I'm refereeing a kid's football game at a playground to earn some extra bucks. And believe me, these kids need a referee.

They're roughing the passer, running into the kicker, clipping, all manner of dangerous stuff. To break them of it, whenever they commit a flagrant penalty I pick them up by the scruff of the neck and give them a little shake. Nothing serious, really, just something to let them know they can't get away with fouls like that. Standing on the sidelines watching me "officiate" is a wiry black dude about my age, checking me out, thinking, I could tell, that I'm a little crazy, but in an interesting way. So after the game he comes up to me and says, "Hey, man, do you want to go out cruising with me tonight?"

JD's version is that we're playing in a pickup touch-football game. He's the quarterback and I'm one of the interchangeable, less important guys on the team. In the huddle he calls a long pass, takes the snap, drops back, sees all his receivers covered, senses the defenders converging on him, and decides to throw it away downfield out of the end zone to avoid the sack. Suddenly, though, he sees a huge, black hand attached to a long, black arm snatch the nose of the ball, and carry it over the goal line for a touchdown. "Hey, man," he calls out, "I was trying to throw it away."

"Yeah," JD says I said, "I catch those too."

"Well, then, do you want to go out cruising tonight?"

I'll bet on my version, but I sure do like JD's.

That night he showed up in a green customized Ford, jacked up a little in the rear. "Come on, man, I'm taking you on a real pleasure cruise." And he did, sort of. Four different girls' apartments. We'd stop in, he'd talk some stuff, they'd produce some food, we'd watch some TV, and then just before things might have gotten really interesting we'd head on off to the next apartment. "Who's your friend, JD?" they'd ask everywhere we stopped, and he'd say, like he was noticing me for the first time, "Oh, this dude? This is Winfield."

But JD was a genius at procuring the basics every poor student needed—free food and entertainment—and soon I became his willing protégé. Besides, it was 1969, white guilt was everywhere, and the two of us were helpless in its wake. At his urging, we used to go to this apartment where four white girls, students at the university, lived. One of them was on to us and would cut out the second we showed up. But the others stuck around, studying us like we were rare specimens. "What's it like," they'd ask, "living in the ghetto?" And JD and I would tell our woeful tale as they fed us and ministered to our needs. JD always kept everybody entertained. If the joke wasn't funny, you'd laugh at JD's cackling laugh. One of them worked as a waitress in a greasy spoon downtown, so once around suppertime we showed up there and told her, "Hey, we want some food and we're not paying for it." It took her a couple of seconds to check both sides of her conscience, then she brought us a couple of huge dinners and charged us only for two Cokes.

Another one of our liberal pals was a white guy in my Afro-American studies class who'd always stop me after class to ask me about the "black experience." I gave him some pithy insights, then asked him what *his* story was. He told me he worked at the Varsity Theater as a ticket taker. "Oh, really?" Taking my lead from the white guilt master, one night JD and I tooled on down to the theater and said to the guy sitting in his little glass cage, "You're interested in helping the black cause, aren't you?"

"Oh, yeah," he said.

"Well, then, let my buddy and me in here for free. That'd be a big help."

He did his part. One time, though, we did our part for him. JD and I were in the theater watching *Night of the Living Dead*, scared to death, when suddenly I felt a tap on my shoulder. I wheeled around, ready to shriek if it would do me any good. It was my man, the ticket taker. He whispered he needed my help, that there were some football players outside, hassling him, demanding that they get in for free or they'd kick his butt. He looked ready to cry. Off in the distance I heard some banging on the windows and doors, threats being called out. "Don't worry about it," I told him, "we'll go out and talk to those guys." So JD and I followed the kid into the lobby where I saw a half-dozen football players plastered against the window. I felt like I was at a zoo.

"Hey, Winnie," one of them called out, "get us in here." But I knew where my loyalties lay.

"What are you doing hassling my buddy?" I said, putting an arm around my classmate.

There was a pause. Then a voice, already in retreat, "We didn't know he was your buddy."

"Why don't you guys just run along, then," I suggested, Mr. Moderation. "Otherwise, the way it's done at the Varsity, you pay to see the picture." JD, standing next to me, chest out and looking as tough as he could, loved it.

David Yale

When I got to the university, Steve, a sophomore, was heavily involved in black student politics. He asked me to attend meetings of the Afro-American Action Committee. Sometimes I would, but for better or worse, I was more interested in sports, not causes.

I also wasn't much of a student, figuring that even though I was going to college to get an education, I could skate through and come out an educated man. Mainly my skating got me C's, and lots of times I didn't even deserve them.

The only teacher who made a real impression on me my freshman year was David Yale, a communications professor. First day he comes to class wearing a coat and tie. After a few minutes, he undoes his tie, takes off his coat and shirt and slacks to reveal more casual clothes underneath. "I'm shedding my outer shell," he says, "to be more the person I *am* instead of the person I'm trying to represent." All semester he encouraged us to do the same, to recognize our own thoughts and feelings, and speak our own mind. While I may have wasted much of my freshman year having fun and sometimes acting like a fool, Yale's lecture did not go wasted on me.

Mulford Q. Sibley

By the time I was a sophomore I was taking my classwork more seriously. I even declared a double major—black studies and political science. Mulford Q. Sibley was my inspiration, though I'm sure he never knew it. He was the grand old man of poly sci at the U, with his baggy, tweed suits, his slightly distant expression, his quavery Walter Brennan–like voice. But he was a real powerhouse, had known, worked for, or advised all the giants in Minnesota politics—Hubert Humphrey, Eugene McCarthy, Walter Mondale, and others. And everyone knew that when Sibley said something, it wasn't Grandpa McCoy talking, but the *real* McCoy.

One day I show up at his office after doing poorly on a midterm. "Professor," I begin, "I've been traveling a lot with the team . . ." He peers out from behind his mountain of books and papers, fixes his distant expression right on me. "Well," he says, "there's not much I can do about that. I'm afraid that to do well in this class, you'll just have to find time to study." This, coming from a guy who is looked up to by some of the most influential people in the country.

So I did find the time, declared my double major, raised my grades from mediocre to dean's list, and became a Williams Scholar, an award given to student athletes who excel in academics.

Aunt Bernice

Aunt Bernice was one of those stickler aunts. You simply could never blow anything by Aunt Bernice. One day after I pitched a particularly good game, a local TV sportscaster comes to do a locker-room interview with me. I'm a hotshot jock, dressed in a gray "Property of the University of Minnesota" T-shirt with cutoff sleeves and a beat-up old hat with a lot of character, the kind that looks like you wore it through a war. Anyway, later that evening we're all sitting around the TV at Grandma Jessie's—Ma, Steve, a host of cousins and aunts and uncles, and, of course, Aunt Bernice—waiting for the sports segment of the news. Finally, my interview comes on and I'm thinking, Winfield, you're handling this real well . . . real well. So when it's over I turn around to get my accolades. Everyone's smiling, I'm smiling, and we all seem to be so overwhelmed by my performance that nobody says a thing. Suddenly Aunt Bernice pipes up, "You said too many 'and's and 'uh's and 'you know's." And she walks off. For a moment, nothing, then it hits me: Hey, this is my *family* for God's sake, the people who are supposed to support me!—meaning, tell me how wonderful I am. And Aunt Bernice just says, "You said too many 'and's and 'uh's and 'you know's," then skedaddles.

I'm pissed, but afterward I think about it, believe me, I think about it. And I come to the conclusion that while she might have been a little too hard-assed, the lady was right. She was right that I didn't present myself all that well, and that as a ballplayer and a role model for other kids, black or white, I had to do better, to give more to those that looked up to me. It was the first time I sensed that maybe I owed something to the game and to those that cared about my playing. Looking back on it, it was probably the seed that would become the Foundation.

THE LAW

It's easy enough to make light of it now, but the fact was that those first years at the university were difficult ones. My half scholarship paid only tuition, nothing else. Not books, not room and board, not transportation. If there were any under-the-table payments to athletes, they were never made under any tables where I was sitting. I'd like to think that I wouldn't have taken them, anyhow, but knowing me then, I might have.

My finances being what they were, the only way I could afford to attend the U was to live at home, twelve miles away, and commute by bus. But playing sports and trying to do well in my courses I always had either late practice or an evening class, or the library to go to, and by the time I got out it was often too late to catch the bus. So I spent a lot of nights on the floors of my friends' dorm rooms, taking the cushions off their chairs and laying them out, covering myself with an extra blanket.

As for my daily bread, when I wasn't out scrounging with JD, I'd often get into the dorm cafeteria line with some of the other ballplayers—big guys in front of me, big guys behind me—and grab a tray. "Hey," a food monitor would inevitably call out, "where's your ID?" and bad dude that I was, I'd hold up a fist and say, "Here!" and they'd let me through. I suppose there was another way, but I was just too big, too cocky; it was just too easy. Plus I was at that age when you feel invulnerable, not governed by rules or law.

So when JD desperately needs tires for the Ford—for weeks we'd had more canvas on the road than rubber—we make the rounds of the big tire stores—Treads 'R Us, and the like—to see if the humongous stacks of tires out front are chained down. They aren't; they're "flowers just waiting to be plucked," according to JD. Trouble is, there's always some serious-looking high school dropout with "Big O Tires" on his khaki work shirt tending the garden. That is, unless there's an unpleasant turn of the weather.

So the plan is to wait until it rains and everyone makes a run for the bays to smoke and fart and tell lies about how they scored that weekend. We endure about a week of unseasonably good weather, when one day while JD and I are playing cards in the kitchen it finally begins to rain. First, just a little pitty-pat on the windows. But soon it's really coming down. Really! It's a *monsoon.* So we look at each other and I don't even remember who or even if *anyone* says a word, but the thought is, Let's go for it! In a second we're out on the street, make a dash for the tire store, JD the lookout and me grabbing the tires we need, then running like hell, each of us with a tire under each arm, and drenched to the skin. Now whenever I pass a tire outlet I see a chain running through the piles of tires out front, just like they put a thick wire through the sleeves of leather coats at even the fanciest stores.

The summer after my freshman year, JD and I manage to get enough money together to move into an apartment in Minneapolis. Late August, the rent is due, we're restless, bored, cruising the area. We stop for some coffee, get back into the car, drive down an alley with warehouses on either side. I spot an open door.

"Hey," I say to JD, wondering now what could have possibly been going through my mind. "Stop the car!" He does and the two of us get out, take a quick look inside the building, and there they are—dozens of snowblowers, nice, expensive-looking pieces of equipment, just sitting there. Rent money! Quick as a flash we pile a couple of 'em into the car, laughing and joking, thinking, Oh, man, fun and games, let's get the f__ outta here!

Soon we're six blocks away, now really laughing and

joking, high on the thrill of doing it, high on having made a clean getaway. Then JD looks into the rearview mirror. "Sonofabitch," he says, "we're being followed." Very uncool, I spin around to check it out myself, see a faceless gray sedan behind us.

"Naw," I insist. JD makes a quick turn, then another, then another. The sedan's still there. "Head down this alley," I tell him, smack dab in the middle of the worst TV show of my life, "then let's get this stuff out of the car."

But they're still behind us. Nothing to do but get back on the main drag and lose them in traffic. Suddenly, the sedan pulls up next to us, a red light flashing on the dash. "All right! Pull over," a loudspeaker blares. JD and I look at each other, both flirting with the ridiculous notion of making a run for it, each of us knowing that we're done for.

"Out of the car with your hands up!" There's a plain-clothes cop at either door, gun drawn. We're pushed up against the car, frisked. "Hands higher, hands higher!" one of them yells. They don't find anything on me. On JD they find a blade—not that he'd ever use it, he just carried one. So they put handcuffs on him and order us both into the back seat of the Ford. A few feet away folks drive by; on the sidewalk a crowd gathers. I wonder if anyone there recognizes me, knows that I've just come off an 8–0, .300+ Metro League season.

Five minutes later we're downtown in the old jailhouse where we're fingerprinted and booked. Snowblowers aren't cheap; this isn't shoplifting for candy, this is a felony. But I still hold on to the notion, idiotic as it may be, that since I never really thought that *taking* the snowblowers was the same as *stealing* them—we were, after all, only poor, dumb college students—everything that's happening is an elaborate joke and soon the cops will let us go, with lots of backslapping and guffawing: Gosh, you guys really had us going there! Soon enough, though, I realize I'll have to call

Ma, that my whole family will know, that it will make the papers, that whatever happens after this, my life will be different, more complicated.

After a while Ma shows up. When I see her coming through the bars of my cell, I try to look tough, like, It's cool, just get me a lawyer. But right away she starts to cry, and so do I. And then Bill Peterson comes by, and later Steve and I don't feel cool at all. I feel embarrassed and awful.

It's also Friday, end of the day. Too late to see the judge, have to wait until Monday. Monday? I think. What happens on Saturday and Sunday? I mean, I have plans for the weekend, one of my cousins is getting married, I'll put a hot comb through my Afro, get it way out there, put on some fine threads, my L.A. shoes, make my appearance, 8–0, a .300+ hitter.

My appearance is canceled. Instead I spend the weekend in jail, wearing green army fatigue pants and a green nylon T-shirt, sitting on a hard wooden bench next to the toilet, with a little light bulb over my head. Nighttime I have to wad up some toilet paper to use as a pillow.

Finally, it's Monday, no toothpaste, no toothbrush, my hair all lopsided, I smell funky; time to see the judge, make a good impression. Since I'm the guy without the concealed weapon I get bargain bail—$3,000, so $300 buys my freedom. That is, until my trial.

But there is no trial. Instead my lawyer negotiates with the DA for a suspended sentence with probation. Still, I have to go back to court—this time dressed for the occasion—for sentencing. I listen as the charges are read: "David Mark Winfield willingly, knowingly, wrongfully . . ." Goddamn, I think, it sounds pretty bad, wondering for a moment whether the judge is really going to buy this suspended sentence deal. Indeed, the next thing out of his mouth is that I've pleaded guilty and that I'm sentenced to three years in the St. Cloud Penitentiary, and then, only after a very, very long pause, he suspends the sentence, gives me three years probation, lays out the rules, and asks what my plans are.

"Anything you say," I tell him, meaning it, realizing just how close I'd come to closing down my life.

Years later, when I was playing on the Padres and the word got to Minnesota about the work I was doing with kids, they cleared my record—JD's too, a few years after that. And I wouldn't end up on the wrong side of the law again until 1982 when I made the mistake of tossing a baseball at a seagull in Toronto.

WOMEN

I went through my first three years of high school without dating much or going steady, and had to endure my friends' kidding—"Man, Winnie, you'd rather play baseball than get laid!" I'd tell them that I didn't play baseball at night, letting them draw their own conclusions. But the fact was I was basically shy around girls. And I wasn't particularly interested in dating. It wasn't until my senior year, in fact, that I had my first serious girlfriend.

It's hard to know what to say about a high school romance that hasn't been said a million times before, but for the first time in my life I felt I could be lover and friend to a girl, felt comfortable just spending time talking, listening. Often, we'd study, talk, listen to music—she introduced me to jazz, Les McCann, Eddie Harris, guys I still listen to—or mess around late into the night at her house (her mother worked a 4 P.M. to midnight shift) after we finally conned her kid brother into leaving us alone around ten. Midnight, her mother would show up and it'd be, "Well, hello, Dave." "Well, hello, Mrs. G." I'm sure she knew what was going on but she was cool about it.

Graduation marked the beginning of the end of the relationship. She went off to college in another state, met new people, made new friends—our worlds diverged, although we kept in touch. I remember telling her once while we were still in high school about the fancy car I'd buy when I signed my first major-league contract. Four years later, after I signed with the Padres she called me and asked, "Did you get it?" I knew just what she was talking about. "No," I told her, "I just got me a regular ol' car, a Pontiac Grand Prix." We laughed about that. It was great to hear from her.

By the time I got to the university I'd definitely come out of my shell in my relationships with members of the opposite sex. There were just too many opportunities for a local sports hero to pass up. I used bravado to cover my shyness, and stopped trying to second-guess why any girl or woman would be interested in me or find me attractive.

The pendulum had swung so fully in the other direction, in fact, that by the time I was a sophomore, JD and I were actively competing to see who could end up with more girlfriends. "How many you got?" he asks me once. I tell him, "About seven or eight," knowing he has a paltry three, four at the most. A few weeks later I'm celebrating my birthday in my bedroom, wearing a pair of shorts, watching a Tarzan movie on TV. Suddenly, there's a knock on my door. I get up to answer it and who's standing in the doorway but one of the aforementioned ladies. She's carrying a little gift. "Happy birthday, Dave," she says. I don't remember telling her anything about my birthday, so it catches me a little off guard.

"Hey, what's happening!" I say. I give her a big hug, and she returns the favor, and then some. I follow her into the living room anticipating more action, but who should be sitting there—each with little presents in their laps—but all my other girlfriends, each trying to figure out what the hell is going on. And the one person who knows, my dear friend JD, is history—gone. Lucky for him, because if he'd been there then, I'd have wrung his scrawny little neck.

Over the next few years I settled down a bit, had a few serious relationships, one with a woman I remained close to for years after we graduated. Thing is, I don't think I ever said I love you to any one of them, though I cared a lot for each of them. In fact, I don't think I've said those words to more than two or three women I've dated in my life. It's simply something I don't take lightly. But I've seen it happen with women—they go out with you a couple of times, and suddenly they say, "I love you." Sure you do, I think, you don't even know who I am.

BOSSES

If successful teams are a measure of a great coach, then the University of Minnesota's Dick Siebert has to be thought of as one of the greatest. Siebert, or "Chief" as he was called, coached the Gophers to nine Big Ten championships, going all the way to win the NCAA title three times. He was an aloof, gruff guy with a gravelly voice who ran his team like a tyrant and rarely had anything pleasant to say to anyone.

I'd come to the university as a pitcher after abandoning

the razzle-dazzle of the infield my senior year in high school for the glory of the mound. Playing on the frosh team I went 4–0 with a microscopic ERA. The summer following I pitched in the St. Paul Metro League, posting an ERA of .091 with eight wins and no losses, to make me 12–0 for the year.

I also hit .373 that summer, but Siebert didn't seem particularly interested. He was only interested in my arm. I remember him once barking at me during batting practice, "Aaargh! Winfield, you're never going to be a hitter, 'cause you got that hitch in your swing." Next day he came by to second his pronouncement. "You, aaargh, don't swing right." And Siebert, it seemed, didn't have the time or inclination to show me how to do it right. But he did show me a lot about pitching. My first year on the varsity I had the lowest ERA in the Big Ten.

THE GAME

Sophomore year, my first on the Minnesota varsity, I went 8–3, posting an ERA of 1.48. Not a whole lot of batters got to me. Looking for more of a challenge, I gave some serious thought to playing another summer of Metro League ball. But my previous summer in the league I'd won every game I'd pitched, hit every pitcher who'd pitched to me. It was time instead, I decided, to put myself to the test. So after finishing out the season for Siebert, I traveled north to Alaska to play in the Alaska Summer League, one of the best semi-pro leagues in the country. Tom Seaver had played there. Dave Kingman had played there. So would Randy

Jones and many others. "Yeah," Siebert said when I asked him about it, his usual talkative self. "They got some good players up there. Aaargh! Sure, I think it's good. Aaargh! Good experience. Don't throw your arm out. Bye."

Seeing Alaska for the first time as the plane dropped below the clouds to land in Anchorage was awesome. To the east there were rugged mountains—gray, snowcapped, formidable; to the west, right at the foot of a chain of palisades, was the Gulf of Alaska. Cradled between the mountains and the sea was a white, white city where we landed, dropped off most of our passengers, picked up a few more, then took off again, for Fairbanks, my final destination, where I'd play for the Fairbanks Goldpanners.

Flying inland, we passed over land incredibly green, where a huge logging site or thousands of acres blackened by a forest fire would just be a speck in all that green. After a while, the green gave way to glaciers on ice-blue rivers that looked like wide, arching roadways heading nowhere. Even from 40,000 feet, the size, the scale of it made me shiver, scared me a little. Where the heck *was* I going?

In 1971 Fairbanks was little more than a good-sized village, one-twentieth the size of St. Paul, not at all formidable. Neither, did it seem, was the Goldpanner coach, Jim Dietz, a serious, straitlaced guy with wire-rimmed glasses. Turned out, Jim *was* formidable, in his own way. He was all business and had little tolerance for his players acting up or carousing. Besides, our schedule—living with a local family, working days at a regular, paying job, and practicing and playing in the long Alaskan evenings—made any hijinks almost impossible. It was Jim's philosophy, in fact, to keep us a little tired—the more tired we were, he figured, the less apt we'd be to get into trouble. Also, since a lot of us were headed for the pros, he felt it was important that we get used to the strain of playing tired, performing well under any circumstance.

"The way you beat the system," Jim would say, "is by

working harder." And unlike some hard-nosed coaches, he practiced what he preached. Once, when he was pitching batting practice, a ball came back at him, hit him right in the eye, knocked his glasses clean off. His eye, his face looked terrible. But he refused to give up the mound. "Get your ass outta here!" he insisted when I tried to relieve him, "I'm going to finish what I started." And he did, though eventually he had to undergo an operation to save the vision in that eye.

That summer—I would return again the next—I boarded with a white family, Patsy and Harry Turner, and their two kids. I don't know how surprised or disappointed they were to see me, this tall, citified, black guy, at the door to their log cabin, but they had asked for a Goldpanner and I was it. Fortunately, they were extremely nice, sincere people, and though we had little in common and not a whole lot to talk about, our time together was rarely strained or uncomfortable. Sometimes we'd go through the photo albums I'd brought along with me and I'd tell them what it was like in St. Paul. Other times they'd ask me questions and I'd answer—like, "Why yes, I've been to jail."

The only real drawback to living with the Turners was that in a town of only 15,000, their cabin was four miles *out* of town. Patsy got the job of driving me to the furniture store where I worked or to and from practice. One time on our way to town, Patsy hit a squirrel that dashed out in the road in front of us—*thump, thump.* Sad, I thought, he was trying to make it, but he didn't. But Patsy was completely undone by it. "I took a life," she said. She had to pull off to the side of the road where we sat for a while until she got herself together. I really couldn't think of anything to say.

Cocky as I had become back in St. Paul, Alaska made me realize that taken out of my element, I was basically very shy and still very unsure of myself, making me an easy mark for Jim's tall tales and practical jokes. It wasn't enough that in the Anchorage airport he pointed out a stuffed grizzly bear bigger than I, with teeth the size of my fingers, but later in the season he took a bunch of us to a friend's cabin in the woods and told scary bear stories all night. After we finally went to bed, I had a powerful need to use the outhouse, but you couldn't pry me out of that cabin for a million bucks. Another time Jim told us how glacier ice never melted and urged us to get some to send back home, and I was one of the guys who next day went up to him to report that my piece had been "stolen."

Realizing just how young and inexperienced I was, Jim didn't push me too hard. I played in 34 games, working mostly as a reliever and a pinch hitter. In my 63 at-bats, I hit about .280, not exactly tearing up the league. Still, when opposing pitchers would throw at me, try to intimidate me, I stood my ground, refusing to let them break me. Thinking back, the most important thing I learned that summer in Alaska was that I would not be intimidated, no matter how good the competition, or how badly they wanted to get to me.

SEASONS: 1971–1972

Much as I loved baseball at the university, in some ways it was frustrating. We rarely saw huge crowds at the games, until we were about to wrap up a Big Ten title, which we did in 1973. But even then they didn't compare to the size and the craziness of the basketball crowds that would fill beat-up old Williams Arena to its wooden rafters—festooned with the maroon-and-gold banners of championships gone by—virtually *every* game night.

While I was still in high school, I'd occasionally go to a game, get there early, and watch the frosh play in the prelim while the varsity team sat, dressed to kill, in a favored section of the stands—gigantic dudes wearing suits, hats, long top-coats. Then, early in the third quarter they'd get up, one man at a time, to make their way downstairs to the locker room. As they did, 12,000 fans (in this 17,000-seat arena) turned away from the game on the floor to see the better "game" in the stands as these dudes sauntered out. Everyone was looking at them and they knew it. Even in the stands they were heroes, on stage, looking very sharp, very, very cool.

I'd always liked the game of basketball, but had never played it growing up. Then the summer between my junior and senior years of high school I began horsing around with some good basketball players on the playground and got hooked, found how much I really loved the game—the con-stant movement, the strategy, the man-on-man. It was, in many ways, the opposite of baseball.

That fall I decide to give it a shot, go out for the Central High varsity. I make the team as a starting forward. All right, I think, let's play some *basket*ball! Trouble is, no one ever bothers to explain the rules. I don't know what consti-tutes a foul, so I foul out of my first game in the third quarter. In another early game, I'm sent off the bench to replace someone and I just run onto the court without checking in at the officials' table. But I finally get the hang of it. The team wins the city championship, and I make All-City.

My first year at the university I go out for the frosh team only to find that *everyone* trying out is All-City, All-State, All-Region, All-This, and All-That. Plus, these guys are *big*—six foot nine, six foot eleven, like that. And *good*. First day of practice the coach puts me man-on-man with future NBA great Jim Brewer. But I'm not about to back off. I make the team, lots of times playing over my head. Still, I'm convinced I'm going to do this *well*. I'm not going to go out there and have anyone slamming it down my throat, outrunning me, scoring on me. No way!

Sophomore year, I decide to focus my energies on my classwork and my first varsity baseball season. But when basketball season rolls around and I see guys running up and down playground courts, their butts dragging, their tongues hanging out, I get lonely for the sport. So, along with Steve, I join an intramural team, the Soulful Strutters, the brainchild of JD. First year out, we wipe up the league, win the intramural championship. We even became the practice team for the junior varsity. The following year we're about to do it again when Jimmy Williams, the assistant varsity basketball coach, sees me dealing against the JV, and invites me to practice with the varsity, with the big boys.

Having played on the frosh team I had some idea how it was for those cool dudes on the varsity who sauntered out of the stands during the frosh games . . .

. . . You make your way down into the maroon-and-gold–painted locker room where you find clean socks draped over your locker, your uniform all laid out. You get taped, walk the halls bathed in that clean smell of adhesive and talcum powder. You're wearing a brand-new jock, a "Bike," right out of the box. Band music and crowd noise filter down, keep the adrenaline flowing, the anxiety high. The game's going to be on TV, so you've got just a little more than the usual butterflies.

"It's going to be a big crowd tonight," the coach says. He's nervous. He's pacing. His brow is furrowed. He goes through his scouting report, his strategy, tells you how important the game is. Then you and the others put your hands together to meld your energies. "Let's go!"

Upstairs, on the court, you warm up like you're a Harlem Globetrotter, to the strains of "Sweet Georgia Brown." The fans eat it up. Warming up on the other end of the court, being just about totally ignored, is the other team.

After your warmup's over, you disappear back downstairs for a few minutes. A quick pep talk, then hands together one more time.

Back up on the court, it's suddenly lights out! The arena goes completely black. A split second later a single spotlight picks out an enormous cutout of a gopher dribbling a giant basketball. The critter's sitting at the edge of the court, and there's an open circle in the basketball big enough for a man to run through. Which is precisely what you do, poised, ready, waiting until they call your name, until 17,000 Minnesota fans cheer for you like maniacs, cheer for you and then each of your teammates, a cheer that builds to a crescendo when you're finally all standing there together on the court. And from that moment on, you've got 'em. Jump ball, tipped to you, drive downcourt, score a basket, YAAAHH! The other guys, they never even have a chance.

"Yeah," I said to Jimmy Williams the day he asked me to practice with the varsity, "I'll give it a try."

That year the varsity had a new head coach, Bill Musselman, who told the athletic department when they hired him that he intended for his team to win the Big Ten title his first year out, though it had been thirty-seven years since Minnesota had done so. "I don't believe in rebuilding seasons," Musselman was quoted in the papers. Gutsy talk, but I liked it, wanted to play for a guy who *knew* he was going all the way.

First thing I learned about Musselman was, while he let his teams warm up like Globetrotters, he never let them *play* like them. His players weren't loosey-goosey shootists and stylists. They were defensive specialists. Defense with a capital "D."

"Put your chest in that guy's face and then move your

feet. Not your hands! Your feet!!" he'd yell. From Musselman I learned to get on that man, to get inside his jersey,
his shorts, his jock. I learned first and foremost to *be* there.
To get up in his face when he tried to dribble, and to stay
there when he tried to shoot. Then to "snatch that rebound,
swing that free arm, clear your space!" Clear your space,
hell. I remember one day we're playing Indiana and a six-
foot-nine guy named Rose goes up against me for a rebound;
I make the snatch, swing the arm, and there's this guy
collapsed on the floor, blood trickling from his forehead like
somebody shot him. I never even knew I'd *hit* the guy, but
that's how "high" I'd get.

More significant than Musselman's concentration on defense was his training philosophy, the "overload principle"
as he called it. And Musselman was a man true to his principle. Often, for example, we'd practice with weight jackets
on, an extra twenty pounds at least. Sometimes we'd practice wearing them on offense, sometimes on defense. Sometimes half court, sometimes full court. Until you dropped.
Really. And if your team lost, he'd make you run. So you
never knew whether to dog it a little and lose, then take your
punishment running, or give it everything you had and take
your punishment playing. Either way, all of us developed
amazing strength and endurance. "Musselman's Musclemen," we were called.

Also part of the overload training regimen was the use of
weighted basketballs to build up our hands and wrists. And
to improve our rebounding and build upper body strength,
there was the McCall Rebounder, an elevated platform that
held a regular or weighted basketball and was rigged with
a lever that made the ball much harder to grab. Forget going
for it with one hand—King Kong couldn't have done it.
The result was absolute, monster rebounds. In fact, during
practice we'd all go for them, see who could come down
with the biggest monster rebound, grab the ball with both

hands, pull it in, spin, elbows out, roarrRRR! I started that roar for fun, and the rest of team followed suit. Musselman loved it.

Playing for the Gophers that year were a half-dozen NBA prospects—Jim Brewer, Ron Behagen, Clyde Turner, Keith Young, Bob Murphy, and Corky Taylor. When I showed up, they didn't exactly put out the welcome mat. Each of these guys had serious hopes of playing pro ball, and they needed to start, needed to shine under the new coach to attract pro scouts. So there I was, not even officially on the team, an interloper from the baseball team, of all places, practicing with them, often outhustling them in scrimmages, threatening to take away someone's job.

From the beginning, no one much liked seeing me run into the arena from the underground tunnel that connected it to the gym where I took baseball practice, but one guy, Ron Behagen, Wild Bee, was downright hostile. Every time play got rough under the boards, Wild Bee might catch me with an elbow or his protégé, Tommy Barker, would stiff-arm me at the hip as I came down with a rebound, sending me sprawling to the hardwood. Rather than discouraging me, though, it just made me tougher, and I'd get up, ignore the foul, outplay 'em some more. But what with two practices a day, classes, wondering every night whether I should crash in a friend's dorm room or shiver outside in the freezing cold and wait for the last bus home, the emotional conflict, the pressure was getting to me.

Then one day, with Behagen banging me up and down and me not giving an inch, it all comes crashing down on me. We're in a rare lull, no one is actually on me, when suddenly I just smash the ball into the floor and fall to my knees in tears. Damnedest thing. I stop after a few seconds, look around to see who's staring at me. They all are, but quickly look away, embarrassed maybe. Musselman comes up, tells me to wait for him in his office. I assume it's to tell me I didn't make the team. But when he finally shows up he says he knows what I'm going through, knows how hard it is, but wants me to keep at it, knows I can. I'm amazed by how much better I feel.

Just a few practices later, Behagen elbows one of the scrubs playing defense on him and knocks a couple of teeth out. I replace the scrub and the next thing I know Behagen elbows me in the chin after a lay-up. This time, though, I don't ignore it, but jump up in his face, push him back, stand chest-to-chest with him, and spit out, "Enough is enough!" I'm prepared to fight him then and there. He runs to the sideline, picks up a folding chair, and starts back at me. The players and coaches grab us, and that pretty much ends it. I don't give a damn if the team likes me, I realize, I'm going to make the team, I'm going to play, and they're going to have to respect me.

A few days before the first game of the season, Musselman calls me aside to tell me how much he likes my intensity, likes the way I pull down rebounds against guys a half foot taller than I, how much he wants me to play for him. I'd made the team! And once that's finally established, the team accepts me and many of the guys become my friends.

That's not all that changes. Making the team, I give up my half baseball scholarship for a full basketball scholarship— basketball being a much larger money-maker for the school, filling Williams Arena for every game. It's no wonder then that the athletic department is freer with dollars for a sec-ond-string forward than for its number one pitcher. Any-way, for the first time I can go to classes, go to practices, live away from home, and not have to worry whether I'll be able to afford my meals, my books, or transportation.

That entire fall and winter are still crazy, though. Come from indoor baseball practice after two or three hours of hitting, throwing, running, sprint through the tunnel to the gym, get my ankles taped, then fun and games with Bill Musselman and his madmen in their weighted vests, fighting the McCall Rebounder for rebounds, and developing wrist strength chucking around super-heavy basketballs. But it's worth it to play with the guys, especially Brewer. We called him "Papa," because he controlled things in the middle. Not a real great shot, with hands so small he couldn't even palm the ball. But he's as strong, as smart, and as agile as they come. A team man, the type of guy you need to go all the way, which is where we're convinced we're headed. And we are, sort of.

On January 25, 1972, at Williams Arena, Musselman's overload reaches critical mass. It's the fourth game of the season. We're playing Ohio State, a game that has been hyped: Ohio State always the team to beat, upstart Minnesota, Musselman and his junior college recruits, blah, blah.

Turns out, the game is pretty boring—tough, but boring—sloooow, tied 33–33 at the half, the fans still waiting for us to come out and dominate. From my vantage point on the bench, I can see a lot going on—Brewer playing defense on Ohio State's Luke Witte, pushing him. Later, Witte giving Brewer an elbow, Brewer giving him a shove, picking up the foul, Witte and his teammates yukking it up, Brewer complaining. Then at the buzzer, with all of us ready to go into the locker room, Witte (seven feet, 220 pounds, a white guy) crosses in front of Bob Nix (our six-foot-three guard, the only white starter on the team) and punches him right in the face. *Bop!* Nix is so stunned he doesn't know what to do, just puts his hands over his face and walks on, reeling from the blow.

But Behagen and a couple of others including Musselman see the whole thing, and as we descend into the two locker rooms, Behagen screams down the hall at Witte, "Hey, you, motherf___er, I'm going to get you!" A bunch of us have to hold him back. In the locker room, though, the word from Musselman is, "Calm down, calm down." Everyone does, and there's no more said about it.

Back up on the court it's a seesaw game for most of the third and fourth quarters. But now there's a whole lot of banging by both teams. One play, with only a minute or so left, they really chop the ball out of one of our guard's hands, take it downcourt, go up for the lay-up. It's so obvious we're still waiting for the foul to be called, but it isn't.

Then with less than forty seconds left to play it happens again. This time it's Ohio State's Hornyak with the chop, and players fan out on the break, as Witte goes downcourt to take the pass for the lay-up. Two of our guys go up with him. One blocks it and the other bangs the ball and Witte hard. Witte falls back, hits his head on the floor. The foul is called on us, though not a flagrant foul. Witte's still lying on the court, hurt maybe, when Corky Taylor reaches down to give him a hand up. The way Taylor tells it, that's when Witte spits at him. And that's when Taylor lifts him right into a knee in the groin.

All hell breaks lose. I'm on the bench when I see one of their guys grab Brewer from behind while another guy winds up to hit him. In a second, both benches clear, everyone heading for the action. And I'm right there, turn a player around who's about to haul off on one of our men and *boom!* knock him down. In the middle of it all, captured in the photograph that made up most people's minds about the incident, there's Witte down on the floor, Behagen trying to step on Witte's head before someone pulls Behagen from behind.

That's when the fans get into the act, climbing from the stands onto the elevated court. At the same time the Ohio State guys and our guys are running the perimeter of the court just to get *out* of there, all of us by now scared of what happens when 17,000 screaming fans are added to the mix.

I was never so happy to be inside a locker room. The game is forfeited at that point, Minnesota to Ohio State, with thirty-three seconds still left to play.

That night the videotape of the fight is played on virtually every newscast in the country. The next week it's a *Sports Illustrated* cover story. A hell of a way to make national news.

Deserved or not, Minnesota takes virtually all the heat for the incident. Behagen is suspended. Taylor is suspended. And in only my fifth game as a varsity player, I'm told that I'll be starting, that I'll be one of the "Iron Five" who'll play virtually every second of every game for the rest of the season. With two starters gone and his eye on a Big Ten title, Musselman isn't about to make substitutions.

The very next game we travel to Iowa to play the archrival Hawkeyes. The second we hit the floor the fans start booing. Musselman—now quieter and even more intense—tells us to ignore it, to play tough and clean. We have a title to win.

Like all our games it's a tight one—Musselman is so stoked on defense, he never really lets us run on offense—and at one point the ball takes a bounce off the court and four guys, two of ours and two of theirs, go for it. Our guy, Keith Young, gets it and their two guys collide in midair, one of them falling to the floor, *bang!* opening up a gash over one eye. He's lying there holding his face and they blow a time-out.

The fans go crazy booing, then get even crazier when the Iowa trainer holds a towel to the guy's head, wipes up some blood, and holds the towel high like a banner for everyone to see. When he does, everyone in the arena breaks loose, booing even louder and stamping so the whole place is shaking. Finally, the injured guy gets up holding the towel over his eye and walks shakily with the trainer to the bench. Just then, an Iowa fan hurls an ice chunk from the bleachers.

For an instant, it's all I can see, the ice chunk coming through the lights, mesmerizing. Then *wham!* it hits the injured guy right in the forehead over his other eye. More blood. The place goes mad! "You motherf___ers!" they scream at us. "Killers!" And a lot worse. Against all odds, we leave Iowa that night with a win. And that's the way it is, *every* game, *every* week—tense, always with the sense that a fight might break out. The referees are in our faces looking for problems. If you hear the whistle you raise your hand, say "Yes, sir," and go about your business.

Last game of the season we face Purdue on the road. We need the win to clinch the title. We've got a two-point lead and there are maybe fifteen seconds left on the clock. The Boilermakers have the ball out of bounds and Musselman calls a time-out.

"We're supposed to be the best defensive team in the league," he says. "Now's the time to prove it!"

Purdue puts the ball in play, ten seconds, eight . . . one shot, two shots, out of bounds. We're all over them. Six seconds, five . . . another shot off a couple of hands, *still* Purdue ball. Finally, out of desperation they take an eighteen-footer. I watch its arc, know in an instant it'll be off the board. And when it hits, I'm in position, know that no one, but no one can take that rebound away from me. And when the buzzer sounds I've got the ball in both hands, my body covering it, a wide grin on my face. I know I'm going to play professional baseball, but damn, today I'm part of the team that won its first Big Ten title in thirty-seven years—in a year we'd barely make it out of some arenas alive. It felt great. More than great. Fantastic!

THE GAME

In the spring of my junior year in a game against Michigan in thirty-degree weather, I threw a pitch and felt a slight pain, just a twinge. I thought about it for a second, then wound up and threw another. This time it really hurt. Simple as that, I'd damaged tendons around my elbow. As it was, Siebert wasn't too happy that I'd spurned his scholarship for basketball. "You were playing that basketball and traveling when you should have been thinking about baseball. Aaargh! You weren't ready. Aargh! That's what happens." I was out for the season.

To Siebert I was a pitcher. To Jim Dietz I was a baseball player. So when I told him about my sore arm he was unfazed, said I should hustle my tail on up to Fairbanks anyway. We had games to play. That summer I headed north again, but making the flight this time I was not so much awed by the scenery as uncertain about my future. I just didn't know what to expect. I couldn't pitch and was afraid I might have screwed up my chance to play major-league ball. When Jim suggested the outfield, it seemed reasonable enough. As he put it, I had the speed and the agility to cover a lot of territory, the height to catch a lot of balls at the fence, and the arm—when it was healthy—to keep base runners honest. Still, early in the season I was nervous, unsure that I could really help the team.

I wasn't about to let on how worried I was. Instead, whenever anyone, particularly Jim, asked how I was doing, my answer would always be, "Everything's cool." It wasn't *all* bluff, though, and I actually learned something from it—staying calm on the outside helps me relax on the inside.

It helps my performance, too, and can often mislead the opposition.

One day, though, I took being cool a step too far. That summer I earned my keep working with Jim on the stadium grounds, and one morning while mowing the outfield, perched atop the big tractor-mower, I nodded off—fell fast asleep actually, dreaming about the big leagues. Jim was working on the pitcher's mound, as he tells it, when he saw me chugging toward the right-field fence, my head bouncing on my chest. He shouted my name a couple of times, then took off after me, tearing across the infield, and through that deep, deep outfield, huffing and puffing to catch me just as I was about to prove that not only could I cut grass with my eyes closed, but I could drive a tractor over an eight-foot fence without missing the game-winning catch I was making in my dream. Jim got there just in time, turned off the tractor, grabbed me by my shoulders, and shook me awake. I blinked a couple of times, trying to scope out the situation. I was still dazed, but when I saw it was Jim and that I was in the outfield—my new position—I told him what I'd been telling him all summer: "Everything's cool." He still kids me about it.

Jim doesn't play me much the first three games, then late in the fourth game he calls on me to pinch-hit. We're down two runs, the bases are loaded. When the opposing coach sees who's coming to the plate he waves his outfielders in. "This guy's a pitcher," he calls to his man on the mound, "just blow it on by him." That's all I need to hear. First worthwhile pitch I see, I take a tremendous cut and blast it out of the park and onto the roof of a bowling alley across the street.

From then on, I'm in the lineup every day, play in fifty games, go 58 for 184, lead the team with a .315 average. Of those 58 hits, 28 are for extra bases—7 doubles, 6 triples, 15 home runs. Also helping the cause, I score 46 runs, drive in 52, steal 6 bases, and, pitching in relief, strike out 36 batters. At the end of the season I'm selected the team's Most Valuable Player.

Two things that happened that summer—beyond the realization that I didn't have to be a pitcher to be of value to my team—stick in my memory. The first is relatively inconsequential, but taught me something important about myself, nonetheless. Before the season began, Jim asked me to shave my mustache—not because it offended him, but because facial hair was not widely accepted in the major leagues in 1972 and Jim was concerned it would jeopardize my status in the draft. I told him it was part of my Afro-American heritage, but he didn't go for the okeydoke. "You're an exceptional talent," he said, "but until you get where you want to go, you'd better play by their rules." I thought about it long and hard and finally decided to keep the mustache, though neatly trimmed.

The other memorable event of the summer took place on a trip I took with the Goldpanners to Holland where we were matched with teams from all over the world. It was my first time out of the States and what I saw surprised me. I mean, here were people eating eight- or ten-inch-long *eels* they bought from what looked like a hot-dog stand—eating these eels with the heads still on them. People, too, who had a language of their own, yet spoke English as well as anybody on the team. And people who, for the most part, had never seen a guy my size, to whom I was some sort of giant. So I hit a bunch of home runs for them and they just went nuts.

A single moment, though, stands out. We're playing the Cuban team. I'm on second base taking a lead when time is called, and for a few seconds I stop concentrating on the game, take my cap off, stretch, and look at the Dutch signs, the people in the stands, the odd, old buildings that surround the stadium. Then with time back in the Cubans start their chatter—in Spanish, of course—and suddenly it dawns on me, all this foreignness in a *baseball* game, in what I thought was "America's pastime." And for the first time I realize how little I know about the world, how little I've actually experienced. Just then, the pitcher throws to second, and I lunge for the bag, barely making it back. I stand up, dust myself off, mind back on the game, but with a new glimmer of how much I have to learn.

SEASONS: 1973

It's hard to know what makes for a championship team, but whatever that elusive chemistry, Musselman's Musclemen didn't have it in 1973, my senior year and the year following the Ohio State "incident," and our successful capture of the Big Ten title. Still, despite losing our last two games, we were a solid contender, finishing in second place, and were asked to play in the National Invitational Tournament in Madison Square Garden in New York.

Mercifully for me, we lost in the early rounds. Had we done any better I would've had to decide whether to finish out the season as a forward and risk Siebert's wrath, or pitch the varsity baseball opener in Texas. To further complicate matters, I'd been voted captain of the baseball team, a real honor and a confidence builder for a guy who had only played a couple of games the season before. As it was, I had to travel directly from the tournament to Texas where those good ol' Longhorns were waiting for us—me in particular, the only black guy on either team. Believe me, they called me just about everything you can and can't imagine, and on every pitch. It was the only game I lost that year, winning 13 with a 2.74 ERA, and hitting .385 with 33 RBIs.

Following this less than auspicious beginning, we went on to wreak havoc on the rest of the competition, winning the Big Ten title, and traveling to Omaha to play in the College World Series. There we bumped heads with all the contenders, then on that fateful, final day lost one to Arizona State, and we met USC in the championship game, a game I'm certain that everyone involved will always remember.

I'm our number one pitcher and given the start. Three days earlier I'd pitched a nine-inning, 1–0 shutout against Oklahoma, striking out 14. Siebert tells me he's looking for more of the same from me today. For eight full innings I give it to him, holding a USC team that features future major-league all-stars Roy Smalley and Freddy Lynn, Rich Dauer, and Heisman Trophy–winner Anthony Davis to only one hit, with 15 strikeouts. We're ahead 7–0. But I've thrown nearly 140 pitches in those first eight innings and in the bottom of the ninth the Trojans finally get to me for a few hits and a couple of runs. There's one out, two men on, and they bring in a reliever, move me to left field. Fine, I figure, the game's over, we win. Then *boom! boom!* a couple of hits off him, bring in another guy; *boom! boom!* and the next thing you know it's 7–5 with men on, still one out.

Siebert's been thrown out of the game on a blown call at first by now, so George Thomas, the assistant coach, jogs from the dugout to talk to the pitcher. Not much hope there, so the next thing I know he's walking toward me, stops at the front edge of the infield, waves me in, and asks if I can pitch again. I tell him the truth. I've got nothing left. So they put in another reliever, and sure enough, *boom! boom!* the game's over, we lose 8–7. I don't think we even got a second out. Small consolation, I'm named Series MVP.

SUCCESS

In my senior year I'm picked by the San Diego Padres in the first round of the major-league draft as an outfielder; picked by the Atlanta Hawks in the fifth round of the National Basketball Association draft; picked by the Utah Stars in the fourth round of the American Basketball Association draft; and picked by the Minnesota Vikings in the sixteenth round of the National Football League draft, though I'd never played a down of high school or college football in my life.

2

The Middle Game

SEASONS: 1973

My first season as a Padre, we had a pitcher from Mexico named Vicente Romo. He was basically a junkball pitcher, but occasionally he'd blow one by you. Then, just when you figured he'd do it again, he'd offer up one of those off-speed Ephus pitches. You'd swing, miss by a yard, and he'd give you this big old smile like, "I fooled you, no?" Romo didn't speak much English and I didn't speak much Spanish but we got to be buddies, developed this routine. Every day I'd ask him, "Vicente, what kind of stuff you got today?" and he'd look back at me real serious and say, "Hey man, I got NOTTIN'!" Over the years it's stuck, and today all the Yankees know that when I ask what the opposing pitcher has that day, the answer down the bench has to be, "NOTTIN'!" Never give 'em any credit.

"Nottin'" was the operative word that first year for me as a major leaguer. I came to San Diego in June directly from St. Paul on a nottin' contract—as the number four draft pick, I was earning $15,000. There was also a $50,000 signing bonus, but my agent took a piece and the stock market swallowed a bigger chunk. My stocks were blue chippers, only the market took a nosedive and I went down for the count with it.

The Padres were also a nottin' team, with no history, no

credibility. A lot of the players were either too old to be any good or too young to be any good. Not that there weren't a number of guys with impressive ability, but as a team we were always tentative, unsure of ourselves. We weren't playing cohesively, we weren't playing with confidence, we never really thought we would win and we rarely ever did.

Playing half our games in San Diego's Jack Murphy Stadium didn't make it any easier. Here we were a last-place team with a home ballpark big enough to fit another stadium in, with a 17-foot wall 330 feet from home plate at the closest and 420 feet at the farthest. It was a park that had the Dick Allens and the Willie Stargells, the George Fosters and the Greg Luzinskis leaving in tears, as they watched their home-run balls become routine outs or long singles, at best.

We had a good manager, though, in Don Zimmer. He knew his baseball, was a "lead-by-example" guy, always hustling, plugging away, running onto the field, running off the field. He reminded me of a little squirrel out there, chewin' tobacco puffing out his cheek, as he did his thing. Zimmer also loved playing cards and going to the track, and his coaches were the kind of guys who lost their money on the horses and wore scuffed patent-leather shoes with turned-up toes and worn-down heels. That's the way it was in San Diego back then. From coaches to players, money was tight and our game wasn't right.

But Zimmer did the right thing with me. He saved me from the batting coaches who took one look at the hitch in my swing—my starter mechanism—and began salivating at the chance to break me of it. Instead, Zimmer worked on developing my confidence, platooning me primarily against left-handed pitchers and sparing me the Tom Seavers and Bob Gibsons who would try to overpower me, knock me down. Up till then I had never seen certain pitches, a Mike Marshall screwball, say, a Phil Niekro knuckleball, or a Jim Lonborg slider. So I spent a lot of the time in the dugout, watching, taking notes, scouting pitchers, and figuring out strategies to hit them. It was a far cry from the experience of rookies on today's Yankees, where a guy who doesn't perform right away, and consistently, soon finds himself on the shuttle to Columbus, or traded to another team.

The first time I actually take the field as a Padre I'm nervous, scared. Scared, scared, scared. It's a home game against Houston and I'm out there in left field with my newly painted cleats—I had to paint my old white cleats from the university black because the Padres didn't have any size thirteens. Can't be more than 10,000 people in the stadium but I'm still thinking I don't want to embarrass myself. What do I do the first time a ball is hit to me? How *do* you play the outfield? Then Doug Rader drills one over third base and right at me. I run like a madman, scoop it up, and throw a bullet to second. Got him! Ten thousand people cheer and I think, Yeah, that's it! Give the drummer some!

Ninth inning, I come up to bat and I smash the ball between short and third. Rader, at third, dives left, knocks it down, scrambles up, and wheels toward Lee May at first. But I need that hit like a hog needs slop, so I *dive* into the bag, beating Rader's throw. Safe! Right after that we lose the game.

Next day I belt a home run, get three hits. I go on to hit safely in my first six games—lots of rookies have done better, I'm sure. But the local press is so hungry for a hero they go crazy, adding to the hype that had begun long before I'd played in my first game. Cito Gaston, one of my teammates, was amused. "With so much ink," he says, "I expected you to be a white guy." And all the while I'm just scared, thinking, this *is* a whole new ball game. What am I going to do, how am I going to get better, what's it take, whom do I talk to?

My fast start notwithstanding, 1973 was really a nottin' season for me, without a doubt the toughest three months of my life till then. I was living in the Sands Hotel, had nowhere to go, no car, no friends. When we played at home I spent most of my time trying to figure how we got beat over the head that day by the opposition. On the road I thought about the same thing, the only difference being I got to talk it over with my roommate, the batboy, or our Venezuelan shortshop, Enzo Hernandez, who barely spoke English. The team was overstocked with outfielders. Everyone was fighting for a job. And since my contract guaranteed I wouldn't be sent down, at least not that year, I was the heavy, the guy taking someone else's job. Not only that, I was seeing pitches I'd never seen before, I was holding my hands too low at the plate, overstriding, opening up, overswinging, legs all tangled up in the outfield, even dropping a few easy fly balls. Terrible!

My first season in the majors is the last for Juan Marichal, one of my idols. I can't wait to bat against him. But the first time we play the Giants in San Francisco and I face him he's throwing nothing but junk—sidearm, twist, overhand, underhand. I finally manage to chop one over the mound for a single. "Hit the ball, hit the ball!" he yells to me after I'm safe at first. But the man let me down, so I yell back, "Throw the ball, throw the ball! I hit it like you threw it!"

THE ROAD

The Padres finish the 1973 season in the cellar and I figure I can take it easy for a while. Padre management has other ideas. They want me to play winter ball in Mexico. Two of my teammates and new pals, Cito Gaston and Nate Colbert, shudder when I tell them. "Don't go," they insist, "it's terrible down there." So I disappear to St. Paul. But eventually the Padres catch up with me. I answer the wrong phone call and get shipped off to Ciudad Obregon, a small town 25 miles inland from the Gulf of California, some 500 miles south of the border. First taxi I take, there's a tarantula as big as a cat in the middle of the road. We drive over it, straddling it with the tires. I look back and it's gone. I figure it's got to be under the car, soon to make its way up my pants leg.

As for the town itself, let me tell you, this place is rough. Scrawny dogs, donkeys, fleas, *la cucarachas*—you place a call, it never goes through; you send a letter, it never arrives. The "hotel" where they put me up has a night club that features an all-night, loud party—every night. Then at eight in the morning little kids come and bang on my door, "Hey, Winf! Winf!" They're there to see *El Gigante Negro*.

I'm on a team called the Yaquis, named after a local Indian tribe. First day they ask me, *"Primera base?"* and I think they're asking me if I'm married so I say no, which is lucky since they're actually asking if I play first base. So they put me in the outfield, which looks like a minefield after a battle, craters everywhere. Tarantulas patrol the infield. At the stadium in Mazatlan, a rat runs through the dugout and our ageless, hunchbacked batboy, *El Arana*—the spider—goes after it with a bat, flailing away like a madman, banging up the lockers, and just missing a half-dozen players as he careens from wall to wall after the squealing rodent. Finally he traps it in a corner, beats it to death, then holds his bloody, mangled prize up by the tail for us to see. I can't believe this scene.

For entertainment the players favor a few raunchy strip joints where they drink the local beer and watch the local women. With no TV or movies and my Stevie Wonder tape worn out, I sometimes go along. At the clubs, the women come out on a little runway, sing a little song, strip, then dance little circles around the men who are down on their knees, wagging their tongues up at them, going crazy. Those who go too crazy, begin to touch and grab, are escorted from the club to the one-room hut down the block they called the police station. Come the weekend, when things really got rowdy at the station, the *rurales* wade in with their billy clubs and you can hear the walls banging *boom! boom! boom!* and the drunks and rowdies crying out in pain.

As for winter ball as a learning experience, the Mexican pitchers threw primarily junk—spitballs, sidearm, screwballs. Junk and more junk. Marichal and my pal Vicente had nothing on these guys. Rarely, in any event, did I see the kind of pitching I'd faced in the majors, the type I had to learn to hit. Also, the Yaqui fans got it in their heads that *El Gigante Negro* should be their home-run king. When I wasn't—wasn't hitting at all—they got pissed and rattled the chicken wire separating them from the field. Or they'd throw bottles and vegetables at me, and anyone else they'd lost patience with. They liked my defensive play, though. I managed some spectacular catches in the outfield, climbing cyclone fences to steal home runs, stuff like that.

But I was getting fed up with my whole south-of-the-border adventure—the all-night party downstairs, the strip joints, the funky fields, the unhittable pitchers, the overly

demonstrative fans, the language barrier, fouled-up communications with home, no girlfriend, and those hot, hot
afternoons. Besides, I'd been playing baseball virtually every
day for over a year. I needed some time off.

Six weeks into my Mexico stay the Yaquis are playing
in the town of Los Mochis. Earlier that morning I'd come
down with my first full-blown case of *turista*, so I'm a
little tentative taking the field, concerned I may have to
make a run for it at any moment. Still, playing left field
in the eighth inning I pull a home-run ball down from
about ten feet in the air to retire the side, act like it's
nothing, flip the ball behind my back to the pitcher's
mound. The fans go wild.

Next inning I single, steal second on a hit-and-run, see the
ball trickle into center, make a run for third, and dive in
headfirst to knock the ball out of the third baseman's hands.
When I do, he drops a knee on me. I jump up and we hook
a couple of times, end up rolling around on the ground until
the umpire breaks us up. I'm safe at third, I'm filthy, my
uniform's ripped, my gut is churning, it's hot, I'm mad.
Next play we try a suicide squeeze, I'm going, but the batter
misses the bunt, and suddenly I'm in a rundown, back and
forth about six times. Finally, I give a stutter step, fake out
the third baseman, dive back safely to the bag. But no, I'm
called out. Now I'm really mad. I'm screaming all over the
umpire. The third baseman's screaming too, the fans are
screaming, we're all screaming, a stadium full of people
yelling their lungs out in Spanish while I uselessly argue my
case in English. In the heat of it I suddenly realize, "Hey,
I'm through with Mexico! Later for this bulls___!"

Walking off the field, already outta here, two things
happen. Somebody in the crowd throws a bottle and *wop!*
it hits the third-base umpire on the head. He's down like
a fallen statue. It's the signal the fans have been waiting

for. Now they throw everything. Apples, oranges, toma-
toes, burritos, a big bouquet of the overripe and the
underdone. I'm walking to the dugout muttering, "F__
you all, I don't want to be here," when suddenly a guy
throws his beer through the chicken wire and right into
my face. It sets me off like a madman. "AHHHHH! I'll
kill you!" I scream, shaking the fence, clawing at the
wire, wanting at this guy, wanting at them all, unaware
that here I am a grown, intelligent man trying to rip my
way through some chicken wire to get at 10,000 people
who, if I did, would tear me limb from limb.

It probably would have happened, too, if I didn't realize
halfway up the chicken wire that I'd pulled a hamstring in
the rundown. So I let myself down gently, decide in a
moment of clarity simply to tell management that afternoon
of my decision to leave. But they beat me to it. The second
I mention the hamstring they tell me they can do without
an injured rookie who's also not hitting—I'm cut. "All
right," I say, trying to salvage some dignity, "then send me
home." "You want to go to Mexico City?" they ask. "No,"
I insist. "Home. All the way home. Minnesota." My winter
in Mexico is over. Talk about a reprieve. Freedom! It felt
great.

LESSONS

In March 1974 I drive to Yuma, Arizona, for my first spring
training, one of thirteen outfielders trying to make the team.
My name isn't high on the list. But I'd worked out all winter
following the Mexican fiasco, am in great shape when I

arrive, and do all they ask. Every day I check the board to see who's made the team, who's being called into the little room. I beat every cut.

Then on one of the last days of spring training we're playing Cleveland in Yuma, one out in the bottom of the ninth, the Padres are losing by three, bases loaded, and John McNamara, the new manager, calls on me to pinch-hit. I'm not really a pinch hitter, but thinking back on my pinch-hit homer in Alaska, *bam!* I drive a double into the gap in right center, clear the bases, tie the score. Next batter hits a ground ball between short and third. The outfield's way in, I get the stop sign as I round third, but I think, Hell, no! I've got a team to make. The catcher's straddling the base path, the ball's on its way into his glove, but the way I see it I'm destined to score. I slam into the catcher, he drops the ball, the game's over, we win. And I'm a Padre.

Of course, it wasn't as easy as all that, even playing for a last-place team. There were a lot of things I had to learn. The most basic was having to play when people were watching, which is what the business of professional sports is all about. Club owners need an audience to realize a return on their investment, and are less concerned with how well you play than how well you play in front of a crowd. Some guys play great college or minor-league ball for the few thousand spectators that show up. But put them in front of 20,000 fans day in and day out, or on national TV, and they can't hack the pressure. I learned how to hack it largely by ignoring the fans, ignoring the press, not reading stories about me, good or bad, and focusing my intensity on the game. Then, as I became more at ease, I started playing *to* the fans, just as I'd done in high school and college. No player, I found, no matter how intense, can ignore the fans forever. It's just human to want to know where you stand. It's like New

York's mayor, Ed Koch, roaming the streets of Manhattan asking the crowds, "How'm I doin'?"

A second thing I had to develop as a pro was the mental toughness to play a 162-game season, virtually a game a day for a full half year. And for a pro, it's not really a game. Every time you take the field it's serious business. Your job is on the line, your reputation, your future. You're out there every day against pitchers who are thinking, not just throwing. So you can't go up there just swinging. And good defensive play takes a lot more than a natural athlete with good instincts. Add to that travel, interviews, distractions, squabbles, different surfaces, weather, injuries, and there's no way you can do well without putting yourself on a rigorous mental regimen—a plan for the brain that only allows certain things in at certain times. I was fortunate to have a head start on some of the players, by having Ma to use as a model for mental toughness. And later, an exceptional man named Al Frohman.

The bitterest lesson of all for me to swallow—there were lots of players better than I was. Sure, on a given day I might make that monster catch, or hit that game winner. But what I saw when I looked at the players I respected was *consistency*. And I knew to develop *that*, to maximize my abilities, would mean I'd really have to work on the fundamentals— the right way to hit, field, run, and think—and to incorporate them into a style that took into account my personal strengths, quirks, and weaknesses as a player.

For some, it never happens. I see players every day— especially during spring training—with tremendous amounts of ability. But a lot of them never seem to get the technical stuff down to do it right again and again.

My first year on the Padres there weren't a lot of coaches with the time or inclination to work with me on the basics and even fewer players to model myself after. So I ended up watching players on other clubs to see what they were doing, and talking to them about the game when I could. I'd watch the Chicago Cubs' Billy Williams, for example, a smart hitter, a great clutch hitter. Pittsburgh's Richie Zisk, too. Not a big, big name, but he was big and strong, hit for power, and put up some impressive numbers. So I analyzed his swing, broke it down into its component parts, tried to incorporate it into my style.

Another player I'd look to was Dick Allen, the Philadelphia Phillies' first baseman. He was a relatively small, muscular man who regularly hit them in the upper deck in San Diego. Hall of Fame hitting ability. What interested me the most about him, though, was that his swing had a starter mechanism built into it even more pronounced than mine. As the pitcher began his motion, Allen would tip the head of the bat forward, then whip it back and forward again for extra momentum to crush the ball. Whenever we played the Phillies I always hit a lot of singles, and Allen would talk to me at first base. "You're getting to be a pretty good hitter, man," he'd say. I felt terrific that someone as good as he was would even notice. As for advice, he once told me, "When they finally pay you, buy yourself some property."

Tony Perez was another hitter I tried to model myself after, a dogged, clutch hitter. They even called him "Doggie," as a matter of fact. Put Tony up with a man on first, and he was dangerous. Dangerous. Year after year he drove in dozens of runs, scored dozens more. I used to kid him, "I'm going to drive in more runs than you this year, maybe even hit more homers." And he'd come back with that deep Cuban accent, "No way! You can't get me, man." He was right.

And then there was Joe Morgan. First time I ever saw him we were in Cincinnati, and here's this little, cocky guy, five foot seven, strutting along, carrying a glove the size of my hand. He walks by and says, "Hey, mullion!" I look him over. Thing is, I'd always followed the American League, don't even know who he is, don't know he's one of the greatest hitters of all time, Hall of Fame second baseman, puts numbers up there I may never reach. Also, I don't know what "mullion" means, and think to myself, Who's this little dude talking this trash to me, "Hey, mullion"? Later, after he feasts on our pitching and sucks up balls in the infield I find out who Joe Morgan is. And I find out that "mullion" is what old-time ballplayers call an unattractive woman, or an unattractive anybody, especially a rookie. The only thing lower is a scullion. Over the years I'd watch Morgan for his smoothness at the plate, his confident, chicken-wing flap of the arm as he stepped in, his consistency, his intelligence for the game, and to marvel at how he'd pepper the entire field with his hits. You never knew where Morgan would go. A perfect example of the "small package" theory.

Another one of the Reds I'd study was Pete Rose, a true hitting machine. And no one ever to play the game was more intense than Charlie Hustle. When Pete Rose stopped your rally to end an inning, he didn't just toss the ball to the mound. He drilled it into the ground like "Take that, motherf___er!" His son, Petey, who's been in locker rooms from the day he could walk, is a chip off the old block.

Not only would I take lessons from how these guys played the game, I'd also check out their gloves and bats. My initial bat philosophy was to go the way of the Pittsburgh Lumber Company, Willie Stargell and his pals—find a big heavy bat and bludgeon the ball all over the park. Hard line drives. "The bigger the bat, the harder the hit," was the theory. Hey, a pitcher from the Midwest, corn in my ears, what do I know? So I started out with a 36-ounce bat, 36 inches long. Trouble was, I couldn't get around on the ball. Major-league pitchers were just too smart and too fast for a guy trying to take them on with a small tree.

So I began my informal study. Joe Morgan, I found, used

a small bat. Tony Perez, a thin handle. And over the years as I continued my bat check, I saw George Hendrick hit them into the upper deck in St. Louis with a 31-ounce, 33-inch bat. And saw George Foster hit 40 home runs with a thin handle. I experimented and finally settled on a 34-ounce, 35.5-inch bat, aware that as I got older and lost some strength or quickness I might have to go to an even shorter, lighter bat. Or finish out my career like George "Boomer" Scott, who had to turn in his ticket when he couldn't bring that heavy old club around anymore. Or like my old Padre teammate, Nate Colbert, I love him but he phased out when he no longer could hit a curveball; though in Nate's case it might have been all that scotch, the Cutty, "the ship" he'd call it, together with all those chocolate-chip cookies.

One teaching tool that the Padres certainly could have used was video, and I suggested it early on because we'd used it a little at the U. They didn't get it until my fourth year, and in retrospect, I know that even then they used it incorrectly. Inevitably, what coaches would stress when we watched tapes was what we were doing *wrong,* rather than what we were doing right. Sure, it's instructional to see what you're doing when you're *not* hitting well. But 90 percent of the tape you watch should be of the times you're doing it right in order to train your body and your mind to make hitting correctly a reflex action. A couple of years ago George Steinbrenner ordered our video coordinator to assemble all the Yankee defensive bloopers from the previous season on one tape and show it in the locker room. He had it shown once, then again, then over and over—so we'd never make the same mistake again, he claimed. And all the time I'm thinking, Talk about a guy who's going about this the wrong way.

Actually, my first exposure to videotape as a teaching tool wasn't with the Padres but in Bill Allen's backyard. Bill was a San Diego policeman who'd never been a coach or a player, but he knew as much about hitting as any guy I'd met till then. Not only did he have video equipment way back in the early seventies when it was terrifically expensive and almost unheard of, he had tons of books and hitting diagrams, plus a batting cage. During the off-season I'd often go over to his place and work with him on hitting techniques. Using video, I'd watch tapes of other players, watch them in stop-motion to see how they held the bat, the angle of their body, hip placement, how they used their legs. I'd watch Reggie Jackson's leg stride, Hank Aaron's wrists and hands, and a dozen other players.

Bill was fairly fanatical about his methods, which put me off, but I learned a number of things from him that enabled me to hit with more power, drive the ball to right with more authority, and bring out more of my ability. One important thing I learned was that all good hitters, whatever their stance or swing, arrive at roughly the same position when they make contact with the ball. Another was to wait to roll my wrists until after I made contact, as I followed through, and then use my right hand on the bat like a karate blow—*biff!* you just punch it on through.

I wasn't Allen's only "project." He worked with lots of guys, Gene Tenace, Ozzie Smith, others. Sad thing was that with all the help he gave us he was really counting on the Padres or some other team to make him a hitting coach. But baseball is really a private club and with his limited experience, no one would hire him. So on his birthday, sitting at home on the couch, he killed himself, blew his brains out with his service revolver. It's a story that in the movies would have had exactly the opposite ending, with Bill going on to manage a major-league team to victory in the World Series. In real life, though, Bill became one of the fatalities of the sport—the guy who for one reason or another didn't make it, and couldn't take it.

While I was able to use video to improve my hitting, I quickly found that the only way to improve as an outfielder was to go out there and *practice* it. And then practice it again. Show up at the stadium a couple of hours early, practice playing the corners, the alleys, the warning track, the wall, practice hitting the cutoff man, working with the other fielders, backing them up, learn who'd make the call, who was in charge. When my teammates took batting practice, I'd take my defensive position for extra fielding.

To master Jack Murphy Stadium's seventeen-foot killer wall, I'd have coaches hit line drives by me that I'd play off the padded and unpadded sections of the wall to see how hard and how far the ball would bounce in any given situation, to check its trajectory. The trick was to hold anything off that wall to no more than a double and quite often a single. A misplay in that huge outfield would result in a certain triple or an inside-the-park home run.

During those early years I had my share of embarrassments. In a game against the Dodgers, Willie Davis is on first, a ground ball is hit to me in left field and Davis scoots like a rabbit to second, rounding the base like he's going for third. I watch him as he does, take my eye off the ball, it bounces off my glove, and now he heads for third in earnest. I finally field the ball, make the throw to third, allowing the hitter to advance to second. Everyone's safe.

Another time we're playing the Mets in San Diego and Ed Kranepool socks one to left. I'm running into the left center field alley for it, it slices back toward me, my feet get tangled, I fall on the warning track, and the ball barely misses conking me on the head as I go down. Kranepool's safe at third.

Of those early embarrassments the most memorable occurs my first season. We're playing Cincinnati and Derrel Thomas, a utility player, is in the Padre lineup that day at shortstop. Derrel was a real style master. When he played center field he'd run the ball down with the best of them, get there, pat his left hip a couple of times with his glove, make a basket catch, throw the ball, look around, and just wait for the applause. Mr. Style, with his tinted glasses, immaculate uniform; a skinny guy, six foot one, 165 pounds or so. Anyway, it rains the day before the game, the field's a little wet, and I'm playing center. There's a man on second and a ground ball up the middle. Derrel's the cutoff man. Fresh out of college where everything's do or die, I'm determined to make the play, stop the guy on second from scoring. So I charge toward the infield, scoop up the ball, knowing I've got the arm to make the throw to the catcher without a cutoff man. Derrel sees what I'm up to and drops down out of my way about 40 feet in front of me just as I let fly with this great bullet throw, and then slip on a muddy patch in the outfield. Next thing I know the ball hits Derrel right in the butt and sticks there between his cheeks like a bumble bee. He squirms around for a couple of seconds, then jumps up, pulls it off, drops his glove, and does a quick dance around the infield, obviously hurting, obviously okay. The guys on the Cincinnati bench laugh themselves silly.

I'd finish out that year with the most outfield errors in the league. Yes, I have an asterisk next to my name in the record books on the negative side. But gradually as the season drew on I began getting the hang of it. Not long after I stung Derrel, the Pirates come to town and Willie Stargell, who always hit these amazing blasts—400-foot drives, not arcing flies, but line drives 60 feet in the air—hits one deep into center off the wall. *Wham, chip!* It takes a piece off the wall and bounces back. I grab it, fire it to second. And there's Willie on first, shaking his fist at me.

Maybe it's still the pitcher in me, but I love firing bullets from the outfield. I see a guy trying to score and I throw a perfect shot—the catcher's there waiting for him. And after the guy gets up, dusts himself off, nine times out of ten he'll glare back at me. Great feeling.

One pro I really learned from during those early years *was* a Padre—Willie McCovey, one of the greatest ballplayers I've ever played with, one of the greatest guys I ever met. There was something special about Willie, and it went beyond baseball. He was dignified, quiet, easygoing, a truly generous human being. I'm not sure why, but the year he came to the Padres he took me under his wing. Once in a while in the evening Willie and I would go out together. We'd talk a little baseball, a little this, a little that. He turned me on to some of his favorites—a Tia Maria and coffee concoction, macadamia nuts by the canful, and his absolute favorite, black-bottom pie. I'll always remember those nights on the road when Willie would turn to me with a wicked gleam in his eye and say, "You know, big guy, right now I'd *kill* for some black-bottom pie."

Willie saved his murderous impulses for the diamond, though. One day he was at bat and I was on deck. I can't remember who we were playing but they were playing him where they almost always did—deep. So Willie took a monster cut to make sure they'd stay there, then laid down a perfect bunt, to get himself on base. "I did it so you could knock me in," he told me later. I did, and learned as much about strategy in that moment as I had in the twenty-one years preceding it.

BOSSES

When I joined the Padres they belonged to C. Arnholt Smith, the first of the unpredictable owners, which is the only kind I seem to get. C. Arnholt Smith wrote the Padres' payroll checks on the U.S. National Bank of San Diego, which he also owned and where I had my account. Then the bank failed! C. Arnholt Smith is paying my salary with checks drawn on a dying bank, and I'm pouring the money right back down the drain. Luckily the Crocker Bank took over U.S. National and my money was safe. But it was quite a shock, and it was part of the reason why the Padres were sold to Ray Kroc, the McDonald's hamburger king, in 1974. He brought financial stability. He also made the team a family operation, naming his wife, Joan, to the board of directors, and his son-in-law, Ballard Smith, president. The hope was that with new ownership things would change, and sure enough, right away we got new uniforms, going from the old, tired Padre yellow to a dazzling white trimmed with yellow and brown stripes.

On opening day, all decked out in our new threads, we were down 9–5 in the eighth when we got our first taste of Ray Kroc's ownership style. He commandeered the PA system microphone and chewed us out—his new acquisition—for all of San Diego Stadium to hear. "I've never," he concluded—right before a streaker zipped across the infield—"I've never seen such stupid ballplaying in all my life." And I thought, Oh, oh, there's trouble on the horizon. A number of the players came down on him, the Players Association came down on him, and the commissioner fined him. What I had no way of knowing, of course, was that Kroc's performance was only a humble dress rehearsal for the ownership I was yet to experience.

THE GAME

The best thing happening with the Padres in the mid-seventies was the San Diego Chicken, a guy dressed in a chicken suit who'd come to the games to spice things up. A number of other teams had mascots, but the chicken was Grade AAA. He'd worked up a terrific act; among other things, running on the field between pitches, wearing a trenchcoat over his chicken suit and puffing on a big cigar, and dropping money on the turf for the umpire, like, "Let me buy you off."

Initially, the chicken was sponsored by a San Diego radio station, but when they thought he was getting too big for his wings, using the act to make money on his own, they decided to clip them, take away his chicken suit. He sued and the judge told him he'd have to redesign his suit if he wanted to remain a chicken. Next time he showed up at the stadium it was in a big egg in a nest atop an armored truck, while the PA blared the music from *2001: A Space Odyssey*. The lights went out, then on again, and he emerged out of the egg in a new chicken suit to a burst of fireworks and applause, born again. He left the game in a limo, a walking stick in his claw, a blond under each wing.

As for the Padres, in the mid-seventies winning was more the exception than the rule. We always played below .500 ball, never threatened to win a pennant, never had a "critical" game after opening day. So though I always played to win, I found—like many young players on losing teams—that I was often playing more to improve, to impress the scouts on the winning teams so that someday they'd consider me in a trade, to put myself in a better bargaining position for my next contract, and to make the All-Star team. Playing, too, in San Diego—millions of miles away from where the national press was based—I often felt I was playing in a vacuum. On Sundays I'd always check the paper to see where I was in the National League standings. Halfway up, I'd see, and my goal for the next week was to inch up a little higher.

But you can't play only for yourself. I wanted what I did, what my team did, to *matter*. So I decided if the Padres weren't going to win the National League West, we'd sure as hell be a force to be contended with, if only as division spoilers. It gave me something extra to play for, especially when we played Los Angeles, who won the division more often than not and never showed us any respect, making us the Rodney Dangerfields of baseball. The Dodger who rubbed our noses in it the most was their right fielder, Willie Crawford, a tough guy with a wad of tobacco in his mouth, who'd always tell me, "We're gonna kick Padre ass today!" I remember once L.A. came to San Diego needing a three-game sweep to make the playoffs and Crawford said to me, "Hey man, why don't you guys take it easy?" So I joked, "How about it, Willie, you gonna give us some of that playoff money?" Willie used the turf between us as his spittoon. "No? Well, later for you!" That day we kicked Dodger ass.

Managing the Padres from '74 through part of '77 was John McNamara, a quiet, thoughtful man you could really talk to. He used to walk around the field with a fungo bat in his hand while we were practicing—walk around the infield, the outfield, talk to all his players. He'd ask you how your family was, how you felt, and what you were thinking. He'd point out any problems with your play, suggest things you might need to work on. But mostly he'd emphasize what you were doing right. It instilled confidence, and even through those lean years, it made me feel good to be playing for him.

McNamara also hated for his people to be taken advantage of, and was always willing to put himself on the line in their defense. Once I was at bat with a man on first and got the signal to bunt to advance the runner. I made contact, but the ball bounced off home plate and went foul. The catcher grabbed it, jumped into fair territory, threw down to second for the force, then the second baseman threw to first. The umpire called it a double play. McNamara was on the field in a flash, chin-to-chin with the man in blue until he was thrown out of the game. On his way out he grabbed a bag of balls and threw them out onto the field. As the young player whose errant bunt started it all, I felt here was a guy I could count on to support me. It made me feel far less alone out there, more inclined to take a chance to make things happen.

I played the first half of the 1974 season as a part-timer, an "irregular" as we were called. But after the All-Star break McNamara said to me, "Kid, I'm going to give you a chance to play every day. Play well and the job is yours."

It was the chance I'd been waiting for. And I sure as hell was going to take advantage of it, no matter what. But right about then an odd thing happened. A guy I once played ball with at the university had recently come from Minneapolis and told me that the woman I'd been dating seriously before I left was going out with another guy, a football player on the Vikings. And though we'd made no promises to each other, I felt deflated, and jealous. I thought about calling her to ask if it were true, but realized it wasn't any of my business. So I ended up staying jealous and distracted. It lasted over a month, affecting my game and cutting down on my concentration. Finally, I just said, "Later for this. I'm on my own down here, I'll figure things out for myself, I'll hang in there and just play as well as I can." I hung in there well enough that year to keep my spot on the roster, batting

.265 in 145 games, with 20 home runs. Only McCovey hit more.

In '75 the Padres started strong and I rode the tide with them, batting .338 by the end of April with 6 home runs. Too many times, though, I got my hits without men on base and would finish out the inning on first or second—no runs, one hit, one man left.

But that was only part of the pain of those years. One day in the early summer of '75 we're playing Montreal and as I slide into second to break up a double play I'm hit in the right wrist with a ball thrown by the Expos' shortstop, Tim Foli. No doubt in my mind, Foli is trying to get back at me for flipping him over on a slide into second a couple of days before. Right away, I know I'm hurt, know it's something I can't just rub off. I end up sitting out eleven games, wanting to play so badly that I put myself back in the lineup still hurting. A few games later I take it on the other wrist from a Charlie Hough pitch in L.A. It clears the benches.

Similar thing happened the previous time I was hit by a pitch in L.A., the year before. But back then I was already in the trainer's room, ice pack on my wrist, listening to the game on radio, when our pitcher, Bill Greif, played Willie Crawford some chin music of his own. "Willie is going wild," the announcer said. "He's charging the mound." I threw off my pack, ran through the clubhouse, the hallway, around the corner, down the runway, up into the dugout, and out onto the field, just as L.A.'s Joe Ferguson dove on top of a huge pile of Dodger and Padre bodies. Slowly, he sifted down to the bottom. All I could see was arms. Off to the side Davey Lopes was itching to get into the fight but was being held back by the batboy. Suddenly, the fight cancels itself out. Everyone gets up from the pile, leaving only Ferguson on the turf, grass stains all over, shirt pulled inside out over his head. You could tell something was wrong. Finally Ferguson stood up, looked around, then muttered, "Oh, shit," and crumpled back to the ground. He'd broken his right forearm.

The mid-seventies Padres had a few bright spots, though, and one of the brightest was Randy Jones, who in 1975 started pitching like he was Cy Young. Here was a guy who'd lost 20 games the previous year with an ERA of 4.46, then did a complete reversal to win 20 games the next with an ERA of 2.24, the lowest in the National League. The San Diego Stopper! It was great watching him work from my vantage point in the outfield. He'd changed his fingering a tiny bit from the year before, as well as his arm angle and pushoff, which caused the bottom to drop out of the ball. It was so effective it looked downright illegal. Even the best hitters were confused. Randy would throw Pete Rose his sinker and Pete's hands would just about fall off. Pete got so flustered he finally gave up trying to hit Randy right-handed. But when he faced him left-handed, Jonesy punched him out with a wicked hook. Next season Randy went on to win the Cy Young Award with 22 wins and a 2.74 ERA. But he never missed a start, pitching over 300 innings—my guess is he was actually being paid by the inning—injured his arm, and was never quite the same after that.

Another interesting case study was Tito Fuentes, not only for his play at second base, but for his unique rituals. He was originally from Cuba and believed in voodoo. He wore lots of jewelry, lots of charms, and painted all manner of Christian, Hebrew, and generic symbols on his chest. Every game before he put on his uniform, he'd stencil a cross on his head with some flour, right in his thick, black hair. It was like the police painting numbers on the tops of patrol cars, so they can be spotted from the air. I guess that Tito wanted to make sure that if God were going by in a whirlybird, he'd know Tito was on his team. While God watched out for Tito well enough, Tito watched out for himself even better. As a second baseman he had one credo—never stand in when they're trying to break up the double play. "You never get me, man," he'd say. Yet he turned the double play as good as anyone, got rid of the ball real quickly, then dodged, ducked, or jumped out of harm's way.

By 1976 things started looking up for me. We opened against L.A.—our first meeting since the time Hough nicked me in the wrist—and I hit a grand slam to win the game before the largest opening crowd ever in Dodger Stadium. Next day, I homered again. A few days later against Montreal, I hit another, then set up a winning rally with an infield hit and a stolen base. Against the Mets I hit a two-run homer to break Tom Seaver's eight-game winning streak against us, and by May I was leading the team in runs scored, home runs, RBIs, walks, and stolen bases. Still, other teams were convinced I was playing over my head so they'd pitch around Willie McCovey to get to me and I'd accommodate them time and again by hitting game winners.

I was also finally getting the hang of the outfield. I was leaping to make monster catches against the wall, diving for balls to keep them from dropping short, and throwing bullets to the infield. Runners rarely challenged my arm.

That year, too, it appeared that things might be looking up for the Padres. We picked up some players with a history of getting on base—Doug Rader from the Astros, and Willie Davis who'd played most of his career on the Dodgers. Roger Craig also came on board as a pitching coach.

Rader—the guy whose throw I beat out for my first major-league hit, and whose potential double into the bullpen was my first putout as a Padre outfielder—was a fine third baseman, a former Gold Glove winner, a regular vacuum cleaner out there with very quick hands. Trouble was he was also a wild man, a real drinker and carouser who loved to be loud and goad his teammates, me especially. And a lot of it was more than just good-natured kidding. One day I was in the training room reading the *Wall Street Journal* and he looked over my shoulder and said, "Hey, Winnie, what ya doing with that? There's no pictures in it." Yuk, yuk. Then a few days after "Roots" was on the tube, Rader started ragging me while I was sitting at my locker. "Hey, Kunta!" he yelled, "Hey, Kunta Kinte!" Enough. I jumped up and glared at him. He glared back, and in that moment I realized that Rader was one of those guys who'd get into a fight and not care what he looked like when it was over. And I was one of those guys who did. But I had a few inches on him and plenty of aggression built up inside, so looking down on him as menacingly as I could I said, "Listen, I never want to hear this s___ from you again!" I never did.

Another guy on the team about that time who loved to get on my case was Dave Freisleben, "Freisey." He was a so-so pitcher with a good curve who managed to squeeze out ten wins in his best year with the Padres. Still, whenever I'd miss a game—which was rarely—Freisey figured I was doggin' it, hiding from the opposition. But rather than accuse me of hiding, he'd suggest I was suffering from a disease. "Winnie, you got Seaveritis today?" Or "a case of Carletonitis," or "Gibsonitis." After hearing this a half-dozen times I finally told him, "You know, I've never seen anyone come down with Freislebenitis. They get up out of their wheel chairs and run to home plate for a shot at you."

By 1977 McCovey was gone, and so were Fuentes and Willie Davis. New on the roster were reliever Rollie Fingers, catcher Gene Tenace, and George Hendrick, an outfielder. The guard was changing, and along with Randy Jones I was just about the only player left on the roster from the team I joined five years before, for better or for worse.

For better, I'll always remember Rollie's first year with
the Padres. He and Randy Jones were two of a kind, pure
"country." They were always playing those sad ol' songs on
their tape players. I used to kid them on the team bus, "My
dog died, my tractor broke." Then Rollie found himself an
Emotions tape, played it for Randy, and the two of them
never set their ears on country again.

Gene Tenace, another former member of the disassem-
bled World Champion Oakland A's, was brought on board
to shore up our hitting. More than hitting, though, Tenace
liked his walks. He would take everything—bases loaded,
men on second and third, no outs, two outs, it didn't matter.
The only way you could get Gene to swing was to throw
into what he called his "itty-bitty box." "Hey, man," he
would say, "that man is going to have to come to old Gino
here, going to have to throw into this itty-bitty box . . . and
then, *bam!* I got him!"

If Gene was the kind of guy who liked to talk about his
game, George Hendrick was his opposite number, a big bat
from Cleveland who never talked to anyone, especially the
press—the Steve Carlton of the outfield. When the Padres
told him that he had to make two appearances for the team
as part of his contract or be fined $500, George said, "You
want cash, check, or money order?" I remember one hot and
miserable day we were in St. Louis—the heat rising in waves
off the Astroturf—and after the game the press came to the
clubhouse to interview George. "Ha!" he told them. "Don't
you know I don't talk to reporters?" Next day the front page
of the sports section carried a banner headline: "Interview
with George Hendrick." So I checked it out, as curious as
anyone about this journalistic first, and there it was, only a
single quote of George's in the entire two-page article: "Ha!
Don't you know I don't talk to reporters?"

In May of that year with a record of 20 wins and 28 losses,
John McNamara gets his walking papers. We're managed

for a single game by Bob Skinner, and then Alvin Dark takes over for the rest of the season. And believe me, Dark takes over. He calls every pitch his pitchers throw, wants to be the defensive instructor, tries to control every aspect of the game. Worst of all, he's always calling signals, driving everyone crazy, taking away everyone's initiative.

This goes on for a couple of months when in a game with the Mets with Jerry Koosman on the mound, I'm on first and Dark gives me the one-way lead and steal signal. This is a kamikaze steal used against a left-handed pitcher with a good move—the second he commits to it, just begins to lift his leg, any movement, you go! It's a low-percentage steal and I never liked it. Anyway Dark gives me the signal, Koosman makes his move, I take off, and Koosman throws a bullet to first. Next thing I know I'm in a rundown, with no chance of avoiding the tag. I come back to the dugout fuming. "One-way lead and steal, my ass!" I say, kicking over the trainer's kit. Band-Aids, pills, scissors, and salves fly everywhere. You could have cooked on my forehead after that for the rest of the game. Next day I tell Dark no more one-way lead and steals. "You can signal all you want. I'm not going anywhere."

This whole business with signals is pretty crazy stuff. It's like the CIA. The opposing team has a guy in their dugout trying to decode your signals, and you've got a guy trying to decode theirs. When they break your code, you've got to change your signals. Some seasons you end up changing them ten times or more. Sometimes they're changed a few minutes before a game, which is when things can really get screwed up. One of the years that Billy Martin was managing the Yankees he made a last-minute change in the squeeze bunt signal. The squeeze would now be on when Martin leaned on the post next to the dugout. Billy forgot, though, because late in the game he accidentally leaned on the post just as the pitcher went into his motion. The third-base coach, Don Zimmer, gave the signal, the batter never saw it, the runner did and ran. He never had a chance. The dust hadn't even cleared before Billy went bananas, screaming and cussing, until Zim told him what he had done. As it is, the squeeze is such a complicated play, depending on split-second timing and the intricate exchange of signals—the opposition's always looking for it, waiting for the sign so they can call a pitchout—that 50 percent of the time it's blown anyway. And to call it by accident . . . it was just too much for Billy to bear.

SUCCESS

The most exciting thing that happened to me in 1977 was playing in my first All-Star Game. I wasn't selected on the ballot, but was picked as a reserve, though that was good enough for me. The game was played in Yankee Stadium, and I'll admit, after listening to all those games on the radio as a kid, I was in awe of the place. Yankee Stadium! Hard for me to believe that I was finally on my way there to play with the very best in the game. Next thing I knew I'd be suiting up alongside the famed Pete Rose, or Steve Carlton.

And I was, signing baseballs, a hundred or more, with Rose, and Joe Morgan, and all the other National League all-stars. The atmosphere in the clubhouse was charged. Dozens of stories were blowing in the wind. How one guy threw a pitch so hard no one could see it. Or how some other guy put bubble bath in the whirlpool. Or what a crazy thing so-and-so's manager did. Or how Luis Tiant, "Roller 'Rilla," would zip around Yankee Stadium on roller skates.

Being my first year, I had no way of knowing that these were the same stories that were swapped at every All-Star Game—in both the National and American League locker rooms. And that there were always first-timers like myself in awe of the established all-stars—young guys full of enthusiasm, who play against you all the time, but think it's terrific just to suit up next to you. "Hey, Big D, good to see you, man. This the bat you use? Oh, man, no wonder you hit that ball so hard. This the glove . . . ?"

Sitting there, taking it all in, you realize, whether you're from Montreal or Houston, you all enjoy the same excitement, the same trials and tribulations, the mishaps, the craziness. And suddenly—it just sneaks up on you—there's a transformation. You're not just a bunch of guys, you're a *team!* And you think that as a team you'd dominate the league, *dominate.* But today there's only one opponent to focus on, so as game time draws near you gather what strength and cohesiveness you can to take them on. You check their lineup, you check your own. You figure you've got it—the speed, the power, the pitching. No way could you lose. Only trouble is, the guys in the other clubhouse feel the same way.

Also common to both clubhouses is that just about everyone is being tended to by one of the trainers the league selects for the game. Wrists are being taped, ankles, thighs, calves. I'd never seen so much tape in a baseball locker room. Seems that the better the ballplayer, the more tape he uses, the more likely he plays in some kind of pain. On the field everyone looks great, but there's always something taped and bandaged under that uniform at the All-Star Game that you can't see.

As for who ends up on the team, as everyone knows, it's not necessarily the guy having the best year in that position—although he'll generally be having a good year. More often it's the guy the fans most want to see—given the choice between Eddie Murray and Joe Blow, they'll go for Eddie, even if he's batting 20 percentage points lower. Also, it's much easier to make the team as an established all-star—making it the first time is definitely the hardest. One thing that's certain, whoever's on the team is going to be hustling. Everyone's trying to play their best, to earn the respect of their teammates, and to show the fans their appreciation for being selected. Plus, this is one of those rare games you can play for fun.

You're certainly not doing it for the money—$200 and two free passes—although for some, selection to the game can mean thousands more in incentive pay. Nor are you doing it for the fringe benefits—a ring with your name on it and a little plaque to put up in your den. No, you're doing it for the thrill of playing with the best. And for me, coming from San Diego, where only a few hundred thousand people *total* had ever seen me play, there was the thrill of playing for an audience of millions—with millions of kids trading a new "Winfield" for a surplus "Rose."

My first at-bat in my first All-Star Game is in the sixth inning against Dave LaRoche. I smash one to the right-field wall. Jim Rice manages to get a glove on it just as it hits the wall, but the ball drops out and I'm credited with a double. Then in the eighth I pull a single into left off Sparky Lyle, who Joe Morgan told me moments before liked to come in with a slider, driving across the two runs that give the National League the final margin of victory.

WOMEN

My first year in San Diego I met two women who would have a great influence on my life. The first was Sandra Renfro, a distant cousin of Duane Anderson's, the Padres' part-time second baseman/shortstop and my roommate for part of that year. She was living with her parents near Houston and was competing for the Black Miss Texas title. She was a nice, gentle-voiced, pretty girl of eighteen, not at all hung up on herself. I liked her right off, but it was strictly platonic. We just enjoyed talking, doing stuff together whenever I'd get to Houston. She'd invite me to join her family for a home-cooked meal or take me shopping in her car. Today she's taking me to court.

After a couple of years of seeing Sandra each time the team passed through Houston, we finally became lovers. By 1977 she was working for Braniff Airlines, and we'd see each other more often. Every few months she'd fly to meet me in San Diego, or we'd go off somewhere together. One time, I remember, she came to visit me in Minnesota in the dead of winter, twenty-below with snow and ice covering everything. Taking her back to the airport, my rental car spun out on an ice-slick freeway. We did three 360-degree turns and then smashed into a guard rail before we were pointed back in the right direction. I should have taken it as a sign, a message from the gods, but I didn't.

Instead, I saw Sandra a few more times that year. We seemed to get along very well, but living so far apart we never demanded faithfulness from each other. Rumor got to me that she was seeing a guy in Dallas, a professional basketball player, but I figured it wasn't any of my business. Besides, remembering my last bout of jealousy, I didn't want to know. Then, a few weeks after one of her visits, she called to tell me that she was pregnant. I asked what I thought were the right questions. "What!?" (She had told me she was on the pill.) "Who?" (I didn't assume it was mine because I wasn't at all sure it was.) And "How much?" (We had gotten pretty close and no matter whose it was, I wanted to help her with the abortion, if that's what she wanted.)

She hemmed and hawed about the "who" question, then said it was probably mine. I suppose she did the same with the other guy, because after she had the baby they moved in together and sometime after that I heard they were married. Still, my adventures with Sandra were far from over.

The second woman I met my first year as a Padre was Dorothy Bowen, one terrific lady. She was in her thirties at the time, ten or fifteen years older than I, already a grandmother, and a real baseball nut. The way she tells it, she became a fan of mine after she'd been let down by her idol, Willie Mays. She and her husband were in Japan, where he was stationed with the navy, when Willie arrived there with the Giants for some exhibition games. The Japanese beat them up and down and Willie skipped town before the series was over. So back in San Diego, Dorothy was on the lookout for a new idol when she came to a Padres game with a friend and saw me in left field. "There he is," she said to her friend. "Just look at him run! Poetry in motion. And look at his booty!"

By coincidence, later that week I was having dinner with her friend's husband at her friend's house when she called Dorothy and said, "Dorothy, put on your diamonds and K-Mart shoes and drag your butt over here. There's somebody I want to show you!"

"This," her friend said when Dorothy arrived, "is Dorothy Bowen, the old, honky grandma from up the street who thinks you're the greatest thing going." I was embarrassed, stood up to shake her hand, banged my head on the chandelier, and we've been great friends ever since. More than friends, it was Dorothy's belief, hard work, and dedication that brought the idea of a Winfield Foundation to fruition.

KIDS

Ever since Aunt Bernice's pronouncement about too many "and"s and "uh"s I've known that being in the public eye, you mean something to people. But it was not until my first year in San Diego when a white guy came up to me after a game and said, "My son wants to be just like you," that it really hit home. I knew then that I couldn't just play ball, draw a salary, and go home. I was going to do something more.

Ma had set the example with her actions and her words. She always did for others and she'd always say, "Give a little when you have a little, give a lot when you have a lot." And though in those early years I certainly didn't have a lot, right after my second pro season I set up a scholarship and award dinner to benefit minority student athletes in St. Paul. Also, around that time, Dorothy and I started a little fan club for disadvantaged kids in the neighborhood. I'd buy a block of bleacher seats, we'd arrange for chaperons and transportation, then round up some kids from an orphanage and head for the stadium. When I could, I'd visit them in the stands before the game. Afterward, we'd have a pot luck dinner for the kids. Other times we'd gather the kids together at Dorothy's before the game and I'd give them a pep talk. I think the kids enjoyed it and benefited from it. I know the game of baseball did. Over the years, many of the kids we took to the games became avid fans and players.

Seeing the expressions on those kids' faces was also great for me. It was like when someone asks, "What's that on your face?" You can't see it yourself, but when you see the fruit of your own efforts and concern reflected in someone else's face—a little kid's face—it's tremendously gratifying.

So we kept at it, turned Dorothy's place into a virtual clearinghouse for kids, volunteers, and chaperons. As Dorothy once said, "I know where every kid in San Diego is. Here." One time her husband came home from a tour in Vietnam to find twenty-five teenagers sleeping on the living room floor. He opted for easier duty and went back to Vietnam.

Over the years Dorothy became my California mother, as she called it, a great friend and confidante who would give me solid, down-to-earth advice. I could talk to her about anything and everything.

PEOPLE

He wasn't a baseball player, he was more than a foot shorter than I was though we weighed about the same, and he had a reputation for being only out for himself, but he was the pro who taught me the most in my eight years in San Diego. His name was Al Frohman and he was a businessman, born and bred in New York, a rabbi's son, a consummate wheeler-dealer who, when I met him, was a retired caterer running a sweater company with his wife. Later he started a company called All-American All-Stars, selling T-shirts and kids' pajamas that bore the likenesses of well-known ballplayers. The rag trade, the "schmatte" business.

Al and I meet through Jerry Koosman, the Mets pitcher. He tells Al that I'm a "comer." Figuring he might use my face on a T-shirt, Al gives me a call and we get together one day in L.A. at his office. I walk in expecting to see a real L.A. business type—silver hair, tan, open shirt, gold chains—but instead, here's a scowling fat guy with smudgy, dark glasses, a ratty golf sweater burned and singed in a half-dozen places, one cigarette in his hand with ashes three inches long, and a couple more going in an ashtray. Everyone had told me, "Watch out for him." But from the moment I walk in we seem to hit it off. I'm offhand, casual, just a little cocky. He's candid, outspoken, direct. Also gruff, opinionated, egotistical, difficult, but I don't condemn him for that. He's a great talker, a real original. And above all, sharp.

The capper, though, as Al tells it—what cements the relationship from his point of view—is on the way out he introduces me to his wife, Bobbie. Right away I like her, she's such a pleasant lady. So when I leave I give her a little kiss on the cheek.

"Dohvid," Al calls after me, taken by the gesture and using the Yiddish pronounciation of my name, "call me if you need some help, some advice."

So, in the off-season I call him, tell him I want to get some work, make some money. "What?" Al shows mock surprise. "You gonna work in a health club? You gonna make an appearance at a sports banquet? You don't know enough yet to do anything and get paid for it."

"So, what do I do?" I'm ready, I'm adaptable, I can learn, I'll be a willing student.

Al laughs a wise-ass laugh. "Wait till next year. Maybe you'll win a World Series, make some money that way."

At the end of the next season I went to work with Al in his clothing business—learning all I could about selling, deal making, and management, traveling with Al and other salesmen from city to city, calling on clients, contacting athletes, checking out stores. It wasn't enough for me just to *do* it. I wanted to understand everything that was happening—the dynamics of a negotiation, *how* a deal is made. So I started reading—buying books on business, checking others out of the library. A couple of years out of college, I'd become a student in a completely new way.

Whether we were on the road or at home, Al and I would spend a lot of time together, talking sometimes six or eight hours at a shot. He woke up late, went to bed late. Spending time with Al flipped my circadian rhythm completely around. He always had a lot of opinions, a lot to say. As brusque and difficult as he was, he was also a cultured man. He'd attended the Juilliard School of Music, had studied with Art Tatum and played the piano in jazz bands around New York City. He was friends with Chink Hines and had seen his sons, Gregory and Maurice, grow up. So if the talk wasn't about baseball, it'd be about music, travel, Asian cultures, or family, or philosophy, people, and always, business.

About business he used to say, "Don't think small, don't think cheap. Think smart and intelligent. Think Jewish," which he was. He was also a great problem solver. Trap him in a room without any doors or windows and he'd get out. Then he'd lecture you on how to build a better trap. I listened and learned, adapted what I could to my style, picking up on Al's tremendous drive. Also on his mental toughness. When Al decided to do something, for better or for worse, he'd let nothing distract him, not Bobbie, not his kids, nothing and no one.

Al and I never had a formal agreement of any sort, even years later when we were negotiating my multimillion-dollar contract with the Yankees. Ours was a relationship based totally on the trust we had in each other. When he could afford it, he would give to me, and when I could afford it I would give to him—no percentages, no fixed fees.

Over the years I've benefited tremendously from our time together. And I'd like to think that Al got something from the relationship as well. Always sick, overweight, distrustful, dishonest when I met him, he changed. He lost weight, he became more positive, he—as he told me—stopped lying and conniving. And while our relationship often took him away from his wife and kids, he started bringing them to ball games and doing more with them as a family. In any event, I had become his "cause," and he had adopted it wholeheartedly. The one good, clean, selfless thing he had done in his business life, he once told me, was working with me. "Besides," he added, "you need me to protect you."

With my first agent having passed away, Al helped me renegotiate my subsequent contracts with the Padres. At first he just advised me from afar; the Padres never knew I had an agent. My salary climbed from $15,000 to $40,000, then to $50,000. Later Al took an active negotiating role and maintained that I should be the good guy and he should be the heavy: David just wants to play was our story, but he's got this s.o.b. working for him that wants to make sure he makes some money.

Hotshot businessman that he was, things didn't always go smoothly for Al. There were times in those early years when I'd end up lending Bobbie money for groceries. More pressing than money problems, though, was Al's health—his aches and pains, some real, some imagined, often manufactured for the occasion. There'd be times, for example, when he'd get excited about something not going well and in thirty seconds he'd work himself up into a frenzy and have an attack, "AHHH! My heart!" Still, eighty pounds overweight, only meat and potatoes in his diet, never any vegetables, high blood pressure, you had to take it seriously. Usually I did.

I remember one time in particular. Al and I are on the

road, in Manhattan. It's freezing out. We hit the street and the wind tears at our clothes. A gripping, biting cold we can't escape even in the crummy hotels where we stay. We're late for an appointment, can't find a cab, and are hustling crosstown on foot. We're at an intersection when Al suddenly stops, all white and chalky. He leans against a signpost for support. I know he's been having chest pains lately, more than usual. Hunched over, he glances at me apologetically, and coughs out a single word, "Nitro." I look down at this small old man, the wind whipping his coattails as he fumbles for his heart pills—nitroglycerin tablets—and for an instant see an expression of dread and fear on his face. I don't know what to do, and then I open my own coat, stand behind him, and wrap it around him as best I can to keep him warm, to protect him.

MONEY

In 1977 Hendrick signed and didn't talk. That year I talked—to the press, to the Padres' general manager, Buzzie Bavasi—but didn't sign. In January Bavasi and I had agreed on total dollars, but we were miles apart on other considerations, "we" being the Padre management on the one hand, and Al and I on the other. For one, Al felt that my contract with the Padres should be guaranteed in case of injury, whether the injury was incurred on or off the field, basically an insurance policy. Nowadays, such guarantees are commonplace for established players, but the Padres were digging in their heels back then. So rather than sign a contract that didn't give me what I wanted, I decided to play without one for the 1977 season—at 80 percent of my 1976 contract. Then, as set forth in the collective bargaining agreement between the owners and the Major League Baseball Players Association, if the Padres and I couldn't come to terms by the season's end, I'd become a free agent.

Once the press got wind of the battle I was having with the front office they wrote about it constantly, stories, I feel, that to a large extent magnified the problem. Most made Bavasi out to be the bad guy, which only made him dig in deeper. He was a baseball man of the old school, and I think the prospect of "giving in" to a player's requests cut against his grain. Buzzie had been in the Dodger organization and he claimed that he'd put Koufax's and Drysdale's contracts behind his back and make 'em guess which was which. I borrowed a diamond ring from Al when I went to negotiate with Buzzie, to show I wasn't begging and couldn't be steamrollered into a bad contract. Meanwhile, more than a few "Keep Dave, Trade Buzzie" banners cropped up in the stands.

The whole affair blew up a flurry of trade talks, the most notable being a straight-up trade with the Mets for Jon Matlack, a hot left-hander who'd won 17 games the previous year. Matlack went on record as being amenable to the move, I was told. But I wasn't. As much as I was tired of losing, I liked San Diego. I liked the friends I'd made, the roots I'd set down. So I gave the Mets my personal answer the next time we played. It was a double-header and we won them both. I homered and hit two singles in the first game to drive in three runs. In the second I had the game-winning hit.

Slightly more than a month into the season, I was leading the club with 36 hits, 24 RBIs, and 5 stolen bases. I was batting .319, clearly demonstrating I was one of the more valuable players on the team. Right about then Al decided to up the ante by asking for a larger base salary. After all, I was taking a chance playing without a contract. And with a team still in the doldrums after signing Tenace, Fingers, and Hendrick for quite a few dollars, I had suddenly become an even more valuable commodity. Besides, I knew that the money they didn't want to pay me they'd pay someone else right after me. It was simply a matter of not wanting to pay for something they already had. Sure, Bavasi had his budgets and had to work within certain parameters, but dangle an appealing free agent in front of Kroc and I knew those parameters would magically change.

My request for more dollars than we agreed on in January really rankled Bavasi, particularly because he thought it was coming from Al, not me. He felt that if Al hadn't interfered I would have been a signed, sealed, and delivered Padre months ago. Also, like almost anyone in a negotiation with Al, Bavasi couldn't stand him. Al would do things like light a cigarette and then rummage through Buzzie's desk in search of an ashtray.

Come July, Al and I are meeting with Bavasi and negotiate our way down to a difference of $100,000 in a $1 million-plus package over a four-year period. We want the dollars, they don't want to give them. At a stalemate, Bavasi leaves the room claiming, "I've gotta ask Mr. Kroc if he'll go the extra hundred thousand." My guess is he's heading for the can. As soon as he's gone I say to Al, "What we've got is more money than I ever had to work with. I'm ready to go with it." But Al says, "No we're not gonna go with this. We're gonna get that hundred thousand. Watch!"

When Bavasi gets back he says, "No, I'm sorry, Mr. Kroc says we can't give you that money."

So Al says, "Look, you give us the money and we'll give it back."

"What?"

"Give us the hundred thousand and we'll buy one hundred thousand tickets in the bleachers at a dollar a ticket over four years. We'll give the tickets to kids who wouldn't otherwise get to go."

Bavasi can't believe it. You can see the gears working in his brain. They never filled the bleachers anyway, so it's not as if they'd lose money on the tickets. It all sounds too good to be true. He thinks it over for what must be five minutes before he decides he can't go wrong on the deal. In fact, the idea excites him so much, he gives us the name of our program, suggesting we call our section of the bleachers the Winfield Pavillion—"pavillion" being the designation given to special sections of the stands in Dodger Stadium by the Los Angeles organization, Bavasi's former employer. Al smiles. Bavasi smiles. I smile. After nearly a half year of negotiations we're suddenly very, very close to a contract.

Occasionally, through all this wheeling and dealing, I'd flash back to the previous year's Cy Young Awards banquet honoring Randy Jones, where the reverend giving the invocation expressed the hope that greed would not spoil the game. I wondered then what Kroc paid the reverend. Then I wondered what he paid Randy Jones. Not a whole lot, I thought, causing me to give the reverend's words some serious thought. But whenever I found myself thinking like that I remembered Rollie Fingers at the banquet, my new millionaire teammate, smiling like the cat that just swallowed Ray Kroc's wallet.

On the Fourth of July I signed a four-year contract with the Padres worth $1.3 million. It made that day's paper and when I was introduced at the stadium the next night and the scoreboard lit up with the contract announcement, the fans greeted me with a standing ovation that continued until I stepped out of the dugout and doffed my cap. Then the opposition beat our brains out.

That winter Al convinced me that we should attend the owners' winter meetings in Hawaii. I had a multi-year contract, I was pretty satisfied, and at first I had no idea what he was up to. I found out soon enough. On the plane he said, "Come on Davey, let's have some fun." He corralled a few reporters who were on board and said, "I have a hunch David is going to be traded." They scribbled all the way to Honolulu.

If planes had had airphones back then, in fact, the press would have burned out the circuits. By the time we landed, the "Winfield trade" had become one of the big stories of the meetings—meetings, incidentally, that can be as dull as dishwater, unless free agency is hot or a strike is looming. When we got there Al kept feeding the trade fever. One of his elaborate hypothetical four-team trades would have landed me with the Yankees. Another would have sent me to the Dodgers. In the midst of all the talk, Al orchestrated a mad scene in the hotel lobby between Ray Kroc and Tommy LaSorda, Al Campanis, and Peter O'Malley from the Dodger organization. Al first asked Kroc how he felt about other teams offering nothing but garbage for his best all-around player. Then he turned to the Dodgers and asked, very serious, why they didn't make a respectable offer, throw in more players, more cash. Did they think they could steal Dave Winfield from the Padres for nottin'?

Before this, I doubt Mr. Kroc would have done what he did next, which was invite me to a cocktail party with all of baseball's movers and shakers. Later that evening, at the main banquet, I sat next to a "source close to the Yankees" who whispered that George Steinbrenner himself was interested in me. The Yankees and other successful teams had tables in the front and middle, where they could flash their championship rings at also-rans like the Padres, who had a table barely within earshot of the podium.

The upshot of it all was that I left Hawaii still a Padre,

but with a vastly different sense of what was possible. Through Al's gift for public relations and hype, all of baseball had been sensitized, I guess you could say, to who I was and what my play might mean to a team. In an atmosphere traditionally focused on division and pennant winners, Al had persuaded people to look in my direction.

A few day later, back in San Diego and still a little heady from the experience, I received a call from a UPI reporter who wanted to know my reaction to being traded to Toronto. "Toronto!!" I was floored. It was the first time I truly felt how out of my control my own life as a player was, what the downside of a trade could be. The "UPI reporter" turned out to be none other than Al, doing a remarkably good job of disguising his voice. My next contract would give me veto power over any trade.

THE GAME

First day of spring training in 1978, the locker room was empty except for an old, balding guy with a few days' gray stubble and a baggy body. Someone's grandfather? Uh-uh, our new ace, Gaylord Perry, just over from the Texas Rangers. I'd heard about him, of course, but I didn't know where he stood, where I would stand with him, what kind of man he was.

What I did know about Perry was that he was wily and fiercely competitive. He'd resort to every trick in the book— Vaseline, tar, rosin, dirt, cutting the baseball, distractions. He'd try to fool you into thinking he was going to throw a spitter—"Aw man," you'd say, "he's loading up"—and then, *boom!* he'd fastball you. I appreciated his ability to win games, but I never liked playing behind him. His games took too long. He'd throw one real hard, then he'd have to recuperate for a minute or so. He'd circle the mound, position people, kick the dirt, then ritually touch every part of his body.

Mostly, though, I remember Perry for his crustiness. Every pitcher wins or loses games because of the defense. A smart pitcher won't blame his teammates for a loss. Gaylord wasn't dumb—no one with his record or style could be—but he tended to give credit or place blame where he thought it was due. Once, against the Cubbies in Chicago, he was in real trouble, and I hit two three-run homers that saved his butt. Next day I found a huge bottle of champagne in my locker, compliments of Gaylord. Another time, though, a guy hit one down the right-field line to me and I caught it okay, but when I stopped, turned, and reached into my glove to make the throw, the ball just stuck there as the hitter ran to second. Gaylord turned toward me and yelled, berating me and making all these faces. When the inning was over I just railed on him. "I don't need your bulls___! Who is helping you win all the time?" I told him. After that there was an unspoken truce between us.

The word from management was that Perry and Rollie Fingers were to be the "glue" to bind a winning team. All through the season Fingers would never let go of it. Ask him anything and he'd say, "I'm the *glue.*" But there was some truth to it. In 1978 the Padres enjoyed their best season to that date, finishing only 11 games out, in fourth place, with an 84–78 record. Fingers chalked up 37 saves, best in the league. And Perry, at forty, won a league-high 21 games, and the Cy Young Award. An amazing accomplishment for a guy who could barely reach home plate with his pitches at the beginning of the season.

Perry's and Fingers' accomplishments, however, are only part of the story of what was actually a tumultuous year. Halfway through spring training Alvin Dark is fired and our pitching coach, Roger Craig—a good ol' country boy that almost everyone respects and likes—is made manager. Terrific! Alvin Dark's effect on the team had never been right. He came to the club with a reputation for not getting along with blacks, for having been a nasty player, for being a drinker. The fact was he had found God, he was born again and he had put the drinking and cursing behind him. But in this game they put a label on you and it sticks. Nobody trusted his born-again religion. He was a divisive influence because he had to oversee every play. He didn't delegate to his coaches, and he had no camaraderie with them because he had stopped drinking.

So as soon as I hear about the change, I drop by Craig's office. He's there along with Ballard Smith, Buzzie Bavasi, and a bunch of coaches around a conference table. I tell him that he can count on me 100 percent, and that I'll do whatever he wants—hit for power, drive in runs, be a leader, bust my hump for him. Then I ask if he can delay practice for about twenty minutes while we have a team meeting. I just know that now—with Dark out and Craig in—is the time to fire up the troops, get everyone to work together for a winning season.

The meeting takes place in center field. I stand up in front of the team and say, "We've got a new manager, we've got a good team, we've got a chance to win if we work together, play hard, believe in one another!" The whole Knute Rockne spiel. Next thing I know Gene Tenace jumps up on my left, Randy Jones on my right—like we've rehearsed the whole thing. "Let's go! Let's do it!" they yell.

And wouldn't you know it, our next Cactus League game we're down three or four runs, two men out in the ninth, and put together a phenomenal rally to win it. It's the win we've been waiting for and we play well the rest of that spring. Then just before the season opener, Craig announces that I'm the captain of the 1978 Padres, the first in the team's history. I'm surprised, pleased, and just a little wary. It's like in the army where they tell you "never volunteer"; only Craig volunteers me. It certainly isn't something I'd asked for.

First game of the season I homer in the eighth to spark a winning rally against the Giants in San Francisco. In our first 23 games I drive in 18 runs and belt 6 homers. But even with my hot bat and all our "glue" we're not winning games, and by mid-June were looking at a 24–32 record. That month I'm tied with Vida Blue as the National League Player of the Month, hitting .333, and tied with George Foster for RBIs for the season with 54.

Still, in a tirade to the press a few days earlier, when Kroc singles out the *only* four players who are pulling their weight, my name is conspicuously absent. As for the rest of the players on the team, he says, "They are demanding major-league salaries and playing like high school kids." Kroc singles out Gene Tenace for a special invective, calling him a "disgrace . . . the most overrated ballplayer on this club." I am, at least, spared that honor.

Somewhere along the line, too, as team captain I'm held accountable for our losing ways, the suggestion being that as captain I should have the cure for what ails us. I finally tell Roger Craig in a finger-pointing, shouting match in the clubhouse, "Being captain of this team is like being captain of the *Titanic!*" In any event, losing again more than we're winning, a guy like Kroc venting his frustration to the press—creating divisiveness among the players—Roger Craig being a nervous first year manager, and our own frustration in not being able to put together some good offense make it tough for us as a team to have any fun or, more important, deliver on the promise of that spring.

No guy on the team probably had less fun that year than Oscar Gamble, our right fielder—that is, he was our right fielder most of the time as I played left back then. The club put tremendous pressure on Oscar to be the team's savior because of his $2 million-plus contract. They didn't consider that Oscar wasn't a great defensive player, that he just wanted to "corkscrew" that bat of his. Of course, what were home runs for Oscar in his previous parks were only long singles and doubles in San Diego. Then, whenever the game was on the line, and a left-handed hitter was up who Craig thought might smash one deep to right, he began to have me switch fields with Oscar because I was the better defensive player. One day, after Craig had made the switch for the third time that week in front of 20,000 fans in the stands, not to mention a radio and TV audience, Oscar laid down the law. "If you ever do this shit again I will not move. You are making a fool of me."

Playing shortstop for the '78 Padres was a rookie, Ozzie Smith, a great fielder who not only played nearly flawless defensive ball, but played with a flair, a real showman. He'd pick bullets off the turf with a flick of his glove, then make his throw smooth as silk. Other guys would struggle just to get near the ball, but for Ozzie it seemed to come naturally. Like all the other special athletes I've known, the ones who amount to anything, that is, Ozzie put in a lot of work to make the most of his quickness and agility.

As it turned out, Ozzie was as smooth off the field as on, as he demonstrated one afternoon in Houston, the day he met his wife. Ozzie and I were leaving the Astrodome together with some other guys, heading for a friend's car, when a woman caught his eye. He stopped, looked her up and down, she saw him, he walked over, and the rest is history.

Also history now is a comment of Mrs. Kroc's after she

heard that Ozzie's agent, working for a new contract, had come up with a plan that would have Ozzie sitting out the year and taking on some other work to make money. Mrs. Kroc suggested that if Ozzie didn't want to play baseball, he could be her yard man. Later, she changed her story. "I have a job for Ozzie. Let him carry Dave Winfield's wallet."

Ah, the indignities. The thing is, the tables have turned. These days Ozzie, according to the papers, makes more than I do, and he has a swimming pool in the shape of a glove. It's a pleasure to see a young blood I played alongside doing well. We talk a lot of trash at the All-Star Game, kidding each other about our appearances on "Lifestyles of the Rich and Famous."

Closing out the '78 season with my best finish ever—hitting .308, the fifth best average in the league, and leading the Padres in hits, doubles, homers, RBIs, and game winners—I started the 1979 season eager but frustrated. Having tasted fourth place, I knew I'd never be satisfied with it again. Playing .500 ball couldn't be a goal of mine *or* of the team—a team, incidentally, that with their new brownish uniforms had taken to calling themselves the "turds." I'd decided in the off-season that 1979 would be a Padre year. And, I hoped, a Winfield year as well.

It begins less than auspiciously. Early in spring training I hurt my knee dodging a line drive leading off second, putting me out of commission for four or five days. First day back we're playing the Cubs in Scottsdale, Arizona, and I hit what could be a broken-bat single to deep short. Still hobbled, I don't beat it out. Limping back to the dugout I see Rollie Fingers and Roger Craig leaning against the wall. "Superstar, my ass," Rollie says. Craig smiles. The combination of my sore knee, Fingers' remark, and Craig's smile infuriates me. I throw my helmet and *bang!* it hits the railing next to Fingers' head. He jumps and I grab him by the shirt, pick him up, and throw him down. Some guys grab me then, break it up. Craig never says a thing, but the smile leaves his face.

Next day we're playing the Mariners in Tempe, Arizona. First time up I hit a bomb, a monster home run way over the fence, halfway up a hill that looks like a moonscape. Coming back into the dugout I see a bunch of guys leaning over Fingers. He's on the floor and they're waving towels over him, like he's passed out. His way of saying "Winnie can hit! I don't believe it!" It breaks the ice, and I have to laugh.

With my contract up in 1980, during the '79 season Padre management is looking for a way of lowering my appeal in the marketplace so they can afford to keep me in San Diego. One of their ploys is to bench me to groom my "replacement," a young player named Jerry Turner. Jerry's from Texas, has a pleasant drawl, and is one of these guys always on the border between making it and not making it. He's a good hitter—held the pinch-hit record in the National League for home runs—he's powerful, compactly built with small hands and large forearms, but he isn't that much of a fielder with an average arm and below-average confidence.

One day I'm benched in favor of Turner and am in the dugout loosening my shoelaces when the opposition's lead-off batter hits a shot to right field over Turner's head and up against the wall. The way to field it is to just turn and play it off the wall. But Turner runs all the way back to the wall, watches the ball carom off, chases it back toward the infield, then as he finally goes to barehand it and make the throw to third he jams his middle finger into the ground and breaks it. It's bent back at almost ninety degrees. I retie my shoelaces.

And I keep them tied, finishing out the season batting .308 and leading the league in RBIs with 118. The Padres, back to their losing ways, finish fifth with a 68–93 record.

I'm in Las Vegas when I get a call from the Padres' front office. They want me back in San Diego to attend a press conference for the MVP Award. "Hey, I'm doubtful I'm going to win it," I say. I simply didn't think that they'd give it to a guy whose team finished in fifth place, no matter how many game winners he had, no matter what kind of year he'd had. "No, no, no," they say, as if they know something I don't. "You gotta come back." So I do, drive all the way across the desert to San Diego. When I finally get there they tell me that Willie Stargell and Keith Hernandez tied for first place in the MVP balloting. But I'm right up there, the very next in line. Second.

KIDS

The David M. Winfield Foundation gained official legal status in 1977 following my re-signing with the Padres. The size of the contract and the likelihood I'd stay in San Diego at least through 1980 was just what we needed to step up the work with kids that my family, Dorothy, Al, and I had begun years before. We weren't exactly the Ford Foundation, though, and in those early years Foundation headquarters was either at my place or Dorothy's. To lend the operation more credibility Dorothy would usually answer the phone in the dining room, then say, "Mr. Winfield? I'll see if he's in." Then, while I ran to the bedroom to pick up the extension, she'd tell whoever was calling, "Mr. Winfield will be with you in just a moment."

Activities were planned through the baseball season, the single most publicized and best attended being our annual

All-Star Game party. In 1978 the game was played in San Diego and well before I knew I'd be on the team, we began planning a huge sports celebration. The party took place the day before the game and was attended by thousands of kids from all over the area. The Foundation provided refreshments, and with the help of Jack Clark, Jim Sundberg, Ross Grimsly, Phil Niekro, Pat Zachry, Ozzie Smith, Bill Almon, Rollie Fingers, and others, we signed autographs and handed out 10,000 baseball photos. My selection to the All-Star team and Ma coming to the party, then staying to watch me play, was the icing on the cake.

The following year the game was played in Seattle, so we held a party there for more than 8,000 local kids. Not wanting San Diego youngsters to miss out on the fun completely, Dorothy, Al and a few volunteers took a busload of kids to Seattle for the festivities. They were on the road for thirty-three hours. The bus broke down, the air conditioner ceased functioning, the heater went crazy. Dorothy, the volunteers, and the kids alternated between freezing and boiling. By party time, though, there were no complaints. Not from the kids, anyhow. Besides, for most of them it was their first time ever out of San Diego and the best adventure they'd ever been on.

With the 1980 All-Star Game to be played in nearby Dodger Stadium, we decided to try something new and more ambitious. Something more in line with the overall goals of the Foundation, which, in addition to bringing disadvantaged kids to games and having them meet players, included providing them with health education and health care. There was a party, of course—over 10,000 kids came on foot, by bus, by car to Elysian Park near Dodger Stadium for hot dogs, milk, autographs, and a chance to meet the players, the commissioner, and Mayor Tom Bradley. In addition to food and entertainment, thousands of kids were given free physical exams. Doctors and technicians also talked to kids and their parents about exercise, diet, and nutrition. While most of the kids examined checked out fine, a number turned out to have serious problems requiring further examination and follow-up. According to the doctors, this early diagnosis probably saved a few lives.

The prognosis for the kids we saw wasn't always that good. Later that season, a gentleman from a nearby orphanage called Dorothy to tell her about a thirteen-year-old named Brian who was dying of cancer and had never been to a Padre game. I was his idol. Dorothy told me about him and I said I'd get together with him in a couple of weeks, after the Padres returned from a road trip. But it turned out Brian didn't *have* a couple of weeks, so without telling me, Dorothy brought him to the stadium that day, the last of our home stand. She wheeled him down to the dugout in a wheelchair just as the game ended. I'll never forget my first look at him. He was bald from chemotherapy and so frail his black skin looked almost translucent. He couldn't have weighed more than forty pounds.

"Hi," Dorothy said, trying to manufacture some cheer, "this is Brian."

"Oh, yeah, Brian. My main man." I could feel my voice crack. Dorothy handed me a baseball she'd brought with her. I autographed it, then ran to the dugout to get everyone else to sign it. When I came back I posed for a picture Brian took with his camera, then borrowed the camera and took a picture of Brian. "Now, when you get these developed, I want the one of you autographed for my locker," I said.

"You want *my* picture?" Brian asked. So I went back into the dugout and brought him a baseball bat and a helmet, just about everything I could find. It was the saddest thing I ever did.

By 1980, the Foundation had become a real force in the community. Hundreds of volunteers had come aboard to help turn Dorothy's and my little postgame parties into huge celebrations and health fairs for kids from all over the area and wherever All-Star games were played. Plus, I'm proud to say, we'd been honored by everyone from the American Legion to the National Asthma Center, from the Chamber of Commerce and the Urban League to the Mormons and the National Conference of Christians and Jews. We were thriving, we were having fun, we were doing more and better than I ever dreamed we could.

The better known we became, though, the more outrageous the requests for help we received. Once when I was on the road I got a telegram in the middle of the night that read "Call this number. Big emergency." It was unsigned. I called the number. It was a guy from a pretty classy neighborhood wanting me to pay off his mortgage.

Another time a guy called for money to build a church. I asked him what kind of church. "Never mind what kind of church," he snapped, "just send the money."

The most outrageous request of all was from a young woman. She stopped by the office one day and asked Dorothy for Foundation money to bankroll her career as a hooker. She wanted us to set her up in a suite of rooms in one of the city's better hotels. She had it all figured out—cash flow, profit and loss, 10 percent back to the Foundation. Dorothy took her name and number. When I finally got up the nerve to call her she told me she had three children and didn't want to go on welfare. I commended her for her industriousness, but told her finally I couldn't get involved in anything like that; that pimping was just not my business. I suppose I was still naive, but I was amazed by the kooks and crazies you attract when you're in the business of giving away money.

PEOPLE

My friendship with Al Frohman was the most important relationship I'd developed since leaving home. We spoke to each other every day, even when I was on the road—about baseball, about business, and more and more often about the future. It was beginning to make me nervous. Sure, I expected Al to play a large part in my life in the years to come, but I was also realizing that *my* future couldn't be *his* version of that future—the little Jewish guy and the big black guy versus the world.

Whether he was doing it consciously or not, Al had become exceedingly possessive, more like father and son than business partners. It bugged him that I wanted to form close relationships with other people. He was often down on Dorothy, the other men I befriended or did business with, and the women I went out with. Inevitably, he'd say something to offend them. "When he talks like that," I would tell people, "don't listen to him." But it was hard not to listen. As it was, people either took to Al right away and forgave him his abrasiveness, or they couldn't stand him. There was no middle ground.

Early on in our relationship, Al would often follow me home from the stadium, checking to see if any undesirable elements—gamblers, pushers, crazy people, whatever—were tagging along. Sometimes I'd arrange for a friend to follow me home or to a party, only to have Al spot him or her and come on like gangbusters. "Where do you think you're going?" "I'm calling the cops!" It got to the point where I told him one day, "Look, after a game, you don't have to follow me to see if anyone is following me. Just let me go out, have a good time."

Still, while we were having our problems, I loved getting together with Al to throw around ideas, particularly putting our creative energy to the problem of making money. One scheme that went well beyond the incubation stage was Superstar Village, a grand plan that would involve me from 1977 till the time I left San Diego, three years later.

Superstar Village, as Al and I conceived it, was to be a family resort where professional athletes who had purchased condominiums would mingle with paying guests and act as superstar counselors, providing sports clinics and the like. When the athletes weren't in residence, their condos would be rented out. We were certain that with enough big names as drawing cards and given the right location, Superstar Village could become a real money-maker. After all, athletes were always a big draw, whether on cruises or at charity functions.

Because of Al's contacts and friendships on the Caribbean island of Curaçao, our first thought was to develop Superstar Village there. Initially, the island government expressed a lot of interest in the plan and flew Al and Bobbie and me and a number of celebrities, including Valerie Perrine and Richard Roundtree, down for a few days. They wined and dined us, the whole island turned out. It was beautiful. Then for some reason they dragged their feet on the deal, so early in 1978 Al and I decided we'd try to build Superstar Village right in our own backyard, in the San Diego area.

As the months passed we refined the concept to include a sports medicine program, and Al came up with the idea of involving Scripps Clinic in the project. Through a doctor I knew, Al and I arranged a meeting with the Clinic's chief financial officer, Bob Erra.

Al came on pretty strong as Bob listened with his arms crossed on his chest and a dubious look in his eye. Al not only hyped the idea of Superstar Village, but also insisted how valuable to Scripps its participation in the project would be. But Bob wasn't buying and told us so. Al got mad. "All right," he said, "if you don't like it, we'll take it to the Mayo Clinic!"

Bob laughed. "Sure," he said, "you just do that. Put a destination resort in the middle of Rochester, Minnesota." Al stormed out in a huff. I threw my hands up in a gesture of mock surrender.

Scripps or not, we weren't about to abandon the San Diego area as a site, and looked into developing the project at a number of locations including nearby Mission Bay, Oceanside, and Escondito, where we ran into expected and unexpected snags—height limitations, political lobbying, and all the coastal rigamarole.

I really liked Erra's candor in the face of Al's overbearing "sell," and not long after our first meeting we became friends. After a while, in fact, he even warmed to the idea of Superstar Village—without Scripps' participation, of course—and said he'd do what he could on our behalf. At a civic round table luncheon he asked Pete Wilson—then the mayor of San Diego and later the junior senator from California—what he thought of the plan. A few days later Bob invited Al and me over to a barbecue after a Padres game to share Wilson's thoughts with us. Bob was uncharacteristically quiet during the meal. Then he sat back and said, "David, I've got to be frank with you guys. Wilson happens to think that the project has merit . . ." He paused. "He thinks it has merit, but that Al is a 'goddamn asshole,' quote, unquote." Al's jaw dropped. "And, that there's no way this town is going to support Superstar Village as long as he's involved with it."

"What do you mean?" I asked, knowing full well.

"Listen, Dave, we can put together a team and we can make this go forward, but Al is simply going to have to take a back seat."

Bob was basically a diplomatic guy, so this wasn't easy for

him, and knowing Al as I did, I was certain it was doubly hard for him to take. And it was hard for me. Al had just negotiated a solid contract for me with the Padres. Plus, Superstar Village was originally more his idea than mine. And most important, there was our friendship to consider. But Wilson's message via Bob was only too clear, so after leaving the barbecue Al and I talked and we agreed that I should run with it and that he'd keep a low profile.

Not long after that, Bob Erra and I assembled a team. We did a feasibility study, put together the financing, even got approval from the city council. We had it all lined up—the concept, the money, but not the political clout. It could have happened, in fact, and been a very successful project, but as my tenure in San Diego was coming to an end, we never took it that final step. I learned a lot from it, though, realizing, too, that more than the bottom line, I liked the process—starting something, working with it, making it happen.

By 1980 I'd been to Hawaii, Curaçao, and virtually every major-league city with Al. The one place I never expected to see him was on the diamond. But Al was a man of surprises. Late in the season we're playing the Astros in Houston. My first at-bat Nolan Ryan brushes me back with a pitch. My next at-bat, he does it again, a real wake-up. Back in the dugout where I'm already pissed for popping up, Willie Montanez, our first baseman, shakes his head and says in his gravelly voice, "I don't know about you, Winnie. Why do you let those pitchers intimidate you? Go out to that mound once and they'll leave you alone, they'll give you some respect."

Now usually, if I get brushed back I just stare back at the pitcher without blinking—like, Your pitch was NOTTIN'!—then take my regular stance at the plate. I rarely lose my concentration. But if I think the guy is really trying to hurt me, then I have no choice but to mix it up, and I don't mind. Ryan's two brush-backs, though, aren't really that outrageous. Still, with Montanez's advice in mind, I decide, Okay, Nolan, one more time and I'm going after you.

Lo and behold, the next time I'm up, Nolan fires a bullet too close to my head, and this is my free agent year. I stiff-arm the catcher to take him out quick, the ump steps in my path and I throw him aside, then charge the mound with my arm cocked to swing. I take a shot, it glances off, and I tackle him. Just when I have a few good licks in, the mound gets crowded with Astros, Padres, umpires, and coaches. With all the bodies, all the yelling and screaming, I can't even tell who's who anymore. So when a hand starts clawing at my face, I bite a finger. It belongs to an Astro, all right, but it's Enos Cabell's, a good friend.

Anyway, just as we're being pulled apart and the umpires are giving us hell, I hear a familiar voice yelling. "Don't let them get you, Davey! Protect yourself!" It's Al, already on the field, being held back by a couple of security guards. He's cussing them out. His pants are torn from climbing over the dugout. I mean, here's a guy with heart disease who can't walk half a block without saying "Where's my nitro?" and he's on his way out to the mound to jump into the fray.

FAMILY

Right before I'd decided to leave San Diego my father got in touch with me to ask how I felt about his moving to the area from Seattle. We'd talked every few months or so, but it was always strained. And somehow, too, whenever we talked my celebrity would get in the way, like he had more interest in my fame than he had in me. I was certain that was a big reason for his wanting to make the move, and I resented him for it. So I told him no, I didn't think he should move down. "You may have had the name first," I said, "but I did something with it."

Later in the season he came down to watch a game and somehow, I don't remember how, it ended up that Al, my father, and I were in the same room together after a game. It was a very odd experience for me—for us all, I imagine—to be there, with the two people that were probably the most important men in my life. I thought as I watched them—my father, tall, black, and lean, athletic physique; and Al—how strange it was to have a, short, white, balding, irascible, sickly guy named Frohman mean so much more to me than my real father. Not much happened, finally, that day. There were no confrontations; there were no words. My father already knew how important Al was to me, and for one of the first times since I'd met him, Al just kind of backed off, let my father and me do what we had to do, which was to talk things over for a good part of the day, not getting close but at least making our feelings known.

MONEY

Dave Parker and I broke into professional baseball the same year, and we were often compared. We were both big, strong, multidimensional players with good arms and good speed, anomalies physically by early seventies baseball standards. But I went to the Padres as a pitcher to be turned into

an outfielder, green, scared, and shy, while Parker went to
the Pirates, where he gained a lot of confidence early on
because he was brash and because he had a better team
around him—more wins, more men on base, more runs,
more people to help him out, and Willie Stargell at his peak.
The day it all hit home was in late 1979 when Parker and
the Pittsburgh Lumber Company raided San Diego Stadium. That year we had a real smart-aleck batboy who
mockingly asked me, "Who's a better player? You or Dave
Parker?"

"Put it this way," I said, "Parker's got a better team."

"Well, I was just over talking to Parker and he said you'll
never be anything as long as you're playing in San Diego."

I glanced quickly toward the visitors' dugout and saw
Stargell, Parker, Omar Moreno, Bill Robinson, and the others having a good ol' time. I knew Parker was right. As
much as I liked the area, the friends, the work with the kids,
I knew then it was time to make a move. With my contract
up in 1980, Ray Kroc had his future in my hands. He could
trade me before the season, pay me enough to make it worth
my while to stay, or dare me to test my worth in the free
agent marketplace.

Early in 1980 the Padres made me an offer. It was a
six-year contract with a $500,000 annual base salary and a
series of six-figure incentive clauses for making the All-Star
team, winning a Gold Glove Award, being chosen MVP,
leading the league in RBIs, etc. A lot of money, but not at
all in line with what was then being paid top players. I
turned it down.

What followed was unfortunate, at best. Al and Ballard
Smith, who'd taken over from Buzzie Bavasi, got into a
shouting match, trading insults, calling each other names.
The press ate it up and printed every word of it. As a result
any fan in San Diego was able to follow the "progress" of

my contract talks. At one point, wanting to justify his offer, Smith released an accounting of the Padres' cash flow to the *Los Angeles Times,* saying that salaries were doing the Padres in. At that time, clubs never revealed that sort of thing. He pointed to the million-dollar signings of Fingers, Tenace, and Gamble, saying that the Padres couldn't afford any more high-ticket players without raising ticket prices. That year, as it happened, the Padres signed pitchers Rich Wise and John Curtis for a bundle, for a free agent payroll of maybe $10 million.

Right before spring training Al and I are having a heated discussion about the state of my negotiations at my place when he clutches his chest and topples to the floor. By now I know Al well enough to know that some of his "attacks," like those of Fred Sanford on "Sanford and Son," often come at his convenience. As usual he won't let me call a doctor or take him to the hospital. "No doctors, no doctors," he pants, writhing and twisting on the floor. Even after I give him some nitro he still looks like he's in serious pain. Maybe it's a heart attack that doesn't respond to the stuff? Now I'm worried. No doctors, no hospitals, so I make tracks for Dorothy's instead, who claims to be an expert in affairs of the heart. It's a ten-minute trip ordinarily, but I make it in three. By the time I get there I'm the one on the verge of a heart attack. "Al's dying," I yell when she opens the door. "He's rolling around on the floor." Dorothy grabs some pain killers and we speed back to my place. Al's still on the floor, but now he's not moving a muscle.

"Al, are you all right?" Dorothy asks.

"Oh, my back!"

"Your back?"

The pain killers Dorothy has brought are suppositories and she does the honors. "If you're not better in ten minutes, we're going to call the hospital," I say.

"No hospital, no doctors," he wails. "I've got to negotiate the contract. I've got to protect you."

"Bulls___!" Ten minutes pass, Al's still on the floor, so I get on the phone to Bob Erra, who arranges for a room at Scripps. Dorothy and I bundle Al into the back seat of the car—no easy task, since his whole body has stiffened—and we take off. As I weave through traffic Al squeezes Dorothy's hand so hard he cracks a bone in it. I'm so upset I almost take the wrong exit, and end up cutting across four lanes of freeway at a hundred miles an hour to get where I need to go. Just then Al lets out a bloodcurdling scream that startles me so much my head hits the roof.

At Scripps the doctors and nurses are waiting. The gurney's ready to wheel Al straight into emergency surgery if he needs it. Only it's not his heart, it's gallstones. Dorothy and I watch as Al disappears down the corridor on a gurney, blood pressure 210/130, and full of morphine to keep him quiet. She's the grandma with the broken hand, but I feel like a rag that's been put through the wringer.

After two days of R&R, it's the weekend. Al suggests that we should capitalize on his condition and present our counteroffer to the Padres while he's still at Scripps. So we call Ballard Smith to a Monday meeting in Al's room, the John Wayne Suite. Pretty much fully recovered when Ballard arrives, Al nevertheless hunches over in a wheelchair, wrapped up in a big robe with a shawl draped across his head and shoulders. Ballard storms in, takes one look at Al, and says, "David, how much money do you want?"

"Keep your voice down, Ballard, the man is sick," I say, "look at him!"

"I don't give a damn. I just want to know how much money you want."

"The man could be dying," I say. "Look at him."

Ballard then turns to Al as he rises from the dead and feebly presents our formal salary request, $1.3 million a year for ten years. You can see it working on Ballard. In his head he knows it's probably a trick, but with Al looking the way he does—sunken eyes, pale, hunched over—it's impossible for him to know for sure. So instead of responding to the offer, he just stands there, taking notes and calcalating on a yellow pad, grinding his teeth.

Finally Ballard says he'll discuss our requests with the other Padres decision makers. Before he leaves, he asks us not to say a word about our meeting to the press. I guess Ballard wanted to get to the reporters first, because the next day my "absurd demands" are the talk of the papers. It's the beginning of the end for me in San Diego. Not only doesn't it bring us any closer to a deal, it brings out of the woodwork all sorts of fans or "anti-fans" who think I'm a greedy malcontent. At the first exhibition game against the Oakland Athletics, when my name is announced all I can hear are boos and catcalls. The boos continue through spring training. After the regular season starts, about a third of the people who come to the games in San Diego come to sit on the right-field line to abuse me, yelling, cursing, booing, chanting "Sign, sign, sign!" There are plenty of better seats to be had at the stadium, but they've come with a message for me. I don't want to hear it. I'm not signing because it isn't good for me to sign. My career is floundering in San Diego, I'm not happy with the team's progress, they're messing with my playing time and I'm not putting up the numbers I know I can. It even gets to the point where I start yelling back at the most vociferous hecklers: "You have a big mouth and a big belly. Look at you!" It breaks the tension sometimes, even has the fans laughing at the guy instead of giving me grief. But they refocus their rancor on me soon enough. Like a lot of players, I used to hope to catch one of these chumps on the street by himself. I knew I had something for him. But you hardly ever see the real brazen ones face-to-face, unless they're drunk or crazy.

Managing the team that year—my sixth coach in my eight years on the Padres—was Jerry Coleman, a former Yankee second baseman, more recently a Padres broadcaster and a master of the malaprop: "There's a long, long drive to right field, Blank's going after it . . . Back, back, back, back! and oh! he hit his head on the wall . . . it's rolling back to second base!" He loved to talk about the weather: "Hey, guys, put a jacket on, it's stiff out there!" Jerry was a nice guy and I had an on-again, off-again year for him. "On" mostly when I was on the road and could just concentrate on baseball. One such "on" time was a seven-day streak when I hit .467 with 2 homers and 10 RBIs, but the Padres failed to nominate me for the National League Player of the Week. My "off" times were mostly at home, where the fans had gotten even more merciless. No way in the world could I stay.

In October I took the field for the last time as a San Diego Padre and became a free agent. I wasn't nostalgic, I wasn't sentimental. I was just glad the season was over.

My mother's parents, Everett and Jessie Allison

With my brother Steve

Cub Scout Pack 51

ST. PAUL CITY MIDGET CHAMPS
1964

RUDY HARTINEZ	STEVE WINFIELD	JIMMY HARTIN
FRED PRICE	RONNIE REED	RONNIE NELSON
JEFF BROWN	TIM McWATT	GREG PEAKES
CHRIS BROWN	DAVID WINFIELD	ART CARROLL
CLYDE WEAVER	LANSING THOMPSON	BILL PETERSON, Coach

Now that's a rebound

All-American pitching form and intensity

I spent seven spring trainings here

A pat on the back from my man Willie McCovey

Talking turkey—I mean hamburgers—with Ray Kroc

A Winfield Pavillion in San Diego

The sign on my right says, "I am bad; I can play; I will kick your butt."

With Al Frohman, planning free-agent strategy in a smoke-filled room (BIG RED NEWS, OZIER MUHAMMAD)

My new teammate

Billy Martin leads the charge (LOUIS REQUENA)

The Bronx Job
Can Dave Winfield get away with it?
(DAILY NEWS, BRUCE STARK)

On top of the big apple in Macy's Parade
(DAILY NEWS)

STUDENTS OF THE GAME:

Talking baseball with Joe DiMaggio

(LOUIS REQUENA)

...Don Baylor

...and Don Mattingly

(TOM MULLANE)

Roaming right field

Spiderman or what?

You can't get 'em all   (BECERRA PHOTO)

I got it

3

*Seventh-Inning
Stretch*

MONEY

I first met George Steinbrenner in my hotel suite in Minneapolis. Just after the 1980 season the University of Minnesota drafted me to work with Bob Hope on a fund raiser. George came a courtin', up from Tampa, Florida. It was already chilly in Minnesota and he hadn't brought an overcoat. Al scolded him. "You should have a coat on," he rasped. "You'll catch something. You can't come out here dressed like that." George was taken aback.

Some celebrities you see on TV shrink when you meet them face-to-face. But in person Steinbrenner seemed even surer of himself, prouder, more aggressive than on the tube. He was clearly a man accustomed to getting his way. Over steaks in the hotel restaurant (it was too cold to go out without a coat) he claimed that he'd been trying to get me for the Yankees since 1977. "We've been watching you for a long time," he said. In the heat of our 1977 contract negotiations the Padres had often threatened a trade, but they'd never threatened me with the Yankees. The key man doing the watching, Steinbrenner went on, was Birdie Tebbets, a longtime Yankee scout. He'd told George that with a good team my batting average would shoot up 30 points. I already knew the Yankees had really been doing their homework. Two years before, Birdie had told me they'd checked up on my life-style, and mentioned a particularly high room-service bill I'd incurred on a road trip to St. Louis a few years back. At dinner George went out of his way to tell me he knew of my foundation's work and was very impressed by it.

One of the glitches in free agency as it existed in 1980 was that it wasn't really free. Sure, I was a lot better off than Curt Flood, the first player to challenge the reserve clause, the owners' weapon to control where a man played, for how long, and for how much money. Flood's challenge of the clause cost him his career, and a few other guys with guts suffered before players like Reggie Jackson and Andy Messersmith and I, and a hundred others after us, could benefit. Still, in 1980 a player couldn't just up and leave his team for any other. Thirteen teams at most could draft him, with the clubs with the worst records given first priority. The 1980 Yankees, with 103 wins and 59 losses, had the best record of baseball's twenty-six teams. So for me to be drafted by the Yankees would require at least half of the clubs to pass on my services. The only other way I could end up in pinstripes would be for the Padres to sign me on the understanding that I'd be traded to the Yankees prior to the free agent draft.

With that in mind, the Padres finally did make noises about upping their offer to a little more than $1 million, but I didn't want to take it. I wanted to test my worth in the semi-free agent market. Besides, the Yankees weren't the only team I was interested in.

In any event, the dollars were big, the game was hardball, and it was time to put together a negotiating team. As good an idea man as Al was, I knew that we'd need some leveler heads to provide both balance and a different perspective. We asked Bob Erra to come on board, and Dick Moss, ex-general counsel for the Players Association and one of the best agents in the game.

The cornerstone of the strategy we devised was to send letters to the teams that we felt would not be able to meet my salary proposals, and to those I just didn't want to play for. In the letters we spelled out a number of considerations. I wanted a long-term contract to play on a winning team, or a team that could win, in a major market, and in a home park with natural turf. I didn't want my career shortened by an injury from playing on an artificial surface for half my games. I was also looking for a club that would provide partial support of the Foundation. "If you're not prepared to meet these conditions," the letters said, in essense, "then on draft day, please pass on Dave Winfield." The letters would, our thinking went, take enough teams out of the bidding to make room for those with good records like the Yankees. It was a strategy Dick Moss had used with success earlier.

A second key element of our plan was to pit team against team in a bidding war. We agreed that if we could get the interest of the Dodgers, for example, that would probably stimulate bidding from the Atlanta Braves and the Houston Astros, all in the National League West. If we got the Yankees to make an offer, we figured the Mets would bid to keep the Yankees from grabbing all the name players in town.

On draft day ten teams threw their caps in the ring: the Mets, Cardinals, Braves, Pirates, Reds, Astros, Orioles, Angels, Yankees, and Indians. Of those, we had tried to warn off the Orioles, Indians, Pirates, and Reds with letters. The Dodgers, my first choice in the National League, passed, having just re-signed Dusty Baker for a lot less than they would have had to pay me.

A few weeks earlier Bob and Al and I had traveled to talk with some club owners and check out the cities where their teams played. One of our first stops was Atlanta, where I met Ted Turner. Though he was cool and quiet, the second I walked into his office I could sense that here was a guy who was part genius and part wild man; the way he talked, looked, his eyes, the energy. Turner was definitely interested. He pitched the Sunbelt, the city of Atlanta, the team, and his TV franchise—SuperStation TBS, which through cable was available all across the country. "You'll grow here, you'll be part of it, you'll have the city's respect, America will love you," he intoned, like a revival preacher. Sounded good to me.

That night we went to a Halloween party at Turner's radio station and had a great time. Afterward, out on the street, a couple of white guys came cruising by in a car and yelled, "Hey, nigger!" I thought, Damn, is this the new South? Is this really what happens here? Not that I'd never heard it before, but all that day I was imagining what it would be like to be part of this community, savoring it, only to end it on that sour note.

Next stop was New York, the Yankees and the Mets. By this time, in addition to salary, terms, and Foundation support, we were also requesting a cost-of-living escalator to adjust my base salary to compensate for any increase in inflation. Having heard that no ballplayer had, or had ever had, one of these clauses in his contract, Al, with his usual chutzpah, immediately decided I should be the first. The second request was that the contract be guaranteed, with the club paying my salary over the term of the contract if I was hurt or disabled, whether on the field or off. It was the provision I had failed to win from the Padres in 1977, but by 1981 it had become a feature of many top players' contracts.

George Steinbrenner, it seemed, had no tolerance for all these details—the fine print, the escalators, the guarantees. He wanted me at any cost, and it resulted in an incredible courtship, with George at his most charming. Flowers, Broadway shows, dinner at the 21 Club, chauffeured limousines. Even telegrams in the middle of the night . . . "We want you in New York." Somewhere, maybe on the way to Elaine's restaurant from Lincoln Center, George said that he liked me a lot because I had class and he could take me places he could never take Reggie. Fantastic! Not only would I play for him, we'd pal around together.

Our mission accomplished, we told both the Yankees and the Mets we'd be back a few days before the draft. When we showed up again my picture had been in all the papers; I was already a celebrity. Only this time Al and I kept the highest profile possible. Everywhere I went there'd be photographers. I'd walk down the street, *click! click!* Go to a Knicks game, *click! click!* Interview, *click!*

All this attention wasn't lost on the public. One poor guy spotted me leaving my hotel and was so intent on shaking my hand that he crashed right into the standard holding up the awning. He had blood on his face, he looked terrible. "Man, are you all right?" I came up to him. "Oh, sure, sure . . . Dave Winfield!!"

No matter where I went the people would stop, talk to me, and usually the message was, We don't care who you go with, the Mets or the Yankees—we just want you in New York. It was refreshing. It was great. It must have been like Walt Frazier's experience in his glory days on the New York Knicks.

By December six of the teams that drafted me had dropped out of the bidding, leaving the Mets, the Yankees, the Braves, and the Astros. Dick Moss convened a meeting at his house to discuss strategy. While we were there the phone rang. Claudell Washington had just signed a five-year pact with the Braves at close to a million dollars annually. The sentiment in the room was unanimous—"God, if Claudell Washington can get that kind of money, then we should be able to get . . ." Not that Claudell wasn't a fine player. He was and is, and he's now a teammate of mine on the Yankees; it was simply that I had an edge in reputation and accomplishments. As a result, big, big numbers were bandied about, numbers that we didn't feel Houston would pay. So Dick invited John McMullen, the Astros owner, to a meeting in his New York apartment. Mr. McMullen's first words to me were, "You know you are going to get more than you are worth." The meeting could have ended then and there, but he apologized and stayed to talk. Nevertheless, after he left it did seem to be a case of just the Yankees and the Mets, the former with the best current record in baseball, the latter with one of the worst—the Padres of the National League East.

To compensate for not being a contender, the Mets were generous. They offered me $1.5 million a year for five years, six maximum, by far the largest contract ever for a professional baseball player. But George wasn't about to be embarrassed on his own turf, so he upped the ante—a $1 million signing bonus, a $1.4 million annual salary, a cost-of-living escalator that would match the rate of inflation up to 10 percent per annum, and a term of *ten* years. All told, if inflation kept running in double digits, it was a contract that could be worth as much as $23 million, the largest contract to that time for a professional athlete. And beyond that there would be support for the Foundation to the tune of $3 million.

It was the contract I eventually signed, but not the contract that George thought he had offered. Toward the tail end of the negotiations George said he wanted the option of buying out the last two years of the contract at 50 percent, or $700,000 a year. Bob and Al and I went into the other room to *bondle*. Bob looked at Al. Al looked at me.

"I can't believe it," Bob said.

"Believe what?" I asked.

"The guy's a big wheeler-dealer, but he doesn't know how a cost-of-living escalator works. He doesn't realize it *compounds.* "

"Meaning?"

"Meaning if inflation's more than ten percent and you compound one-point-four million at ten percent a year, the eighth year of the contract your base salary could be two-point-five million, and a fifty percent buyout would be . . ."

So we went back to George. "Sure," Bob said, "we'll agree to give you the option of buying out the contract at fifty percent over the last two years." George thought that was just fine.

Next day, after the particulars of the contract had been released to the press, Murray Chass of the *New York Times* came out with an analysis of the deal. Chass *did* know, however, how a cost-of-living escalator worked and he called Steinbrenner to confirm that he had signed me to a $23 million contract. Naw, that ain't the deal, George probably said, thinking he'd signed a contract worth more like $16 million. Six in the morning California time he called Bob Erra, and said, more or less, "Erra! What's going on here? We don't have a $23 million deal!"

Still in bed, Bob said, "You're in the shipbuilding business. When you give your employees a cost-of-living increase, doesn't it compound?" No comment. "Well, the compounding effect of a cap of ten percent could make Dave's contract worth twenty-three million." George hung up, fuming. He knew he'd screwed up.

What George may not have known, and what Al and Bob and I certainly didn't know, was that my signed contract wasn't worth the paper it was printed on until it reached the Players Association offices, which meant that George could still have pulled the plug on us that morning if it weren't for the fact that Dick Moss *did* know—and had hand-delivered the contract to the Players Association immediately after it was signed. Thanks, Dick.

When Bob called us with the news of George's furor Al

and I went into a panic. I didn't want to start off a ten-year hitch on the wrong foot. I suggested that maybe we should renegotiate some of the clauses. Dick Moss said I was nuts, that George had shafted enough people. It was time that someone shafted him. Al and I discussed it long and hard. Finally, I decided we should renegotiate. We didn't relinquish the dollar amounts, but we did allow the cost-of-living payments to be deferred, and at an interest rate calculated every second year, which brought the total potential payout down a little. George flew back to New York from Tampa, and it all went very amicably. That was probably the last time I heard George say, "Thank-you."

Thinking we had a done deal and that I was a Yankee, I flew back to San Diego to settle my affairs. That's when the commissioner's office put a stop on my contract at the request of the Padres. It had to do with the 100,000 one-dollar tickets that I was supposed to have bought from them—a remnant from my contract of four years ago. They told the commissioner that I'd only bought 25,000 tickets and I still owed them $75,000. "Where's the money?" That was the cry, like we had cheated them. The fact was that we'd had trouble finding enough takers for our tickets because the Padres were so godawful. Then they decided to rebuild the bleachers, which is where we were to buy our dollar-a-pop tickets, and we lost half a season's games. The Padres never offered to sell us better seats for a buck, but that was okay, we didn't hold it against them. We just thought they should be a little less insistent about the money. After all, the purpose of the deal was for disadvantaged kids to get to games, and if we couldn't put kids in the seats, it wasn't right for the foundation to just hand the money back to the Padres.

The Padres had actually been hounding me for the cash since early 1980. Then later in the season they decided to lighten up, give me an incentive to stay a Padre. So they offered us more time to buy the tickets and we accepted. But when the season ended, and I became a free agent instead of re-signing with the Padres, they wanted to forget the new agreement existed. Ballard Smith chased me to New York, crying out for the money, the money, the money, and we had to present our arguments to the Supreme Court of baseball, Commissioner Bowie Kuhn. We hammered out a new agreement. Everything was cool. Then right after I signed with the Yankees, Ballard got anxious all over again, wanted to be paid immediately. Once again Kuhn intervened, and the Foundation was given two seasons to buy the remaining tickets.

I'd finally satisfied the Padres. I'd placated George. Things were settled once and for all. I figured ten years now of smooth sailing. Little did I know that an agreement George had signed with the vice president of the Foundation, Bob Erra—totally separate from my baseball contract—would not only rock the boat for me in New York, but would at times threaten to sink everyone on it. The agreement was a promise that George Steinbrenner would contribute, or cause to be contributed, $3 million to the David M. Winfield Foundation, at a minimum rate of $300,000 a year over ten years. Not only had Steinbrenner signed the agreement, he'd actually gone into his office with Bob Erra and typed it up himself. There was no mention of the Yankees on the document, or of any of George's businesses. It was a personal agreement.

Why Steinbrenner signed as a private individual rather than on behalf of the Yankees is open to conjecture. I suspect it's because he didn't want the press or his partners on the Yankees to know the sum total of what he was paying. As it was, it was probably tough enough for them to swallow $23 million. In any event, after making his first few payments, George balked. And I've had to go to court twice to get him to live up to his obligation.

But those problems were still a year or more down the

line. By the close of 1980 I was feeling great, headed toward a team with a winning tradition, knowing that with a good club around me, I'd be able to realize my potential. Besides, when you're the top dog—as I was in San Diego—you get ulcers. I'd had enough of that grief. It was time now to play with players who played as well as I did or even better.

On December 15, at Jimmy Weston's Cafe, George Steinbrenner—in the company of Yankees Reggie Jackson, Rick Cerone, Willie Randolph, general manager Gene Michael, and others—officially introduced me to the New York sporting press as the Yankees' newest acquisition.

SEASONS: 1981

I arrive at the stadium for my first game as a Yankee dressed in cowboy boots, jeans, leather jacket, a ten-gallon hat, and $700 in my sock—it's too big a wad for my wallet. My plan is to get to my locker, change into my uniform, and put my money in the safe deposit box (there's one for each player, and you keep the key in your locker). Instead, I have to wade through a crowd of about forty reporters, twice as many as I'd ever seen in San Diego. I'm eager to get on the field, so rather than b.s. with them outside, I answer their questions while I change. As I pull off my right boot, though, the $700 flies out of my sock, the bills fluttering down around me. "Don't write about this," I beseech them, "or everyone in New York will be looking to grab my right leg."

They could have written about it, though. Nothing could have changed how good that day felt. I knew the Yankees had an excellent chance of going all the way, and I knew I could help make it happen. I also felt that I could add something of my own to the great Yankee tradition, a tradition I was introduced to as a kid in St. Paul listening to the games, and the names—Mickey Mantle, Roger Maris, Yogi Berra, Elston Howard, Whitey Ford, Billy Martin, and more recently Reggie, Catfish, Gator, Willie, and the others. It was a thrill just putting on the uniform.

Of course, a decade earlier, in the late sixties and early seventies, the Yankee mystique was on the wane. They had become a nottin' team, almost as disrespected in the AL East as the Padres in the NL West. Young players on other teams would come into Yankee Stadium and say, "Screw the Yankees. Screw the mystique. Screw the tradition. I'm here to win, to make a living." Sacrilege.

But Steinbrenner had swooped down from the heavens with his limited partnership, bought the team from CBS, and revitalized the tradition by being brash and spending cash, and with an ownership "style" that might loosely be referred to as mouth open and hands on. Interestingly enough, when he and his partners bought the team he told the *New York Times,* "We've applied for absentee ownership. I'll stick to building ships."

Anyway, by the time I had arrived, following two World Series victories in '77 and '78, and the best record in baseball in '80 despite losing the playoff to Kansas City, the mystique was back. To prove anything to my teammates or to the New York fans, I knew I'd have to be pretty damn good.

The '81 Yankees picked up where the '80 team left off. Managing the club for most of my first season was tall, lean Gene Michael, nicknamed "Stick." He replaced Dick Howser, who had won 103 games the previous year, but failed to deliver George his pennant. Stick wasn't an active manager like Billy Martin, nor was he a "character" like Yogi

Berra. He was a simple, low-key, hands-off kind of guy. He was *so* hands off, in fact, and we did so well the first half of the 1981 season that it made me question the importance given to who manages a club. Nowadays, having worked for a dozen different managers in my pro career, I give a manager credit for 5 to 7 percent of a team's result on the upside and slightly more on the downside, if his team flounders and quits on him.

I learned that first season with the Yankees that the real key to a winning team is not who's managing, but who's playing and how well they play together—no real surprise. From Little League to high school to college, I saw one or two exceptional players carry a team. But in the pros, with so many talented players, you need a teamful of talent that can play in synch. That's what we had on the 1981 Yankees—Reggie Jackson, Goose Gossage, Ron Guidry, Willie Randolph, Dave Righetti, Lou Piniella, and plenty of others.

Of course, a roster like that meant a lot of egos in the locker room, a lot of temperament. Guys who'd scream, who'd yell, who'd curse, who'd joke, or who'd just talk. But guys who knew they were good, and knew that together they were even better.

The most long-winded talker that year was Tommy John, a syllable in front of Rudy May. Tommy had the real scoop on anybody and everybody that ever played ball. The guy was just filled with trivia and it was impossible to keep him quiet. He'd just go on and on and on, talking even when no one was in the room, about how Lanny Wadkins lipped the cup on the 13th green of the 1973 Bing Crosby Open, for example. But I liked him a lot. He had the damnedest attitude. He could pitch a game, get blasted all over the park, get pulled, and it wouldn't stay with him for more than a day. Even throwing as he was with a reconstructed arm, Tommy would pitch forever if he could, I think. When he left the Yankees in 1983 I think there were some hard feelings, though. Something the Yankees said or didn't say when Tommy's son fell off a ledge at home and went into a coma. But that was then and now is now and today Tommy is talking and pitching for us again. And his son Travis recovered and is fine.

Rudy May—the "Dude." They say being left-handed tilts you a bit, and they had Rudy in mind. He had a great curve for a left-handed pitcher that he called his "yacker." "Man," he'd say, "I threw this yacker, I locked his bowels, and he absolutely dumped on himself." A black guy, Rudy was okay with everybody on the team, black or white. We only lived a block from each other and he'd call on a whim, anytime night or day. "Hey, Dave," he'd say, "let's go to the shooting range and shoot guns." So we'd get into his van, drive to the range, shoot guns. Another time he'd call just to tell me what he was up to. "You know, man, I was on my ham radio last night and I was talkin' to China and New Zealand, and you know I'm going to Tasmania in the off-season to go fishing, you know." That was Rudy, all right, off in his private world. And he was always in a great mood. "HAAAA! HAAAAA!" he'd grab me, put an arm around my shoulder. "Big Blood" was what he nicknamed me.

Another guy who was a talker, but not to the press, was Willie Randolph, the guy I got the closest to that first year, and one of the few players, along with Dave Righetti, Tommy John, and Ron Guidry, still left from the 1981 team. Willie was respected, low-key, a family man, no-nonsense on the field, a true professional all the way. If there were "wrong" people and "right" people to hang around with, Willie would definitely be one of the rightest. We'd talk about different things—the Yankees, personal life, family, baseball, business, anything. Talking to Willie was like coming home.

For talk of another kind there was Larry Milbourne, a utility player who'd been all over and did pretty well wherever they put him that year, especially at the plate, where he hit .313 to lead the team. In a town and on a team where stories and rumors were constantly flying, Milbourne fit right in. Usually a serious guy, he was also a prankster, specializing in the rumor as humor. He'd come up to you and quietly say, "You know what Cerone said about you?" Then he'd go up to Cerone and say, "You know what Winfield said about you?" You'd listen—most often it was outrageous, but sometimes it had the ring of truth. Then just as you started taking it seriously, Milbourne would let out a demented cackle.

But once practice or the game started, the screaming, the cursing, the joking, and the talking were put to bed, and being a Yankee meant working hard, playing together, and winning. There was no dilly-dallying, no fooling around about maybe being too tired. Even with injuries, you'd do your best to be in there and perform. We were a team of seasoned veterans who knew what it would take to come out on top.

From my vantage point in the outfield, I'd watch the infield make the routine plays, and the clutch plays, day in and day out. I'd savor the teamwork of Graig Nettles, Bucky Dent, Willie Randolph, and Bob Watson: Wow! I'd say to myself. Look at that play. They made the play! Two men on, the ball hit in the hole, and they threw 'em out. Double play! They were diving and leaping to catch the ball, throwing people out from all corners of the field. We were getting the same performance from the outfield, too. Up and down through the lineup, we were making the defensive play nine times out of ten that other teams would make only seven times.

We were getting similar results on the mound and from the bullpen. Our pitchers were crafty, strong, and courageous. A tight game never rattled them. Ron Guidry was firing the ball pretty doggone hard, Rudy May and Tommy

John were throwing their outrageous curves, and Dave Righetti was having his first solid year as a starter. For middle relief Ron Davis, RD, was slinging it in to set it up for the Goose to close out the game. And close out the game he would! While a teddy bear in real life with his chubby cheeks—nice guy, wife, kids, lived in Colorado, didn't go for big-city stuff—on the mound Goose Gossage was simply awesome. Sweating and spitting, fuming and flailing and hurling, Fu Manchu mustache, he was a fearful competitor. There are only a few pitchers guys really hate to see coming, and the Goose was one.

We were equally effective on offense. Willie regularly got on base, and sooner or later someone would drive him in. Nettles didn't hit much for average, but he had the knack of pivoting up on a high fastball and driving it out of the park just when we needed it. Reggie was struggling that year, but he could still do his thing. Bob Watson generated some offense and level-headed leadership in the locker room. Jerry Mumphrey and Larry Milbourne hit well. Off the bench or DHing we had Lou Piniella and Oscar Gamble, lofting balls far and wide. His next to last year as a player, Lou was still as volatile as he was when he played minor-league ball—where, rumor has it, one day he'd hit into his third double play to end the game and was so pissed that he ran to first base and down the line, jumped the right-field fence, and disappeared into the sunset. He showed up at the hotel that night still in his uniform. Years later you could count on Lou to storm into the clubhouse, turn over a table, tomahawk a helmet with a bat, break the water cooler, or curse out an umpire. Lou just *did* the stuff many players always wanted to. All told, we were a team worth the price of admission.

As for me, I loved playing that year. We were a winning machine, and after some adjustment—the new pitchers, the new team rivalries—I fit right in, felt at home. Initially, I wanted to blend in, not make any waves. But I soon realized that blending in wasn't possible. I looked different. I acted different. I was too big and too well paid. The sportswriters wanted more, the fans demanded more, and finally *I* wanted more. I wanted to be myself, play to my ability, and, above all, have fun. So after a few games I started taking chances—stealing bases when I wanted to, taking extra bases, daring to take the initiative, be different, make things happen, win. I did it for the team. I did it for myself.

Best thing about it was I didn't have to carry the team. No ulcer here. All I had to do was contribute my share, which I did, though I didn't hit my first home run until the end of April, in Detroit. Actually, it was the first home run I'd hit since the end of my 1980 season with the Padres. I'd gone all through spring training without one, much to George's consternation. One day in Fort Lauderdale he came up to Al, followed by the usual gaggle of reporters, and said, "You better tell your boy to start hitting." Al replied, "He's not a boy. Go f__ yourself." End of conversation. The press had been on my case about the drought for weeks, but in a quiet way. So that day in Detroit, figuring if I had to be on the spot I might as well be the one to put myself there, I put a sign up on my locker that read "Press Conference Here After Game." I hit a homer to right that provided the winning margin. That home-run ball ended up bronzed. It wasn't my idea, actually. Someone who wanted to do business with me down the line had it done, then gave it to me.

But even with my first home run so long in coming, by the end of the first week in June I was tied for the club lead in home runs with seven, and was batting .328, eighth highest in the American League. I was also leading the Yankees with 67 hits, 13 doubles, and 40 RBIs, and had scored 32 runs, only one off the pace of Willie Randolph, our leadoff batter. I'd played in every game, including fourteen as a center fielder, and had not made an error. It was a performance that prompted none other than Reggie Jackson to say that I was the most valuable Yankee. It was a tremendous compliment, particularly coming from Reggie. With strokes like that I felt I could play at that level forever.

On June 12, with the Yankees leading the Orioles in the American League East by two games, the Major League Baseball Players Association went on strike, the central issue being compensation for those clubs losing one of their stars to free agency. All the athletes across the board shut it down. Calling the shots for the Players Association was Marvin Miller, a highly knowledgeable, dignified man and a savvy negotiator who had pretty much on his own built the Association into the most powerful union in professional sports.

I didn't anticipate a strike and I stood to lose more than anyone else in the game with my new free agent pact. But when the decision was made there was never any doubt in my mind that I would abide by it. I knew that without Miller and the Players Association I would have never gotten to where I was. None of us would have, from the highest-paid free agent to the lowest-paid rookie. While I regretted leaving strike insurance out of the compensation package we had negotiated with the Yankees, you can't cover everything. I put my loss in perspective by calculating that Ma would have to work more than two years to make as much as I was losing in one week. The fans were less philosophical. They were pissed.

Fifty days later, on July 31, with a total of 706 games unplayed across the leagues, an agreement to end the players' strike was reached between the Players Association and the club owners. The teams leading their divisions before the strike, the Yankees among them, would play those teams with the best records following the strike for the divisional championship. After a little more than two months of New York baseball, I was on a playoff team.

Not one of the four teams leading their divisions prior to the strike went on to lead their divisions in the strike-shortened second season. I suppose knowing they'd be in the playoffs anyway took a little edge off their game after play resumed. Still, I felt that the Yankees maintained the look of a team that was legitimately playoff bound.

Steinbrenner, however, felt otherwise. Three weeks after play resumed, Michael, thought by many to be George's "man," was given his walking papers and Bob Lemon came in to manage the last 28 games. It was Lemon's second stint as a relief manager, having taken over for Billy Martin in 1978.

To wrap up the 1981 American League East championship, we have to take the best of five from the hard-charging and hungry Milwaukee Brewers, the club with the best second-season record. Coming off only a fair second season ourselves, we approach the series with a very workmanlike attitude. We know the only way to climb the next rung of the ladder is to beat these guys, so we hype our play up another level. We're both excited and sure of ourselves.

We win the first two games in Milwaukee, then come home to Yankee Stadium to finish them off. But the Brewers have a plan of their own, and instead of laying down for us, they beat us in two tough games. After the second loss Steinbrenner storms into the locker room, the first time I've ever seen him there. He curses everybody, screams and shouts about how the Milwaukee owners were guests in his private box, and how we're embarrassing him, eliminating ourselves with unprofessional play. Every guy on the team thinks the same thing: You think we're not trying, huh? You think we want to play extra games, so you and the Milwaukee owners can split another gate? It doesn't put any money in our pockets, it doesn't do anything for our pride or our morale to lose a tough game by one run and have to listen to *this*.

But nobody says a word as the boss sputters and fumes

until he turns all his wrath on Rick Cerone, getting on him about his defense. Cerone is pointed in his response. "F___ you, you fat s.o.b.! You ain't on the field. I don't want to hear your s___. Get out of here!"

Despite Steinbrenner's harangue, we come back to win the series in the fifth and final game. All that stands in the way now of an American League championship is Billy Martin's Oakland Athletics, a losing team two seasons before that Billy recharged with Billy Ball: aggressive, gambling on the base paths, bellowing from the dugout, kicking dirt onto home plate face to face with the umpires. They beat Kansas City in three straight in the American League West playoffs, but we figure they're playing over their heads and won't give us too much trouble. We matched up well, and the swaggering didn't phase us.

The first league championship game, everywhere you look there are TV cameras whirring, photographers clicking away, reporters asking you for interviews. Fine with me. My uniform's right, I'm proud. When my name is called, I run out and join my teammates on the first-base line. Each one gives me some energy, and I do the same for them. I can see in their faces they're winners. The opposing team faces off against us on the third-base line, and I think, Okay, that's your best? *Here's* our best. Let's go! It's a rare feeling. I mean, John Deere salesmen don't run out the front door every morning and pump each other up—Let's kick some butt selling those tractors!

The big story of the series is Graig Nettles. He's awesome at the plate, drives in nine runs and scores a few as we take the series in three straight games. I had been batting well enough through the year, finishing the season with the second-highest average on the team among the regulars, and hitting .350 against Milwaukee in the divisional championship. But against Oakland the ball stops dropping for me. At first, I don't really think much about it. Anything can hap-

pen in a series, and as long as my team does well it doesn't
bother me. I don't feel any less of a contributor. We're
winning, the machine is rolling, that's all I care about.

The one hit I do get is memorable, though. The bases are
loaded in the second game and I smash a bullet hard and low
down the third-base line. It looks like certain extra bases, but
suddenly it caroms off the bag and pops high into the air.
I'm running to first, but all the air has gone out of my lungs.
Easy money now looks dangerously like an easy out. Luckily the Athletics' third baseman, with the improbable name
of Mickey Klutts, can't make the play. I'm safe and one run
scores.

The same game I also make one of the toughest catches
in my career. Tony Armas comes to the plate with men on
first and third, and smashes one deep over my head into the
sun. I race the ball back to the left-field fence, plant my foot,
and leap. Chest parallel to the wall, I twist my head back to
follow the ball, see it like a black meteor fired from the
middle of the sun, get my arm up, higher, higher, higher,
smash into the wall, and snag the ball with the very tip of
my glove. Three Oakland runs disappear into the last inch
of its webbing.

You could see it was over for Oakland when Rickey
Henderson and Dale Murphy went down with injuries. The
A's were like a raft in the ocean with no oars. But the big
story of that league series still is Nettles. He destroys them.
And then after he seals their fate, he tries to seal Reggie's.
It happens in Oakland at a postgame party. Oakland is Reggie's turf, his hometown, and he invites more than his share
of celebrants. When Nettles tries to reclaim some of the
chairs occupied by Reggie's people, there are words, Reggie
and Nettles put up their fists, and Nettles socks him, *pow!*
They grab each other, start rolling around on the floor, and
all hell breaks lose. Bob Watson, the Goose, and I have to
jump from tabletop to tabletop just to get to the fracas to

break it up. I can't believe it. Guys from the same team on the way to the World Series duking it out. Not at all what I expected.

For me, winning the pennant after nine years as a pro feels great. I'm elated. It's a tremendously satisfying experience, and also a kind of justification because some people had said, "Yeah, Winfield is okay in a small pond like San Diego, but throw him into deep water on the Yankees and he'll drown." I've shown I can contribute to making the playoffs and winning them. I've led the team in RBIs, I'm second among the regulars in home runs and hitting. I've proven I belong at the top of the league.

But that doesn't mean I pour champagne all night. I figured we'd steamroller Oakland because of how we matched up against them. But the Dodgers, the team we'd have to beat to come out of the season world champions, are a much more even matchup. So my attitude that day, and the attitude of most of the team, is more one of preparing for the Series than celebrating the pennant. Time to kick some Dodger ass.

The first game of the Series is like the first game of the league championship, only more so. The TV cameras are on you nonstop. You want a drink of water, a sunflower seed to chew? Drink it or chew it while you answer this question. You want to go to the bathroom? Fine, but speak into the microphone as you sit down.

The first two games of the Series are played in Yankee Stadium. We beat the Dodgers in Game 1, and then again the next day in Game 2. The first game I don't get a hit, but no big deal, I'm just happy we win. I go hitless again in the second, and now I begin to get irritated. Damn! I think; how'd they get me out? I'm not frustrated or depressed, but the press are on me like glue, asking me how I feel. All the while the TV cameras whir, the flashbulbs pop. Stepping up at the plate in the second game I can imagine the announcer saying, He must be worried about not hitting—did you see him twitch? But I'm fine, I'm not going to let it get to me. I'm making good contact. It's just one of those Series when, no matter where I hit it or how hard I hit it, the fielder is there.

Instead of dwelling on it I psych myself up for the next game, get myself ready to show what I can do when the Series moves to Los Angeles. Game 3 I go hitless and we lose. A couple of times we have Fernando Valenzuela on the ropes and can't put him away. Then finally in Game 4 I hit a little jam shot to left field that falls in front of Dusty Baker. With so much having been made in the press about my not hitting since the Milwaukee series, I call time at first base and ask that the ball be thrown in, something usually done to commemorate a milestone in a player's career. Only I'm doing it ironically, as a way of saying, Let's lighten up; let's not make more of this than it is. When Dusty Baker tosses in the ball from left field, the Yankees crack up, and the Dodgers laugh, too. It's a nice moment.

I reckon now that I've broken the ice there'll be more hits and we'll win the game. But we don't. The Dodgers go on to win that day and the next for a home park sweep and a 3–2 lead. Furious, Steinbrenner punches an elevator. Well, he punches something or someone in an elevator—two burly Dodger fans that he sends packing, by his account. Waiting for George to come out to the team bus with his bandaged hand the guys are skeptical; nobody figures George for actually belting someone.

In any event, we come back to New York for Game 6, intent on winning two at home to take the Series. We don't do that either. The Dodgers wrap it up in six. And my hit in Game 4 is my first and last in the Series.

Reflection time. I'm disappointed, real disappointed. But not shattered. Like the other guys, I'm proud of what the team had done, proud of my contribution. Hitting .045 in the World Series is no picnic, but a lot of great players have put up low numbers in the World Series, and I know I'll have to wait till the next time to do better.

In that spirit, I ride the elevator up, stop by Steinbrenner's office on my way back home for the off-season. His chin is in his hands, he's so disappointed about losing to the Dodgers. I tell him I appreciate the chance he's given me to play in New York, that I love being a Yankee, and that I'm not satisfied with second place either. On the way out, with a smile, I say, "I owe you one," not to apologize for my performance at the plate, as some reporters had it, but simply to say, Wait till next year—we'll get it then.

Early in November while we were relaxing in Las Vegas Al got a phone call from John Campi, head of advertising and promotion for the New York *Daily News.* He asked Al if I wanted to be on the *Daily News* float in the Macy's Thanksgiving Day Parade. "Yeah!" Al said, "that would be nice," which was true. Next he asked Al if I could sing. "Yeah!" Al said again, which was terribly, terribly false. Finally he asked Al how it was that he could attest to my singing ability. "I went to Juilliard," Al said, which was again true. Two out of three. Then Al hung up and told me what I was in for.

The *Daily News* float was in the shape of an enormous red apple with a platform where the stem would be and a skinny railing and a strap to keep me from tumbling onto the street. It was from this lofty perch, according to Al and John Campi's plan, that I would stand and sing "I'll take Manhattan, the Bronx, and Staten Island . . ." to a live audience of one million lining the curbs and a televised audience of maybe forty million more.

"You must be kidding," I told Al. "I do all my singing in the shower."

"Hey, Diana Ross did it. Julio Iglesias."

"They're singers!"

Al had no patience for the obvious. The day before the parade we rehearsed in Radio City Music Hall. Al and one of the cast members from *Sugar Babies* helped me out. After forty minutes of rehearsal it was decided it'd be best to tape the song, and just have me lip-synch the words on the float. I'd made hour-long speeches without notes, but I was so afraid I'd forget the words to this two-minute song and screw up the lip-synching that I carried a Walkman with me in my coat all day, listening to the lyrics. I even slept with it.

The World Series outcome still fresh in Al's mind he decided I should be outfitted with a bullet-proof vest— "Nothing to worry about, really, just a precaution." It was okay by me. I'd be an easy target traveling the parade route down Fifth Avenue. And I knew that lots of bettors had parted with big bucks on the Yankee loss. Finally, though, I went with my long underwear under my uniform and a Yankee jacket for protection. The vest they came up with wouldn't have fit Spud Webb.

No matter. Less than a year after I signed with the Yankees, there I was, rolling down Fifth Avenue lip-synching a New York song, on top of the "Big Apple." And when, after an hour-long, butt-freezing ride, the float finally stopped in front of Macy's and the red light on the camera went on to indicate I was on the air worldwide, I figured, What the hell! and went for it, rocking and finger-popping to the beat and singing my lungs out.

PEOPLE

As much as I wanted to play on a winner, I never set out to be "the straw that stirs the drink," as Reggie Jackson defined his intended role on the Yankees. Maybe just the lime on the lip of the glass. But then again, Reggie and I are cut from a different mold.

At that time Reggie was the kind of guy who'd show up late at your party, then act like you're the one who didn't belong. Once, before we were teammates and just after he hit three home runs in a single World Series game against the Dodgers, I invited him to a Lakers game in Los Angeles. At first Reggie wanted to know where I got the tickets—from Jack Kent Cooke, who owned the team then—and then he acted surprised, like he didn't believe I had that kind of pull. As we were walking up to the entrance of the Forum—at halftime because Reggie had to stop at a friend's along the way—he said, "You got the tickets?" I reached into my pocket for them. "Doesn't make any difference anyhow," he said, " 'cause I can get us in free." As if I didn't matter, and all that mattered was Reggie and Reggie's fame.

But as I got to know him I found there was a lot more to Reggie than just ego. Sure, he loved to be seen and heard. He had a sharp, quick wit. But he could also be easygoing, unassuming, friendly, and generous. And then suddenly he'd go off—on fans, on the press, on teammates, or on friends, without any apparent provocation. Clearly, beneath both versions he was a complex man with a lot going on.

On the one hand, Reggie was probably pleased to see me on the Yankees. My large contract could potentially put him into a stronger bargaining position when he renegotiated his own contract at the end of the 1981 season. On the other hand, my earning more than three times his own salary could only have rankled him. Plus, the press was definitely trying to create a rivalry, pitting us against each other, article after article about who should be batting cleanup or who the better all-around player was.

Since I wasn't the guy trying to stir the drink, it didn't get to me. But I think it got to Reggie. There were even times when I'd be in the on-deck circle and Reggie would come up behind me, say "Come on!" then hit me on the butt with a bat a little harder than you'd expect a guy on your team would.

The biggest problem between us had nothing to do with my being there. It was that Reggie was having a bad year. His timing was off, he was striking out a lot, he stayed in one of his funks. And Steinbrenner was dogging him in the papers, making him go for eye tests, degrading stuff like that. I remember once when the team was in Chicago for a series with the White Sox I had a long lunch with him, trying to buoy his spirits. But Reggie was inconsolable, wondering whether his career was over. He must also have been concerned about his upcoming free agency, wondering whether he'd get the respect and the money that other free agents would get. And that I had already gotten.

Since he left the Yankees, Reggie and I don't see each other off the field much, but whenever we played the Angels—and later the Athletics—we'd get together on the field and talk. Once when I was batting a miserable .240, was way behind the pack in RBIs, and groaned to him about it, he said, "That's all right. Next time you come through town you'll be right up there with the leaders." Another time when my hitting was off he said, "No matter what you hit, you're still Dave Winfield. Just don't ever let 'em catch you not hustling." That was Reggie in a nutshell. Always was.

It was only a few years back that Reggie seriously

broached the subject of retirement to me. He said that when the time came, he could do it; it would be easy enough to contemplate the few million he had in the bank and say, "Thanks for the ride, adios!" Still, it didn't surprise me when he signed with the A's in 1987 to return to the scene of some of his greatest glories, and in a way again to be the straw that stirred the drink. And I'm glad he finally retired when he did. He was still strong, scary, set a good example for his team and the league. I sure would have hated for him to flicker out of the game like a candle starved for oxygen.

KIDS

In February 1981 the David M. Winfield Foundation opened its doors in Fort Lee, New Jersey. Our goals were the same as they had been in San Diego—to share what I'd learned as a professional athlete with less fortunate kids and their families, to bring them to games and sports celebrations, and to introduce them to opportunities in health and education. To make it happen in our new location, we'd sponsor health fairs, nutritional counseling, field trips and parties, computer literacy and scholarship programs, and a major drug awareness program aimed at getting elementary and high school students to "say no to drugs" and later helping entire communities to take action against drug abuse and related problems in their midst. This was an ambitious plan of action and it would take money to bring it to fruition—most of it to come initially from the $300,000 Steinbrenner had agreed to pay annually, and later from the Foundation's own fund-raising activities and corporate support.

We kicked off our new Foundation in grand style on August 8, 1981, with a party to celebrate the reopening of the season following the strike, and the playing of the All-Star Game. The game had been scheduled to win back baseball fans after the fifty-day hiatus, and was to be played the next day in Cleveland. The party was held at Randall's Island Park in New York. A total of 13,000 kids whose names were furnished by the Boy Scouts, the Girl Scouts, the Police Athletic League, the YMCA, and other organizations were invited from the greater New York area. We were expecting maybe 11,000, but nearly 20,000 showed up for a free baseball clinic, autographs, and a bag lunch. We also gave away hundreds of pairs of shoes, grooming products donated by Vidal Sassoon, T-shirts, and a number of kids received free medical exams.

I flew to Cleveland that night for the game, where I played center field in front of 80,000 fans on a very muggy night, and had a home-run ball bounce back into the park off the top of the wall. My old friends from the National League spoiled my American League All-Star debut by squeaking by us, 5–4.

BOSSES

There's a lot been written about George Steinbrenner. He's the guy who loves kids, the benefactor, the sportsman, the self-made multimillionaire, the man who loves Shakespeare. There are stories about him footing the bill for a weekend in New York for a Cleveland high school basketball team, funding scholarships, starting the Silver Shield Foundation for the children of New York policemen killed in action, hosting the annual Whitney Young football classic at Yankee Stadium to benefit black colleges, and quietly paying Elston Howard's medical bills after he passed away. Howard was the first black Yankee. George as the kindly, munificent Dr. Jekyll.

But then there's Mr. Hyde, the guy who screams at his employees whether they're in pinstriped uniforms or pinstriped suits—the guy who likes to make things difficult. And I mean difficult. Once during the 1981 holiday season, the Foundation organized a Christmas turkey and trimmings giveaway for two thousand needy families. Yankee Stadium was to be the pickup point. It was all arranged a month in advance. Folks from the nearby community were selected at random from a list provided by social service organizations to determine who'd get the turkeys, and the recipients had been told to meet us at the stadium at 9 A.M. The afternoon before the giveaway, with a blizzard on its way, we went to the stadium for a final run-through only to have stadium security tell me we couldn't use the stadium, but if we wanted we could use the parking lot. The parking lot! I looked out my window, thought ahead, and foresaw snow building in huge drifts in the yard. "The parking lot!" The turkey truck was already loaded, ready to make the drop-off. "Whose decision was that?" I asked, knowing full well where it must have come from, because no one else has the authority at the stadium—Old Scrooge himself.

At first we tried to find a spot in the lot out of the wind and snow where people could wait in line for their turkeys. There wasn't one. We searched the neighborhood frantically for a place to use for an hour before dusk. Finally, we got permission to use the elementary school behind Yankee Stadium, where we could unload and where people would be sheltered from the cold.

Making things even more difficult, though, was George's

failure to make his payments to the Foundation. The initial payment was made on Steinbrenner's behalf by WPIX, the New York television station that broadcasts Yankee games. Steinbrenner made two more payments, then stopped in the fourth quarter of 1981. Beyond difficult, it was irritating and embarrassing because there were bills and salaries to be paid, which I eventually had to advance the Foundation out of my own pocket. Right around that time I read in the papers that Steinbrenner said, "Winfield's not a winner, not the guy I'd hoped for." I didn't respond to George's mouthing off, and the only action I took to get him to adhere to his payment schedule to the Foundation was to make a few courteous phone calls. They were ignored, and publicly he became more blustery and offensive.

I wasn't sure then, and I'm still not, what his gripe is with me. Part of it is, I think, as a frustrated athlete with marginal ability, George wants to "own" his players, wants them up on their flippers barking for fish like trained seals. And from the beginning I refused to bark. Maybe he's also bothered by the fact that, because of the Foundation, I have a credibility and respect in the community that encroaches on what he thinks is owners' territory. After all, why's this guy he "owns" doing public service spots on TV, appearing before high school assemblies, talking to executives, being presented awards at City Hall, receiving honorary degrees? You'd think he'd welcome it all as good public relations for the team. Eventually you realize that George Steinbrenner is George Steinbrenner and stop trying to figure him out. You prepare for the worst, so that anything less is a bonus.

In any event, when I arrive in Fort Lauderdale for 1982 spring training, George is already there, holding court like a potentate in his long, long trailer. In it he has a desk with all these phones, and on the wall, pictures of himself with the rich and famous. "Look," I say, finally gaining an audience with him, "let's get together and settle this . . ." But

George waves me off, gets the governor of Florida on the line. I sit down. When he finally hangs up I ask him, "Why don't you pay the money?"

"I'm not going to pay," he snaps like a spiteful kid.

"I don't get it."

"That's just the way it goes."

"The way it goes?"

"Yes." George turns back to the phone. Our meeting is over. I walk out furious, not caring if I ever play another inning of Yankee baseball. From that moment on I'm committed to only one thing—making George keep his part of the bargain.

Weeks later, after reporters begin asking about the payments, he schedules a second meeting. Sitting with him are a bunch of administrators he's flown down from New York for the occasion. My lawyer, Al, and I are sitting across from them in the trailer at a conference room table. The administrators are eager, with the freshly scrubbed look of a boys' choir—except we never hear a peep from any one of them, they're buttoned up in a corner waiting for a cue that never comes. Probably because they don't know a thing about the agreement to begin with. Once again I ask George to pay and once again he says he won't. So I get up and say, "I'm going to let you gentlemen finish this talk. I have to practice." Minutes later, my lawyer and Al are shown the door— end of discussion.

Early in the 1982 season Steinbrenner concedes to the papers that "Winfield's a good athlete," then adds, "but he's no Reggie," referring to the guy whom not too long ago he was hustling off to the eye doctor. Right about the time those pearls appear, Reggie's new team, the Angels, comes to town for a stand against the Yankees. It's a pleasant evening, the lights in the stadium glisten in the mist as Reggie steps up to bat against Ron Guidry, "Gator." Reggie takes one look at Gator's fastball and cold-cocks it over the right-field fence and into the bleachers. Steinbrenner is in his box and everyone in the stadium knows it. As Reggie rounds the bases the chant goes up: "Reg-gie! Reg-gie! Reg-gie!" And then, like it's been rehearsed: "STEINBREN-NER SUCKS! STEINBRENNER SUCKS!" for three minutes or so.

A couple of days later I'm talking to Dick Young, a New York sportswriter, and Steinbrenner's name comes up. I warm to it, foolishly thinking what I'm saying is off the record. "This guy gets on everyone's case," I say, "and when it gets tough, he leaves town. He's the one that can't take the heat!" Next day the headline reads "Winfield Rips Steinbrenner," a picture of both of us above. Same day one of Steinbrenner's lackeys comes up to me and says, "Ooooh, he's mad!" I find out later that's what his people always say, like 'fraidy-cat kids on the playground talking about some bully.

Finally I stop pussyfooting around and take the offense in my battles with my boss. Though people tell me "No one sues George Steinbrenner," I bring suit on behalf of the Foundation. George tries to slip out of it, scurrying around for legal loopholes, but we finally reach a settlement. In return for paying what he owes, he gets a spot on the board of directors and a new payment schedule. No problem. So much dirt, money, and animosity for that.

For some odd reason George sees settlement of the suit as a photo opportunity, which is okay with me. But rather than a shot of the two of us with business suits on, shaking hands, he has me come up to Billy Martin's office at the stadium in my uniform. There are at least a dozen reporters waiting. Just before any pictures are snapped, he jumps up on a coffee table. I look up to see where he's standing, and suddenly *flash! flash! flash!* It's the picture they all print. Big, tall George, and me in my uniform, like I'm his little boy.

BUSINESS

Not long after I signed with the Yankees, when George and I were still on the best of terms, we put together a company called Top Hat to market my services as a spokesperson for products and businesses. The plan was for George and my people to split the proceeds fifty-fifty. George favored the idea because he knew he could capitalize on my popularity to earn back some of the bucks he'd spent to sign me. I liked it because with Steinbrenner involved it would give me an even better entrée into the New York business community.

Things didn't run smoothly from the outset. It was agreed that Al would do the marketing, but his style was too unorthodox and too grating to appeal to the upscale organizations we were talking to, Citibank and Equitable Life Insurance, to name a few. Aggravating the problem was that George couldn't stand Al, and whenever Al put together a deal that required George's blessing, he turned it down. I'm not sure what his thinking was, but I do know it cost us both a bundle.

Also, by the end of 1981—with George bad-mouthing me to the press following our World Series loss, and later with the lawsuits I'd had to bring to get him to make his payments to the Foundation—the business community and some fair-weather friends soured on me. All they ever remembered hearing in the press was that I was feuding with Steinbrenner and was embroiled with him in a legal tangle. It was the kiss of death for endorsements for quite a while. No matter how popular I was, I couldn't be the one to present a company's image to the public.

So deals fell to the wayside, deals that could have easily earned George back the $300,000 annual payments to the

Foundation and a lot more. His mouth and his refusal to pay cost us both, and thwarted my potential and my growth. All I really wanted was for George to let me do what I could. And that I be respected for my play on the field and my work off the field, whether as a businessman or as a contributor to the community. But for some reason he'd chosen to make it very difficult for me.

If I couldn't do it with George, I decided, I'd do it without him. I obtained a few endorsements on my own. I also built up an off-season career as a motivational and after-dinner speaker. My career as a businessman, however, didn't develop until the mid-eighties with my fast-food franchises, my art galleries, and Specific Sports Training—a fledgling company that could revolutionize training and conditioning for serious athletes and the general public. In the early eighties, though, I was still a student, taking business one careful step at a time.

The rumor was that when I came to New York Al was pushing all the buttons. But he wasn't and he couldn't. I soon realized, in fact, through my experience with Top Hat, that while Al may have been the consummate New Yorker, he'd been away too long. Times and styles had changed. He didn't know the New York of the eighties. He didn't know Wall Street, he didn't know Madison Avenue. He was street smart, but the streets had changed. So I spent time learning as much about business, New York style, as I could from others. I talked to a lot of people—corporate, political, financial—I did a lot of reading, I traveled. I did a number of things right, I made some mistakes.

One of the most significant lessons connects back to Al. While I was still in San Diego he introduced me to a father-and-son team of lawyers who practiced in New York—let's call them Papa Bear and Baby Bear. They'd never represented a ballplayer before but were savvy about law and business. So when I got to New York and needed legal assistance, I turned to them. Stupidly, we never signed a contract, and I never even asked how much they charged per hour. "David, we're friends," Papa Bear said whenever the subject of money was broached.

A few years later, following the Bears' involvement in setting up the Foundation, negotiating a handful of endorsements, and the institution of my first lawsuit against Steinbrenner, there were some rumblings about money from the Bear camp. So I decided to settle my account. One afternoon I stopped by their office in Rockefeller Center to see what I owed them.

I found Papa Bear in the office, but it would have been the same with Baby Bear, I'm sure. You talk to one, you're talking to the other. One time one of them is nice, the next time the other. "Let's put it this way," Papa Bear said. "What would you like to give me?"

"What do you mean, 'give you'?"

Papa Bear smiled. We were, after all, such good friends. "You know, David, *give* me. For the work we've done. Money."

"If I owe you something, tell me what your rates are, when we started working together, what you've accomplished. But don't ask me what I want to give you. Just tell me exactly how much I owe you."

Still smiling, Papa Bear told me I owed him $3.5 million. I couldn't believe it. For an instant I considered picking the old bear up and just throwing him out the window, nineteen floors down into the skating rink. I could have picked him up and been done with it. But a saner voice prevailed. "Show me," I said. "Show me what you've done to earn it."

After my meeting with Papa Bear, it was clear I needed a lawyer to protect me from my lawyers. I hired Weil, Gotshal & Manges, a big firm, and worked mainly with Jeff Klein, a young associate. At the time Weil, Gotshal was representing the Players Association in its litigation with the owners about television revenues. Their professionalism in that case impressed me.

My new lawyers asked the Bears to account for all their charges. They had no time sheets or other billing records to show. After lots of meetings—where inevitably one Bear or the other would storm out—we whittled down their $3.5 million blue sky request and finally settled on a payment of $35,000.

Lawyers certainly aren't the only ones out to make a buck on a poor, dumb jock. Agents, stock brokers, investment counselors, real estate developers have all been to the trough. You just have to read the papers to find out who's losing the real money. Ron Guidry makes big, big bucks, and one day you read in the *Wall Street Journal* he's lost over $3 million, he's nearly broke. George Foster earns $2 million a year, a big investment goes belly-up, and suddenly he's hurting. That doesn't necessarily mean that Guidry or Foster or others were ripped off or foolish. But it does demonstrate that if it's your money, you'd be smart to watch it carefully, to know where it is and what it's doing. Aware I could fall prey to scams and Shylocks, I've made myself knowledgeable in handling money. One thing is for sure, I don't want to do it like some guys—give my salary to an individual or a group and have them take care of my finances, pay my taxes, pay my bills, make my investments, and dole out my allowance. Let the mistakes be mine, and the successes too.

WOMEN

Not long after Sandra had her baby, she and her pro basket-ball player husband split up and she went back to work for the airlines. She visited me once or twice with her son, Ira Sharad, while I was still in San Diego, and we talked on the phone a few times after I moved to New York. Early in 1982 she called. We found we both had some time free and decided to travel together. She suggested Brazil. I'd always liked spending time with Sandra, I'd never been to South America, so I took her up on it.

About six weeks later she called me at spring training and told me she was pregnant again, though she had again supposedly been on the pill. I asked her what she wanted to do and she said she was going to have the baby. As before, I wasn't certain it was mine, but even if it were, I wasn't ready to settle down and have kids, and I told her so. A few days later she showed up in Florida, "just to talk a minute about this"—the luxury of working for an airline. I repeated what I'd told her on the phone. Al was also there and tried in his inimitable way to charm her into not having the baby, but she was adamant.

After she left, I felt pretty lousy about the whole thing. I'd always liked women, always liked sex, but I was never the type of guy who would want to father children outside marriage. But suddenly here I was in the position hundreds of thousands of guys find themselves in. A lot of things went through my mind—not me?!? I was doing my best to set a good example, be a role model. I knew, working with disadvantaged youngsters, that there were already far too many kids in the world with negative home lives. And I knew I was not emotionally ready to provide a good environment for a kid *or* a wife, though some day I wanted to marry, have a family. What I *didn't* want was to spend a few days with somebody after seeing her infrequently for years, and suddenly have no choice about my future with her. Among other things, it made me suspicious of Sandra's motives—made me wonder if she'd actually planned it all, dropping back into my life, spending an idyllic week together, getting pregnant, insisting on having the baby.

The bottom line, though, was that Sandra's urgent visit and her being pregnant touched me. As the season went on I came to believe that it was my child. And so to make the best out of a bad situation, I acknowledged that I was the father.

On September 29, 1982, Lauren Shanel Winfield was born in Houston. I chose Lauren, and Sandra picked the name Shanel. I was on the road with the club in Cleveland when I got a phone call early in the morning telling me that Sandra had gone into labor. And though I tried not to think too much about it, tried to concentrate instead on my game, I found myself smiling a little and dwelling on the importance of that day. I knew I wanted to do something special for my child, since I couldn't see the birth. So I did, hit a tremendous home run. I've got it on videotape and when our relationship develops I intend to show it to her. A few days later I flew to Texas to see Lauren. I still remember the feeling of touching her for the first time. I was a little clumsy about it, but there she was all bundled up in a pink-and-white comforter. You wanna see a picture?

PEOPLE

Not long after the '82 season began Al had a stroke, the real McCoy. It happened while he was at the races and they rushed him to the hospital. I was on the road when Bobbie called to tell me, reassuring me that it wasn't a big deal, and that I should wait for the team to come back to New York before trying to see him. I took her advice, but called every day to check on his progress. "He's getting better," Bobbie would tell me. But since I wasn't allowed to talk to him, I figured it was worse than she let on. Ten days later I walked into the hospital. If this is what "better" was, he must have been dead before. I was shocked. He looked terrible. He was in a wheelchair, his face haggard, his body caved in like a half-empty sack of grain. Tears filled my eyes. He saw me. At first there was just the recognition, but then he grabbed the arms of the wheelchair and slowly propped himself up on his arms. His legs were useless. I walked over to him and hugged him tight, as both of us wept.

It was, I was told, the first real sign of hope for Al since the stroke. His recovery began with my visit. As the weeks passed he started to come back. Each time I'd visit him he insisted on demonstrating his progress, however basic—lifting a finger, pushing a button, writing on a pad, and even later getting around with a walker and then a cane. "I'll show you," he said when he finally had enough language to do so, "I'm not going to leave you, Davey. I'm not finished." Sadly, in some ways he was.

If there were any questions about Al's ability to make things happen in New York before his stroke, afterward there was no question. He was sick, he couldn't keep up the pace. I could tell it was killing him. Still, he'd call 'most every night, sometimes with an idea for a new deal that we couldn't possibly bring off, other times with off-the-wall schemes—a real estate development in partnership with an Arizona Indian tribe, "Son of Superstar Village." Long before the stroke, though, I'd told him that I needed more people in my life, other influences, told him I wanted to get involved with projects that didn't necessarily involve him. He listened, but I'm not sure he heard.

In 1983 he and Bobbie moved back to California. We continued talking a few times a week. I always asked him for advice, and he was still more than eager to give it to me. He died in November 1987 after a final, massive stroke. When Bobbie called me with the news, her voice full of tears, I closed the door to my office and prayed for Al. No man has ever meant or will ever mean as much to me as Al Frohman.

The morning of Al's funeral I sat down to write a eulogy, words that flowed straight from my heart.

Dear Lord,

Before we commit the body of Albert S. Frohman to you I want to share these things with his family and friends. Al Frohman took me into the flesh and blood of his own family. He spent more time with me than any other grown man ever did. Under him and with him I grew in wisdom, ability, and stature. Things that can never be taken away from me, and that I hope will be passed down in my own family for generations to come.

You are gone from us, Al Frohman, but you are not forgotten. How could anyone who knew you ever forget you? To the man who was my closest friend. . . .

We have shared our last meal, our last journey, our last negotiation, our last battle. Anyone who knew you knows you lived for the challenge of it all.

There are plenty of challenges ahead for me, and I'm going to take you with me wherever I go. We loved, cared, shared most everything for fifteen years. You taught me many things, Al Frohman. You taught me to never quit. You never quit, time just ran out.

I loved you, Al. I'll miss you. Rest in peace, my man.

THE GAME

The Yankees' 1982 season was like a three-ring circus with a different manager for each ring. We started out with the guy who took us through the Series, Bob Lemon. He never said a lot, was not a real motivator. He lasted fourteen games before Steinbrenner gave him the axe and replaced him with the guy Lemon had taken over from the year before, Gene Michael. But this time Stick was gun-shy. He'd still talk a good, aggressive game, but you could tell he was nervous about what Steinbrenner might do next. He posted a 44–42 record for the first half of the season, and was canned.

Next, Steinbrenner brought in Clyde King, an old-time baseball man and reputedly one of the only men in the game that George respected. He was older than George, had been around the block more than once, though he favored front office work to managing. I liked Clyde King as a person because I felt he honestly tried to get the best out of the players on the field. And he respected me, would ask me what I felt about some of our younger players, stuff like that. But he was only there as a caretaker and the Yankees didn't do any better with Clyde at the helm than we did with either of his predecessors. We played under .500 ball that year, finishing out the season with a 79–83 record.

The problem of that mediocre season wasn't so much managers as it was philosophy. We were playing without a workable plan. I say "workable" because there *was* a plan—the 1982 Yankees, we were told, were going for speed instead of power. This was fine with me, but for the most part we didn't have the right players to execute the plan. We were an older ball club with lots of veterans unable to make the transition at that point in their careers. Management was attempting to make players into something they weren't. It was a disaster.

Trying to import some speed, they picked up Dave Collins from Cincinnati. Get him to first and he was a scooter on the base paths. But he rarely hit with authority, and blooping the ball, no matter what the plan, just isn't the Yankee style. His tenure on the team was further jeopardized by the fact that he didn't have a position, was one of three guys slated to play first base.

They also picked up John Mayberry, past his prime. John was a big, big, southern guy who liked his ham hocks and black-eyed peas. They tried to put him on a diet to shed a couple of pounds, but Mayberry was big all his life and wasn't about to change, though he'd always order Diet Cokes with his five-course southern feasts.

In a losing season with few high points, Bobby Murcer gave the fans something to cheer about. Bobby had originally come to the Yankees in '65 as the guy who was supposed to replace Mickey Mantle. He never filled those shoes, but played hard for the club through all the lean years until he was traded to the Giants a decade later. The Yankees brought him back in '79 as a designated hitter, and in '82 he punched in 30 runs in only 141 at-bats. The New Yorkers loved him.

That season was my last in left field and I was happy to

make the switch to right. I never felt comfortable throwing from left in Yankee Stadium, the angle was odd and I'd actually end up playing deep left center, rather than honest left. I also missed a few games that year with a hamstring injury. Phil Rizzuto, the "Voice of the Yankees," was quick to point out my absence from the lineup, adding, "I wonder if Winfield gets paid today?" Like at my salary I damn well better play every game. The thing was, I guess, that Scooter and a lot of other people hadn't adjusted to the new stratosphere of salaries.

In any event, I finished out the season leading the team with 37 home runs and 106 RBIs. It was the first in what would be a string of five consecutive 100+ RBI seasons.

My first encounter with Billy Martin was in Oakland in 1981 while Billy was managing the A's. He loved to get the psychological edge on his opponents. My first at-bat I hit a cheap single, so when I came to the plate again he stepped out of the dugout and waved his outfielders in to play me shallow.

Later in the game I hit a bloop single in the ninth to drive in the winning run and Billy told the papers I had a "soft bat." Back in New York against them I went out and ripped the ball, including a 430-foot double off the wall. When the press asked me what I thought of Martin I said, "I'm not worried about him because I'm not a marshmallow salesman, and because I don't work for him. But if he needs a loan, he can call me for an appointment."

Two years later, in 1983, I *was* working for Billy Martin. Seeking to break us of our losing ways, George brought Billy back to take over for the failed triumvirate of Lemon, Michael, and King. Once on the same team, Billy and I got along fine. I hit well for him, drove in a lot of runs, stole a lot of bases. He tended to overplay his guys, but if I asked him for a day off, he'd give it to me. He is a master tactician, a motivator, and he favors an aggressive brand of baseball that I like to play.

Billy's tenure with us that year was a qualified success. We went from 79 wins the year before to 91. But we still finished seven games out, in third place. One of the problem areas was the outfield—'83 was the year that management decided that Jerry Mumphrey, a three-year man and a center fielder, was to take charge of the outfield. Only "Mumph" wasn't a take-charge kind of guy. He was a fleet-footed switch-hitter from Texas who could really put some pop on the ball. But he talked slow, almost mumbled, would get right up next to you and plant soft words in your ear. To take charge in the outfield you can't mumble. You've got to be assertive—"I've got it! I've got it!"—and there were a number of times that year when the ball would fall between fielders because no one had taken charge.

At one point Billy asked me how I felt about playing center field. I told Billy I didn't think it was a good idea to have a six-foot-six, 235-pound, thirty-three-year-old center fielder out there shagging flies. "Get one of them young bloods to chase that ball and cover the big field." It wasn't that I couldn't do it. I'd played center field for the Yankees before when they'd asked and I'd played it well. I just didn't think it was the best use of the team's manpower. Better defense, but probably less offense, and we still come up short. Billy never hassled me about it, but not long after our talk I read in the papers that George said, "Winfield doesn't want to play center field because he's scared of the ghost of Joe DiMaggio." Yankee Stadium was full of ghosts, to be sure, but begging off playing center as a regular thing I never even gave Joltin' Joe a thought.

THE LAW

It had been thirteen years since I'd had a run-in with the law. But then, in 1983, I traveled with the Yankees to Toronto . . .

It's a night game, I'm playing center, Don Baylor is in left. We'd just taken the field in the bottom of the third inning and Don and I are playing catch, when I see this seagull sitting way over to my left, about thirty yards this side of the foul line. I'd seen it there earlier, had thought then, What's that big bird doing here? Now, as the Blue Jay half of the inning is about to start, I throw the ball to the ball boy, but I throw it right in front of the bird to scare it off. The ball takes a short hop off the artificial turf and *wop!* it flattens the bird. Right away I know he's a goner. I feel awful. He was a big, old seagull and now he's a big white pile, just lying there with his feathers scattered around him. As the ball boy comes onto the field with a white towel, a murmur starts up in the crowd. He picks the bird up, puts it on the towel, and makes a show of carrying it off. The murmur turns to a rumble, then to massive booing as the guy makes his way to the sidelines. By the time he gets there, the booing has built to a roar. Everyone is yelling, throwing stuff onto the field, and rattling the fences at me.

They boo me the rest of the game. To add insult to injury we win and I'm the key man with a homer. After the game I go right into the dugout to do a radio interview. Halfway through Billy Martin comes by and says, "Why don't you hurry it up. The police are waiting for you in the clubhouse and we've got a plane to catch." "Aw, come on, Billy, don't bulls__ me."

He isn't. I'm taken down to the station in a squad car and booked. Someone has filed a complaint against me, cruelty to animals. So here I am; it's near midnight, and next to me on a table is "Exhibit A," its feet sticking up in the air. It's stiff now, and lying on a handkerchief. Bail is set at $500, which the Blue Jays pay, I believe, but I have to come back for a trial. At one point I peek through a window to see what's happening outside and a dozen flashbulbs go off. I feel like John Dillinger holed up with the hostages. Finally, after about an hour and a half, they let me go. When I'm escorted into the squad car to take me from the station to the airport, flashbulbs pop all over the place again and I hide my face with my briefcase, just like those white-collar criminals do on TV.

"First time he hit the cutoff man all year," Billy tells the press. And in a rare show of solidarity, Steinbrenner rises to my defense with, "This is ridiculous! My people are being harassed."

The next day I show up at Yankee Stadium and I need a police escort to get in because of all the press and the enormous crowd. They're screaming "He killed a seagull!!! He killed a seagull!!!" Like it really made a difference to them. Face it, if it had happened in New York, everyone would have laughed, they'd have thrown it off the field and never said another thing about it.

The next road trip we were in Detroit, and every game of the series 40,000+ fans flapped their arms like birds whenever I came to bat. A whole stadium taunting me. Everything I hit that series was a rocket. I put us in the lead three times the final game, but Alan Trammel spoiled a perfect series with a home run I missed catching by inches. More people probably still remember the seagull incident than anything else I've ever done on the field.

I tried to make it right, though, with the fans in Toronto. I went back during the off-season to speak at an Easter Seals dinner and auction off a painting I'd contributed to their fund raiser.

Before the auction I gave a little speech: "When I told my friends I'd been invited to Toronto, they asked, 'Invited or extradited?'" The crowd gave me a good laugh, easing the tension. So I went on: "But I told them that the Torontonians were good folks. They knew it was an accident, a mistake. And that they were willing to forgive. Still, here I am on the plane, on my way to this fund raiser—mink coat, leather pants, lizard belt, alligator briefcase—and it suddenly occurs to me, Man, the way they protect their natural resources up here, this time I'm liable to get five to ten!" The audience broke up. An international incident had been defused.

The painting sold for $32,000. In fact, the auction was so successful, the feelings so good, that I flew up the following year and donated another painting that sold for $38,000. And now whenever I play in Toronto and a seagull flaps by, the crowd laughs and applauds, like the gulls are coming to get me—"The Revenge of the Birds."

THE ROAD

By the mid-eighties, with George breathing down my neck every time I took the field in Yankee Stadium and the New York press always out with their microscopes, it had gotten so I enjoyed playing more on the road than I did at home. I played better. I relaxed more. Besides, I've always loved just getting into a plane and taking off, and I'd started early—as a kid flying to L.A. for a day, San Francisco, visiting my father in Seattle, flying to Alaska. In college, playing two varsity sports, I'd travel all the time. By the time I was in my late teens I'd developed the ability to just pack and go, changing my surroundings as often as some guys would change their shorts. I don't think I've spent three weeks in the same place in years.

Still, there are guys in the pros who just hate traveling, hate leaving home, hate flying. Mike Ivie, a teammate of mine on the Padres, absolutely dreaded getting on planes. Once aboard, he'd grab hold of the armrests till his fingers turned white. They'd stay white until we got where we were going. No wonder Ivie quit the Padres three times that year.

For me a plane ride is like a vacation, particularly when I travel with the team. On road trips I'll always stock up on reading material—a half-dozen books and magazines, typically books about business or biographies, occasionally sports books, and rarely novels. I grab a whole row, put my briefcase on one side of me, and my food and drink on the other. On long trips everybody on the team takes a row of his own, then drapes a blanket over the seat top for privacy so the whole back of the cabin looks like tent city.

Early in the flight a traveling secretary hands out our per-diem cash in an envelope—about $40+ a day to pay for our meals and tips to the bellman, the clubhouse man, and so on, the same amount for a rookie as for a million-dollar-a-year veteran. Not long after that the card games start—hearts, spades, poker, blackjack. Inevitably, someone loses all their meal money. Joe Cowley, for example, was a notorious loser to Rickey Henderson, incurring the Big Debt. But no matter how much he lost, he never gave up. The second he got on the plane he started raining dollars in Rickey's direction. Rickey called him his personal chump.

The more conservative guys will hoard their per-diem—considered income by the IRS—but I'll always spend way more than they give me. My phone bill alone often runs more than $30 per day, plus overnight mail, FAX, messenger services. And like most veterans, I always spring for a single room, paying the difference over and above the double-room cost provided by the team.

On the road, all the major-league teams are booked into first-class hotels, but that can mean different things in different places. In California and Texas it means nice, open, airy hotels filled with attractive people, while in Cleveland for years it meant the Bond Court with filthy, shag carpeting so old and full of junk I was afraid to walk barefoot on it. With the pile all flattened in one direction it looked like a bay when the tide has gone out.

Whenever we arrive at a hotel, no matter what time of night or day, there are people hanging around, waiting for autographs. We're checked in already, so that hassle is avoided, and bellmen swoop down on us like vultures. They always loved to see Oscar Gamble, who never traveled light and would jokingly request a second bellman to help him carry up his messages.

Once I get to my room, I usually spend all day there, up until game time. Leave the room and the autograph hustle begins—not just one or two requests, but every kid who's been writing me for autographs now has twenty cards for me to sign. In most cases these are not autographs for autographs' sake, but to support the kid's thriving autograph industry. The boldest autograph seekers come up to my room and beat on the door till I yell at them or answer it. I ask them where their mothers are, why they aren't taking care of them? Sometimes the mothers will be beating on the door with their kids.

Leave the room, too, and sometimes your valuables get stolen, though most hotels are pretty good with security. Occasionally, things are stolen from the clubhouse. A genuine, pre-worn Yankee shirt with number "23," "24," "30," or "31" might be worth $750 on the open market, twice that for the whole uniform. In the last month of the '81 season and the playoffs I lost three uniforms. At the end I was wearing Tommy John's pants. The customers for this stuff never wear it, they just "show" it. You can also buy used— read "stolen"—Yankee bats around the corner from Yankee Stadium for $125. I never knew how valuable my equipment and uniform were until I started playing for the Yankees. In San Diego I'd have to bundle it up and take it to Goodwill to get rid of it.

A few guys take advantage of being flown around the country for free with the team and develop side businesses. My friend Dominic Scala, former bullpen coach, started a jewelry business, for example, and he'd take his sample case and make appointments in every city we'd play in. He didn't make a whole lot as a coach, but add his jewelry business earnings and he did okay. Still, Dom was definitely not all work and no play. Whatever party I'd go to, whomever I'd visit when I was on the road, I'd usually find Dom already there, having a good time.

High-profile ballplayers tend to get hassled when they're out in public, particularly on the road when their sole purpose in being there is to wreak havoc on the local heroes. A Reggie Jackson or a Billy Martin is a prime target. I don't have it quite as bad, but now and then someone, somewhere wants to mix it up with me. So I've found a few places where I can go and be left alone. In Kansas City there's the Long Branch owned in part by Lou Piniella. It's light and bright and comfortable. You just order your fried catfish and beers and watch TV and no one gets on your case. In Milwaukee it's Perkins', in Chicago Rush Street, in Seattle I cover the waterfront—where they have great seafood.

Another thing I run into on the road occasionally is discrimination. A couple of times I was treated pretty shabbily in Boston. One restaurant gave me the real runaround, like

I wasn't good enough to be there. Another time in Boston four of us—two white guys and two black guys—went to a wrestling match at Boston Garden and afterward tried to hail a cab. The white guys got the cab, but when the cabby saw us with them he wanted out. "No, no, no, no," he said as he pulled away with the door still open.

Another time, in Houston, I went with a couple of white guys to a western bar, a real hoot 'n' holler kind of place with a mechanical bull and the accompanying b.s. Not only was I black, I also wasn't wearing the requisite jeans and boots. It was clear I didn't belong. One drink and I was gone. It's like Eddie Murphy says in *48 Hours:* "All you got to do is hear one little 'Yee ha!' and the hair stands up on the back of your neck." If I'd known what the place was going to be like, I'd never have gone. I've got enough trouble without looking for it.

Besides, I'm not a hoot 'n' holler kind of guy. When I do go out at night it's to sit, have dinner, maybe a drink, and listen to some good jazz.

All nights must come to an end and Willie McCovey once told me the classic story of how one of those nights ended when he was still playing for San Francisco. During spring training in the early sixties the Giants had a curfew with a $100 fine if you broke it. A lot of guys ignored it, figuring they'd never be caught. They just stayed out to all hours, came back to the hotel, where the elevator man asked for their autographs on a baseball. They signed, then dragged their tired butts to bed. Next day they got to practice and the manager came up to each of them and said, "That's one hundred from you, one hundred from you . . ." And when they protested, he showed them their signatures. The moral of the story? Never sign anything after curfew.

Like alcohol, like drugs, like money and agents and publicity, women are a big part of the professional sports scene.

In baseball, they're waiting at the game, waiting outside the tunnel, in the parking lot, at the hotel. Some attractive, some not, some nice, some otherwise. They're in every city. Some know who you are—your name, at least—but to others it doesn't make a difference. I am sent letters, pictures, erotic statues, cassette tapes, underwear, everything you can imagine. When I reach a city there'll be phone calls, messages. They'll want to talk about business, volunteer for the Foundation, just be a friend. A lot of them will tell me I am the greatest-looking guy in the world. The money makes me even better looking. The fact we're ballplayers makes us *all* better looking.

Some guys ignore it. Some guys dabble in it. Lots of guys just eat it up. Single guys, married guys, players, coaches, traveling secretaries, it doesn't matter. I used to room next to a coach, for example, a respected family man, yet just about every night on the road I could hear through the walls "Oh, baby. Oh, baby!" It's a ritual that's part of the sport.

Some guys brag about it the next day, others try to be cool, make believe it never happened. Once when the team was in Toronto I was having trouble sleeping. We were staying in one of those hotels where the rooms surround a garden courtyard, so I decided I'd take a midnight stroll. Out in the garden I couldn't help but notice a player getting it on in the next room. The curtains were drawn but the TV was on so I could see inside. Man, they were doing *everything.* Next day I asked him how his date was and he said, "Well, she was a very pleasant girl but nothing really happened . . ."

"Oh, she was a nice lady, all right," I interrupted. I was right on him. "She had some beautiful legs and . . . you didn't scrape your knees, did you?" He was a black guy but he turned red. Then we laughed and laughed and laughed about it.

The women never seem to worry about being discreet.

They'll linger by the stadium entrance in flashy clothes, or in the hotel lobby. I've seen a mother and her grown-up daughter out chasing players together, and women with young kids in tow that maybe they'll park in the other room while they're with an athlete.

Some of the sexually more enterprising players will actually "import" women to follow them around on road trips. Others will relegate certain women to certain regions of the country, imposing import quotas. Still others—the more prominent players on the team—will take two rooms at a hotel and split a series with an "import" and with someone local.

Occasionally, too, when we're on the road there'll be a team party and a stripper might be hired to take off her stuff, or a prostitute to do her thing. The most outrageous party I ever attended as a Yankee was in 1984 in Detroit. We invited nearly 100 women to this huge penthouse overlooking the Detroit River. I was in charge of the food and got some local friends to cater it, a varied spread including Cajun and Creole specialties. But they also bought the booze and made the mistake of not buying Stolichnaya vodka. Instead, they bought an off-brand, Mohawk vodka. Yogi Berra, our manager that year, took one look at it and said, "Whaddya mean, Winfield? This is supposed to be a party and you got *Mohawk* vodka? What are you trying to do to us?" He rode me something fierce, until he and the coaches left.

Anyway, 100 woman showed up and about 40 guys. People were having a good time, dancing, talking, the ratio was right. A few guys were going around whispering into people's ears, "Vapor Man's gonna be here tonight, Vapor Man's gonna be here tonight!" I knew something was planned for midnight, but I had missed his earlier appearance and had no idea who "Vapor Man" was. Neither did any of the women, and most of them met the fact of his imminent arrival with a puzzled look. A few, I could tell, were downright nervous. At exactly 12 A.M., the witching hour, all the doors were locked, the lights were turned down real low, and Michael Jackson's "Thriller" blasted over the stereo, DUNH, DUNH, DUNH, DUNH, DUNH. Suddenly from the back room emerged Vapor Man and his sidekick, two players to go unnamed, stark naked and covered only with shaving cream, each wearing an enormous dildo. A few women demanded to be left out, and they bolted right then. Others shrieked—in distress or pleasure—as the guys went after them, getting shaving cream all over their dresses and hair. Still others held their ground, just stared at the dildos and said, "Are those real? What do you think?" It was true mayhem there for a few minutes. At some point one of the guys slid and scraped all the shaving cream from his butt, so his behind hung out like a globe. No one had ever seen anything like it before, and they might never again. Not long after that we unlocked the doors and everyone who wanted to went home.

To some extent the lure of women has always been there for me since late in high school and through college, with the possibilities increasing over time. And while I admit to a large share of experiences, as far as random sexual encounters go these days, I'll pass. There's just too much stuff going around. And not only disease, but lawsuits, paternity suits. Besides, I've gone through my cycle where everything was free and easy, where I felt frivolous with women and sought out these encounters. Nowadays, and for the last handful of years, in fact, I've simply been more serious about what I've wanted from women, and how I spend my time.

Women, boredom, the aggravations of travel may do a number on you. But you can't forget that you've got to do a number on the opposing team. It's almost as important as the game itself, an art that I've refined over the years. It starts with batting practice. No matter whether I'm in what they call a slump or I'm hitting .350, I make it a point during practice to hit the ball to all fields and hit it hard, out of the stadium at least once or twice. That way they can't develop a strategy to pitch to you. Also, when I'm up to bat—even if I'm feeling weak and lousy—chances are, if they're afraid to give me anything good to hit and walk me with the bases loaded for a cheap RBI, I'll throw my bat down in disgust like I was dying to get a piece of the ball.

Then, when I take practice in the outfield, I never dog it, but go after everything, throw the ball smoothly on target or, on the first day in town when everyone's watching, throw the stuffing out of the ball. It's like posting a warning: Don't take liberties with Winfield's arm! That way when it's game time no one is even going to think about taking an extra base on me. It's all part of the game that starts before the game.

Where I'm playing on the road often dictates how well I play. I love being let loose in the Kingdome in Seattle, for example, a homerdome, a tremendous place to hit. If you hit it there, it's gone; if you don't hit it, it's gone. As for playing on the artificial surface in the Kingdome—or anywhere— it's the usual occupational hazard. You can throw your back out, incur all sorts of injuries, shorten your career. As a hitter it may help your average one year or two, but over the long term I'm convinced it's not good for anyone.

A couple of other American League parks I favor are Cleveland and Toronto. Cleveland's got this big, old, damp, and often empty park—not a nice field, really, but I always seem to do a lot of damage there. Same with Toronto where I've got a .300+ lifetime average. Texas is a pleasant place to play in, well manicured with a soft outfield that soaks up the ball. They helped the hitters tremendously when they enclosed the outfield stands. The ball travels legitimately now. Standing out there in the heat, though, you're always praying for a breeze.

The prettiest park in the American League—in all of baseball—is in Kansas City. I always do okay there, but no one liked it better than the guy Steinbrenner brought in to play first base for us in 1982, Big John Mayberry. Out beyond the center-field fence there's a big waterfall with lights playing off the swirling water and John, who talked as slow as he was big, would always say, "You know, Winnie, every time I play here, I stays in the water," referring to the monster drives he'd hit. No matter how he was hitting, whenever Big John got to Kansas City he'd really turn on the ball.

Anaheim is a good hitter's park, with the best weather and the prettiest fans. But they have pitched me well over the years. Minnesota has a nice, clean stadium, the people are friendly, and it's still home.

Worst American League park honors go to Detroit's Tiger Stadium, not for the field but for the dugout, which is so old and small that I have to bend down when I walk around. One time I forgot where I was, jumped up to cheer one of my guys, and just about knocked myself cold. The clubhouse is tiny too. Comiskey Park in Chicago is another one of those old parks with not enough room in the clubhouse, but they did enlarge the smallest dugouts in the league.

In the National League I liked playing in L.A., Atlanta, Philadelphia, and Cincinnati. For some reason the ball really travels in Dodger Stadium. It's a cozy, well-manicured ballpark, great weather, nice for hitters. Same thing in Atlanta. San Diego is a nice park but much, much too big. And while I don't have a lot of distinctive memories of Busch Memorial Stadium in St. Louis, I'll never forget a series the Padres played there one long, hot summer, years ago. It was so hot you could see the convection currents coming off the artificial turf, distorting your vision. We had these huge tubs of shaved ice in the dugout that we used literally to cool our heels. Whenever we'd come off the field, we'd just take off our cleats, or leave 'em on, and soak our feet in the ice. That day I threw my only snowball ever at an umpire. He turned and thanked me.

One of the courtesies afforded a visiting team by its host team is food in the clubhouse following a game. When I was in the National League the Dodgers were infamous for putting out absolutely the worst spread, fried chicken and hot dogs, hot dogs and fried chicken. You were there for four days, you would eat the same thing every day. I expected more imagination next door to Hollywood. Atlanta was the same, just add hamburger. One of the Mets' specialties for visiting teams back then was often cold pizza that we'd warm up by putting it back in the box and giving it a few minutes in the same dryer that was used to dry the towels and jocks. If I made it to "Kiner's Korner," Ralph Kiner's postgame show, as the star of the game, I'd be glad for the extra $50 to buy a slice of something tastier in the Big Apple.

In the American League for a long time the Yankee clubhouse was the worst; cold meat and hot bread. Now it's very good. Though last year as we slipped from first to fourth, so did the food. Best food in the league is definitely in Anaheim. No one does it better than the Angels. You want something special, they'll try to get it for you. Nowadays, they've even got a wine bar, making the Anaheim clubhouse the classiest catering operation in the majors.

SEASONS: 1984

The story of my 1984 season with the Yankees was as much about my legal battles with Steinbrenner as with baseball, though I went into the last game batting .341—my best average ever in the majors. Once again, George had fallen delinquent in his payments to the Foundation and we had filed a second lawsuit against him. By spring training he still hadn't paid and we were incurring heavy legal fees. As a result, a number of the programs we'd been supporting—a neighborhood youth project in the Bronx, for example, a computer literacy program in Brooklyn, the Pavillions at Yankee Stadium—were put on hold or forced to close down.

It's well into spring training that Steinbrenner calls the lunch meeting at Bennigan's restaurant to present his "plan," and where I present mine, suggesting he both pay the money and make me the team captain so that he can look like a good guy. As we talk over sandwiches a woman loaded to the gills stumbles over with a napkin and places it on the table in front of me. I give her the autograph I think she wants and hand it back to her.

"No," she says, pointing at it. "Not an autograph, a sea-gull!"

"What?" She's weaving around, the napkin shredding in her hand.

"I'm from Toronto and I want you to draw me a seagull."

"Are you crazy, lady?"

"I'm serious."

"Well, I'm serious too," I say. "Get out of here!"

No one got what they wanted at Bennigan's that day.

George's counsel, Roy Cohn, was arguably the sleaziest lawyer in the country. I'd heard a lot about Cohn from Al, who told me the man was shrewd and dangerous, a notorious bad guy who'd become prominent as Joe McCarthy's lawyer in the Army-McCarthy hearings. I even read Roy's book, *How to Stand Up for Your Rights and Win!* But I was confident in my new lawyers, including Jeff Klein, and in the strength of our position. It would take a lot more than shrewdness for George to win this round.

What I never really understood was why George was so intent on winning, on getting his point across. And what *was* that point? That a ballplayer didn't deserve to have a foundation? That a black ballplayer didn't deserve to have a foundation? Or that he couldn't run it properly? With no clear point in mind, it seemed that George's team decided to wing it, making up points as the 1984 season dragged on.

And if they weren't making up points, they were making up stories. They filed affidavits about events that supposedly occurred at our meetings but never actually happened. They'd back out of commitments at the last second, make claims they couldn't substantiate, say one thing at a meeting, another thing in court. George Steinbrenner was so uncooperative about giving his deposition to my lawyers, that the judge assessed him $4100 to pay for my lawyer's wasted time.

Cohn never made an appearance in court himself. Just about the only time we'd meet face-to-face was in his townhouse-office. Walking in the first time I remember him saying a somber and slightly effeminate hello. In the middle of the business day he had on a silk smoking jacket, ascot, and slippers. His face was drawn and sunken. Easy to say now, but just looking at him, it was clear he was dying, though maybe he didn't know it yet himself.

Most of the time we didn't deal with Cohn, we dealt with his underlings. One run-in we had was particularly satisfy-

ing. After months of delaying tactics some of Cohn's lawyers wanted to take my deposition. Trouble was I was in
spring training and the Yankees wouldn't allow me a day to
go back to New York, so Jeff convinced the court that since
I was representing a charitable organization the lawyers—
the three working on George's behalf, plus Jeff—should be
brought down to Fort Lauderdale for the deposition. The
whole tab—time, travel expenses, and per-diem for four
high-ticket New York lawyers, including Jeff—was picked
up by George.

To make it even more costly—not in terms of dollars, but
embarrassment—one of the lawyers, who prior to making
the trip had appeared in court on George's behalf, was not
a licensed member of the bar, something we had just found
out. At the start of the deposition, when their team did their
introductions, Jeff interrupted, "And Mr. ——," he asked,
"is he a member of the bar?" There was some stuttering
from George's people and Jeff called for a short break. "I'm
deeply troubled," Jeff told the elegant attorney who was the
leader of George's crew, "that your man has appeared on
Mr. Steinbrenner's behalf holding himself up as a member
of the bar when, in fact, he isn't. And I feel I have an ethical
obligation to the court to . . ." After that the opposition
never did hit their stride.

The arrangement Jeff and I had concerning publicity was
that he'd be the only one on our side to talk to the press. We
knew that the fans would get tired of listening to a guy
making a million and a half dollars with a money gripe
against his boss. Our story was that the litigation was eating
up money that might otherwise be going to kids. It was the
party line, but it was true. Still, in the midst of the hassle,
it was hard to know whether we were making our point. So
it was truly satisfying when the judge strongly chastised
George's lawyers, saying that it was the kids who were the

real losers in this battle. Amen! In August 1984, the final settlement was signed; with it came a check for the David M. Winfield Foundation for $375,000, all the money George owed.

The 1984 season was not only turbulent for me, it was turbulent for the Yankees as a team, with guys coming up, going down, getting traded, being released—much like it would be in 1987. The Yankee roster usually changes more than anybody's in baseball, and that year it changed more than ever. Except for the fact that Steinbrenner stuck with Yogi Berra as his manager the full season, it was business as usual in the big business of Yankee baseball.

All this roster movement made for some odd bedfellows. First year I was on the Yankees we were playing Cleveland and their third baseman, Toby Harrah, worked himself into a frenzy, hollering at me from the dugout, "Winfield, you ain't shit. You can't hit. You're a National Leaguer, nobody wants you . . . million dollars, my ass!" My new teammates were listening, wondering what I'd do. I turned and started hollering back. It went back and forth like that for a few innings with the umpires stopping the game twice. Come 1984, Harrah was on the Yankees. I walked into the locker room the first day he was there and heard Don Baylor say, "Hey, Toby. Winnie's here now. You still got something to say to him?" "Oh, no, no, no . . ." We're good friends now.

Tim Foli—the second baseman who'd been around, worn two or three uniforms in each league, and who I'm convinced purposely injured me on a double play when I was still on the Padres and cost me a poor second half—also showed up in pinstripes that year. We got along okay, but he was just too intense for me and for his own good, I think. He wasn't with us long.

Neither was Steve Kemp, a heralded free agent from the White Sox who reputedly could hit the long ball, and who'd been signed by the Yankees for big bucks in '83. With big-dollar free agency contracts more common than when I came to the Yankees, players like Kemp weren't under the microscope as much. It made things a lot easier for him, since although he hustled he wasn't hitting balls long enough for Yankee Stadium. He was gone by the end of '84 after a series of injuries altered his swing and his throw.

Making his debut as a regular in '84 was Bobby Meacham, as our starting shortstop. To maximize their investment in him, the Yankees were trying to get Bobby to switch-hit. All the work on hitting made him tentative on the field, where he made nineteen errors. That's about average for a short-stop, but Bobby saved his errors for absolutely the most critical situations, a fact that didn't go unnoticed by Yankee fans and management alike. In his seasons with the Yankees, Bobby's been sent down more times than I can remember.

And '84 was Oscar Gamble's swan song year with the Yankees. We called him the "Ratio Man" because of the number of home runs he hit per at-bat, one for every twelve in his last season. He seldom hit for average, but could always put the ball over the fence. He was like a corkscrew at the plate, winding up and generating a lot of torque from a relatively small frame. A good player, a clutch player, a quick talker with a ready laugh. New York was really his kind of town, but the Yankees finally ran out of use for him.

New York was certainly not our catcher's, Butch Wyne-gar's, kind of town. He was a shy, quiet guy who always shunned the limelight. Two years later, in the middle of the '86 season, he'd break down. The fans, the media, the pressure from the top, the pressure from his family to spend more time at home all finally got to him.

Of course, there were Yankees from that 1984 team that weathered the storm and are still with the club today. Willie Randolph, Mike Pagliarulo, Ron Guidry, Dave Righetti, and Bobby Meacham—the last time I checked. And, of course, Don Mattingly, the guy I played tag with most of '84 for the batting title. For me, from the courtroom to the locker room, the pressure was on.

Because of their movie-star salaries and status, professional athletes are under more scrutiny than ever before. But Tom Cruise only makes one or two film appearances a year. A baseball player can be the hero or the goat 162 times a year. It's no wonder then that, given the tensions of the game, so many athletes turn to drugs or alcohol or women or food—have family trouble, get fat and out of shape. It's an escape, and for many, the only way.

No stranger to pressure myself—from the fans, the media, the "man"—my way has always been to stay positive, to concentrate on my job. But during the 1984 season that was damn near impossible. Just about every day there'd be some garbage from George Steinbrenner in the newspaper. Not a week would go by where I wasn't called into the front office and threatened with a trade. Then there were the countless meetings, sessions with lawyers, depositions. One day after I gave a three-hour deposition Steinbrenner came up to me and said, "You got me in there for two hours yesterday, I got you in there for three hours today." On top of that, on George's orders, I was getting the silent treatment from the coaches. It even got to the point that some of my own teammates were nervous about talking to me. I'd become a pariah, and for no other reason than trying to keep Steinbrenner to his commitment. I tell you, as the year went on, I came to appreciate more and more what Jackie Robinson did in standing up to enormous pressure day in and day out.

The Yankees go into the final game of the season mathematically eliminated by a week's worth of games. It's a lost cause for the team and all that's left to be decided is which of us, Donnie or I, will win the batting crown. Our last outing is a home game with Detroit, the division champs. Mattingly and I come into the game with virtually the same average. By then, though, the attacks in the press, the fans' impatience with my battles with Steinbrenner, and the strong positive press Donnie had been getting have done their work. Every time Donnie steps up to bat cheers fill the stadium, standing O's in fact. Every time I step up to bat there are boos. Every time but the last, when Donnie has already won and the boos gradually give way to a few cheers. Stuff like that hurts, believe me. It stays with you.

That day Donnie gets his hits. I get one, where I had to throw my bat to reach it. Not only that, I groundout to make my last out of the game, my final out of the 1984 season. Though I hit .340, with more hits and scoring more runs for my team than ever before or since, it's my most difficult year in baseball. And in some sense, my least rewarding.

After my groundout Donnie and I put our arms around each other, doff our caps, and walk off the field together. Because it is the bottom of the eighth when we leave the field, the press is not waiting for us. They'll want to talk to me about how I feel about losing. But I decide not to talk to them at all, because I feel so many things about it. First, I don't feel so much that I "lost" as that both of us have done a great deal for the team, for New York, and for George Steinbrenner, keeping people coming to the stadium even when the Yankees were finished. And then there are all those other pent-up feelings, building from the time in Steinbrenner's trailer in Florida when he said, "That's the way it goes."

So I shower, congratulate Donnie, and leave the clubhouse, knowing that if I talk to the press I'll say something I'll regret. Besides, I don't want to take anything away from Donnie. Opting for silence is the most gracious thing I can do.

I wasn't going to read any of the postmortems, but a couple of days later I change my mind. I need to seal the season off, once and for all. That's when I see my manager's appraisal of my performance that year in the press, the first and only time I knew where I stood with my manager or coaches: "Winfield," Yogi Berra is quoted, "was my most valuable player."

There were plenty of times in 1984 when I wanted to quit, take the trade they kept pressuring me to take. But I told myself to stick it out, work harder. I'll honestly never know whether the intense duress improved some numbers or cut ten to fifteen percent from my performance.

A few weeks after the end of the season I'm on my way to Hong Kong and I get this burning feeling in my stomach. What's going on? I wonder. I eat and it bothers me. I don't eat and it bothers me. When I get back to New York ten days later I go for a checkup. I've got an ulcer. Me?!? Aw, no.

Playing the hot corner

(LOUIS REQUENA)

You shouldn't have done that

(NEW YORK POST, NURY HERNANDEZ)

(AP WIDE WORLD, SUSAN C. RAGAN)

A hit and a miss

Out?! (UPI INTERNATIONAL PHOTO, JACK BALLETTI)

Safe! (NEW YORK POST, BOB OLEN)

A salami, a grand slam (JOHN BELLISSIMO)

INFORMATION of *MELVIN DUNFORD SERGEANT 3063* 26

of   Metropolitan Toronto Police Officer   3

Police Officer   (occupation). The informant says

that   he has reasonable and probable grounds to believe and does believe

CANADA
PROVINCE OF ONTARIO
JUDICIAL DISTRICT OF YORK

(1)   that   David Mark WINFIELD

on or about the _____4 th_____ day of _____August_____ 19 83 , at the Municipality of

Metropolitan Toronto in the Judicial District of York, unlawfully did wilfully cause unnecessary injury to

a bird, to wit: a Gull, by using a ball,

CONTRARY TO THE CRIMINAL CODE.

Sworn before me at the Municipality of Metropolitan Toronto in the Judicial

District of York this _____4TH_____ day of _____AUGUST_____ 19 *83*

Mel Dunford.

A Justice of the Peace in and for the Province of Ontario   Informant

☐ Appearance Notice ☐ Promise to Appear ☒ Recognizance For *AUGUST 16,* 19 *83* Confirmed on *AUGUST 11, 1986*

Date		
Crown Elects to Proceed ☐ Summarily ☐ By Indictment ☐ Summary Conviction Offence (s)
Accused Elects Trial by ☐ Judge ☐ Judge and Jury
☐ Discharged ☐ Committed – ☐ Ordered to Stand Trial – ☐ With Consent of Accused and Prosecutor,
Without Taking or Recording – ☐ Any Evidence (or) – ☐ Further Evidence. Bail $
☐ Accused Elects Trial by a Magistrate (Provincial Judge) ☐ Absolute Jurisdiction
Pleads ☐ Guilty ☐ Not Guilty ☐ Withdrawn
Found ☐ Guilty ☐ Not Guilty ☑ In Absentia
☐ Absolute Discharge ☐ Conditional Discharge
Fined $ _____ AUG 18 1983 _____ costs. Time to pay	Day	Mo.	Yr.
WITHDRAWN
or _____ Date of Birth
Probation for
Sentenced to
Imprisonment for

Provincial Judge
C.S. CANNON

AG 177
MT 626 (Short Form – Single Accsd. – Not More Than Two Charges) (6/76)

"…unlawfully did willfully cause unnecessary
injury to a bird, to wit: a Gull, by using a ball,
CONTRARY TO THE CRIMINAL CODE."

HEY WINFIELD... YA KNOW DAT SEAGULL YA HIT IN TORONTO... WELL HIS MOTHER'S HERE!

DONATO

With Martina Navratilova and Nancy Lieberman ()

...Jesse Jackson

With Tina Turner …Eddie Murphy

Schmoozing at the White House with President Reagan and my mother

Training with the Justice Department

Hoofing it at a City Hall ceremony for the Foundation

(JOAN VITALE STRONG)

Tymark enterprises with my partner Gil Bland

With my daughter Lauren Shanel

Brothers and friends

Another side of Al Frohman

Who's the lady? My wife

Back to spring training

4

Late Innings

SEASONS: 1985

By the close of spring training, the 1985 Yankees were the closest knit team I'd ever been on. There wasn't a bad apple in the bunch. It was also a team capable of scoring a lot of runs, creating havoc for the opposition. There were Mattingly, Randolph, Baylor, and George's newest acquisition, Rickey Henderson. Plus, the strongest pitching staff since I'd joined the team—Guidry, Phil Niekro, Righetti. You could just sense the excitement. Let's go! Let's go!!!

You could also feel the pressure. Steinbrenner had fielded an *expensive* team, he said, and we'd have to earn our keep right out of the starting gate or the crap would really hit the fan. It did. After the first few games, Yogi, who always did his damnedest to protect himself and the team from outside pressures, could sense things coming down around him. Sixteen games into the season Steinbrenner fired him and brought back Billy Martin for his fourth stint at the helm. Many players were pissed, not just that Billy was coming in, but that Yogi was on his way out. Most of them felt that the team would have righted itself, but our opinions didn't count. Steinbrenner responded in the press by saying that if we liked Yogi so much, we should have won for him.

Billy was cool about it, though. The players' reaction, the press, public opinion, he shrugged it all off. He knew how we felt. "Yogi understands," he told us the first day he was back on the job. "He's a great guy but it happens to all of us. He stepped in for me once. Now I'm stepping in for him. If we lose it, I'll be the one to take the blame. If we win it, everyone gets the credit, including Yogi."

Class. But that wasn't the feeling in the clubhouse. Everyone knew that things were going to be different. First, because it was Billy, there'd be even more reporters hanging around, looking for dirt. Next, a lot of the guys feared they'd be in Billy's doghouse. After all, he had his reputation as a disciplinarian to uphold. Billy's arrival didn't matter to me, though. While their styles were markedly different, I'd play the same for either Yogi or Billy; which is to say, after my experiences in 1984, I'd run, hit, and throw as well as I could, and help the team win, but I wasn't going to kill myself emotionally. Also, I knew that Billy respected my play and would back me up. That's all I really wanted from a manager.

Like any season with Billy in charge, 1985 sees a lot of hustle, a lot of wins. But there's also the psychological toll Billy's presence takes on the players and some coaches, coming from the tacit pressure from the top. Will Billy make it through the year? What happens if we drop a key series? How much slack before the noose tightens?

In 1985 the noose tightens in August. We're having a terrific month, are really on a tear, with the best record for August in professional baseball. We're only two games behind the division-leading Blue Jays, who are coming to Yankee Stadium for a series. But we're ready. We're hot, we're confident, we're cruising.

Then Steinbrenner shows up in the locker room: "This is the most important series of the year. We've got to sweep. This is a test of Yankee heart and Yankee pride. We can't let Toronto shame us in our own ballpark. This is the whole season right here."

That sure relaxes everyone on the team. Especially Billy

who—known for his laid-back style—goes on a spree issuing contradictory commands and cussin' people out right and left. Willie Horton, one of our coaches, takes the worst of it. It's Willie do this, Willie do that. Billy resented Willie to begin with because rumor was that Steinbrenner had hired him to be Billy's chaperon. But that plan misfired because Willie didn't drink, leaving Billy to his own devices during off-hours.

Anyway, we take the first game—a Friday nighter—a sloppy win, but a win. Saturday we lose a close one. The locker room is pretty subdued afterward, the sentiment being: We're not ashamed, we played hard; they're a good team, the Yankees don't own all the talent; we'll win tomorrow.

Then Steinbrenner blasts into the locker room again, a single reporter in tow. George looks around and says, "The pitching's okay, but the hitting sucks!" Soon he's on a roll. We've got no Yankee pride. We should be ashamed to pick up our paychecks. We'd better not count on getting those paychecks indefinitely. Nobody looks at anybody else, everybody stares into his own locker.

Sunday morning we read in the paper that Steinbrenner says the Yankees are being "outplayed, outhustled, outmanaged, and outowned." Steinbrenner also names a few players, all black, who've really let him down. I'm number one on the list, "Mr. May." He wants "Mr. October" back.

Okay, my average is a little low, but I'm still driving in runs at a rate of 100+ a year for the fourth year in a row. The only guy to match me in the eighties was Eddie Murray.

Come the third game the team is disorganized and demoralized. Toronto knows it and kicks our butts all over the field. Steinbrenner's strategy was, I suppose, Let me just whip my guys and they'll perform. That kind of rah-rah Vince Lombardi tactic might work in football, but not in baseball. We're whipped in the papers and Toronto comes in for the kill. After that, we get into a losing groove, although we eventually come back to make it close. But as far as I'm concerned, *that* was the season, right there.

The mindset of a team, I feel, is absolutely crucial to how the players will perform. Professionals or not, there has to be some joy in it, if only to relieve the pressure that builds over a 162-game season. A team doing well can have a lot of fun, talk some outrageous trash in the locker room, on the bus, on the plane. There's fun to be had on the field, too. Hitting back-to-back home runs. Stealing bases, sliding, scoring. Throwing the other guy out at the plate. You can have a *great* time. With Steinbrenner, though, it's win or lose, live or die. The man shows up and the fun's gone, the pressure's on.

George wants controversy in New York; he creates it because he thinks it brings fans into the stadium. Billy is used to seeing his name in boldface so everyone will know who's really responsible for those wins when they come. The New York reporters are always sniffing around hoping for the apocalypse. Most guys in the league think a year in New York is worth three anywhere else. The attention can make a career take off, the pressure can shorten it. In Detroit if you play well for three weeks they let you slide for a month. In New York, performance isn't even judged day to day; it's play to play. And George Steinbrenner's got the shortest memory in town.

PEOPLE

The myth is yesterday's ballplayers were better than today's, but that's bunk. There are just as many great ballplayers now as there were then. Take Rickey Henderson, on the Yankee roster for the first time in 1985. All you have to do is watch Rickey, see what he does at the plate or on the base paths, to be convinced that here's a guy who matches up with the best of any era. He's a tremendous talent. He's strong, in terrific physical shape, low body fat, well muscled, well proportioned, and flexible. No question, he's the fastest guy on the team, probably in the league. You watch him steal and you can see he's almost at full speed from his first step.

Rickey can just about steal a base at will. He's so fast, so smart, so cunning, he'll make it 95 percent of the time. Lou Brock, whose all-time record he's chasing, wasn't quite as fast, and an advocate of the pop-up slide into second, coming in on his seat, then popping up to go to third. Rickey's so fast, so coordinated, he can hit the dirt headfirst, scramble up in an instant, and keep on going. Risky business, but Rickey knows what he's doing, though a couple of times he's jammed his arms and shoulders. As long as he stays healthy, I feel, it's not so much a question of *if* he'll break Lou's record as when.

At the plate, Rickey also can do pretty much what he wants. He can hit for power or for average. If he wants to hit home runs, he does. If he wants to get on base and steal, he does that. He creates his own challenges. I suppose he could help the team even more if he hit fewer lead-off home runs and concentrated more on getting on base. But I'm sure that if he saw his getting on base made the difference between our winning and losing, he'd stop swinging for the fences. In the meanwhile, the homers may not always help the team, but they certainly don't hurt us.

Overall, Rickey does better on offense than defense, and is more effective in left field than center. In 1985 he brought the "Snatch" to Yankee Stadium, Rickey's way of pulling the ball out of the air like a lizard does his prey. It's the first lighthearted thing to happen in Yankee Stadium in years.

Coaches find him an enigma. They don't know how to relate to someone of his caliber and personality. He's always had an independent style, never had to do things the conventional way to succeed. Talent and savvy have put him way above most players.

From time to time people question Rickey's motivation and his day-to-day hustle. It's true that Rickey's not a completely self-winding player, and occasionally he needs to be challenged in a friendly, positive way. One day in the middle of the 1985 season we were really in the thick of it, trying to move up a crucial game in the standings, when Rickey said, "I don't feel like playing today. I'm hurting. I'm tired. I have to recuperate." We all understood "tired," but we needed him in there. The day before he'd stolen maybe three bases, got two or three hits, scored a couple of runs. I sat down next to him on the blue leather couch in front of our lockers. "Come on, man, you've got to play. We need to kick these guys' butts. We *need* you in there!" Rickey finally acquiesced. "All right," he said. "I'm in there." And he was, stole three more bases, got three more hits, made the difference in the game.

THE GAME

I've been a player representative in the Major League Base-ball Players Association for half my years in the pros. I've always liked knowing what might happen before it does, and getting involved in the Association while I was still a Padre was one way of accomplishing this. Most players, however, only turn to the Association when they're in trouble. They don't take a personal interest in what's going on. It's usually the same players who don't get involved in their own contract negotiations. They let their agents handle it, and then if there's a problem, they get on the phone.

As a player rep I urge players to get to know the Association, suggesting they visit our headquarters and meet the staff. I tell the new guys each year that it's better to know them and not need them, than to need them and not know them. And sooner or later every player does need them. I also urge players to act in their own best interests, and talk to them about a variety of issues, particularly drugs. Early on a number of guys questioned my knowledge because I'd never used drugs myself. They wanted to know where I was getting my information. But gradually, as they came to know me and became aware of the Foundation's work, they came to respect what I had to say.

Over the years my relationship with the Association has helped me get where I am. Not only financially—my large contract was a direct outgrowth of hard-won Association advances on behalf of players' rights—but in the education I've received in negotiation, collective bargaining, and interacting with management. It's an education I owe largely to Marvin Miller, the Association's executive director for seventeen years and one of the most impressive persons I've ever met. Originally with the steel workers' union, Marvin was soft-spoken, intelligent, accomplished, and thoughtful, yet with ice water in his veins. He is a distinguished-looking man with graying hair and a slight physical handicap—his right arm is shorter than his left and malformed. But once you see him in action, you never think twice about it, he is so charismatic. With his subtle but commanding style, he had a way of presenting a plan, to players *or* owners, that made it seem the only way to go.

More than impressive, Marvin was a visionary, taking the Association from virtually nothing and making it one of the finest organizations in the country. He commanded unity in the ranks, broke new ground, reached unprecedented goals. Through his efforts players won meaningful pensions, a comprehensive benefits package, salary arbitration guidelines, grievance procedures, and an average salary in excess of $400,000. Not only did the players become well paid and well protected, the Association itself became highly stable. So solid, in fact, that during the 1985 NFL strike, the Association was able to lend the National Football League Players Association funds to help them through tough times.

Above all, Marvin won the Association respect from the owners. And fear. He demonstrated that we would take a stand if the situation demanded, and if we had to, we'd go on strike. We proved to ourselves, to the owners, and to the fans that there are positions worth defending. It made us a stronger association in the process.

To illustrate the begrudging respect owners had for Marvin, in 1984, after he had stepped down as executive director, we went into collective bargaining with the owners. Don Fehr, for many years the Association's legal counsel, was our acting director. Marvin was hired as a consultant to the Association. During the meetings, though, it seemed that the owners were consulting more with Marvin than the Association was. Whenever they didn't like something that

Fehr was saying they'd defer to Marvin and ask him what he thought rather than hash it out with their own people. As for the fear Marvin's presence brought to the table, Marvin had been ill and throughout the negotiations he looked very, very tired. His eyes were watery and red, and we were concerned that when things got really trying, he might not hold up. Clearly, the owners saw it too and you could tell they were hoping he wouldn't. They were probably thinking, Why don't you drop dead so we have a chance. We could kick everybody else's butt, but *you*, we can't get a thing past you . . . NOTTIN'!

Getting someone to replace Marvin in 1984 was going to be difficult and Don Fehr was by no means a shoe-in. We interviewed a number of candidates for the job, and chose Ken Moffett of the Federal Mediation Service. He turned out to be an interim choice, and a year and a half later Don was finally voted in. I wasn't among those who voted for him. He's smart, he's capable, he knows the Association. But I don't think he has Marvin's vision, and I think we still need that more than anything.

Which is not to say that Don isn't up to the job. A number of important victories have already been won under his directorship, the most notable being the action brought against the owners claiming collusion in the hands-off manner teams suddenly adopted in the treatment of free agents. Top players would come on the market and there'd be no takers for them except their old teams, and then at bargain prices. Or when a contract would be offered, it never exceeded three years. In the summer of 1987 a decision was reached by the baseball arbitrator that, indeed, the owners had been in collusion.

Like any organization, the Association has a ways to go. In the years to come it needs to focus more on marketing the sport to the greater benefit of the players. Right now, for example, the Association negotiates the bubble-gum-card contracts and a score or so other relationships—board games, soft drinks, electronics—on behalf of the players, and each player derives income from the dollars generated. More, and more imaginative, promotions need to be developed.

A second direction I feel the Association should be moving in is to educate all the current players on the history of the Association. It's hard to know where you are going if you don't know where you've been. And career counseling is needed to help players find valuable and rewarding work after their playing days are over.

The Association also needs to develop a more positive image with the public. Baseball players could be a potent force for good, like musicians were on "We Are the World." Following the 1984 cocaine trials involving players from St. Louis, Pittsburgh, and Kansas City, the Association was caught between helping the players involved—coming out strongly against the commissioner's sanctions of the players, particularly in light of the fact that the courts let them off without penalty—and trying to take a general position on drug use by members. The need today is, first, to make our image conform with the reality that drug use is not rampant in baseball and that most ballplayers are too smart and too concerned about their conditioning and performance to take illicit drugs. And second, to let the public know that the Association does not condone use of illicit drugs by any player. The best way to accomplish both, I feel, is through Association-sponsored activity in the community.

The sanctions imposed by the commissioner following the trials, incidentally, were a pay-or-don't-play deal, requiring the players involved to give a percentage of their salary to fund anti-drug programs, and for them to spend a number of hours in anti-drug public service work. The sanctions established a precedent and elicited a variety of responses among those penalized.

On the one hand there was Dale Berra, who was like the

kid who knew he'd been bad and said, "Okay, whatever you say. I've embarrassed myself, my dad. Let's just get it over with." On the other hand there was Keith Hernandez, the best known of the guys involved. He was the most vocal critic, particularly about doing public service work. I suppose it's because he's a very private guy and probably felt that for him it was a punishment that exceeded the crime.

Personally, I feel that sanctions were pretty fair, and could have been even tougher. If Bowie Kuhn had been in office they probably would have been. I know from the years I've worked with kids, particularly in the field of drugs and drug abuse prevention, how influential a sports figure can be. A ballplayer is expected to be a role model, it's a demand that goes along with the fame and the money: Behave or pay the price.

I'm a little concerned, though, about athletes being placed at the very top of the role model list. What about parents as number one, teachers as number two, and then athletes? That's a more realistic ranking, I feel. A kid whose parents and teachers are good role models is not going to do drugs because Keith Hernandez did.

I also question the good that's done forcing a guy into doing public service if he's unwilling. Finally, I'm concerned about the effect that ex-drug users, or ex-convicts, or ex-whatever, have on young people. The kids meet a guy who tells them about some scary stuff, sure, but there's a thrill in that, too, and that's the downside. After all, the guy's still around to talk, which conveys the implicit message that you can experiment, have some excitement, and then move on. It's for this reason that, rather than go the "ex-" route, the Foundation tries to present kids with role models who've found success and excitement in healthy ways. It's a much more positive message.

Selected by the owners, Peter Ueberroth came on board as commissioner of baseball following the end of the 1984 regular season, in time to help settle the umpires' strike threatening the playoffs, to ride herd on the cocaine trials that winter, and to steer the sport through the players' strike of 1985. Through it all it's clear he's been the owners' man, but I think he's been pretty good for the game as a whole. Some give him credit for shortening the strike, others downplay his impact. Nevertheless, during his tenure attendance has risen in both leagues. Corporate sponsorship of major-league baseball has increased dramatically. He's a maverick, he's shrewd, he's successful, and he knows marketing. When he came into office he shook the cobwebs, brought in some good people, and noted that he was disenchanted by the fact that there weren't enough black people in professional baseball's front offices. He's the type of guy who, if you're good, he'll give you a chance. But unlike Pete Rozelle, the NFL commissioner, I don't think that Peter Ueberroth is going to be around baseball forever. The commissioner's office is a stepping stone for him, and I wouldn't be surprised to see him in any important capacity five years from now.

BOSSES

On September 23, 1985, Peter Ueberroth's office releases a letter to all major-league players. In it he calls for individual participation in a league-sponsored drug-testing program. Rather than being sent directly to players, the letter is given to each club's front office to distribute. Next day, five o'clock in the afternoon, Steinbrenner is in the Yankee locker room with a copy of the letter for each of us, along with his cadre of vice-presidents, the complete coaching staff, and all the players. I walk into the meeting just minutes after it begins, having heard about the letter earlier that afternoon from Don Fehr, who on behalf of the Players Association had been negotiating with Ueberroth for a drug-testing program. Don feels this individual appeal constitutes union busting, and asks the player reps to tell the players that the only appropriate response is a vote to refer the issue to the Association.

But Steinbrenner wants action today, now. He's headed for Chicago to an owners' meeting in a few days and he wants to be able to tell everyone that the Yankees support drug testing 100 percent. "The Mets," he says, "have already voted one hundred percent in favor," not at all the case, as I later find out. Then to show us what a straight shooter he is he announces that he'll stand up there with us at the urinal and piss in the bottle himself. In closing, he says he assumes everyone on his team is in favor of drug testing, and that if we aren't we should call him personally by 1 P.M. the next day and tell him. "And keep in mind, I'm the guy who signs your paychecks." The implication is clear. It's our butts if we don't go along with it. Besides, aside from a few established players, most of the guys on the team have never even spoken to Steinbrenner, so for them to call him with a dissenting vote is out of the question.

As Steinbrenner starts passing out copies of the letter I say, "Excuse me," stand up, and tell him that his request that we support the commissioner's letter is circumventing the Association. Steinbrenner glares at me. I offer to pass out the letters, saying that it's my responsibility as the Yankee player rep.

"Not for long," he says.

"Oh, yeah? Well, I'm not worried about it. Because you know and I know where I'm going to be next year, and that's right here!"

"We'll see about that!"

"Yeah, we will."

With that Steinbrenner tosses the letters in Gene Michael's direction onto the picnic table in the center of the clubhouse and storms out of the room. "Excuse me," I tell Michael, who's back that year as a coach, "but we're going to have our meeting now." All the coaches and the front office people leave. The meeting is short, Don Baylor, the American League player rep, backs me all the way, and the players vote unanimously to refer the issue of drug testing to the Association.

It's the Association's stand, incidentally, that drug testing might be possible as part of a comprehensive program that includes player education, rehabilitation, and confidentiality. Confidentiality is crucial, we feel, because the tests are far from 100 percent accurate, and in any event, the results should not be left to the owners as a weapon to use against the players. As it turned out, by 1985 many players had already signed contracts with drug clauses—permitting teams to test the player for drugs at any time—often without even knowing it. Mike Pagliarulo or Bobby Meacham, for example. Bobby's agent didn't show up from California for his contract signing, and the front office presented Bobby with a contract that had the numbers the agent had negotiated over the phone. Bobby checked the numbers, saw that they were right, and signed. Ten minutes later the cameras were on him and reporters were asking, "How do you feel about signing the drug clause?" It was the first he'd heard of it.

By March 1986 it had gotten to the point that nearly half the players who signed new contracts that year had signed contracts with drug clauses. The Association called for action on the issue and soon enough the clauses were invalidated by a Major League Baseball arbitrator.

After my meeting with the team where we refer the issue of drug testing to the Association, I get word that Steinbrenner wants to see me in Billy Martin's office. He's pissed, they tell me.

"There can't be any more confrontations like this," he says, ushering me in and closing the door behind me. I agree, no need for it! I repeat that I think the issue is an Association issue and that the commissioner can't go directly to the players with it. But Steinbrenner could care less. He's far more concerned with what he sees as a confrontation between us. "It's not good for the team," he goes on.

"Not good for the team!?" That gets me. I flash to all he's done to undermine us, make us skittery and nervous. "I'll tell you what's not good for the team . . ." And I light into him about his locker-room chat prior to the Toronto series a few weeks back and his subsequent blasting of the team in the clubhouse and in the papers. "You may employ us, but I'm in that locker room every day. I see what that stuff does to a team."

When I finish, Steinbrenner is oddly quiet. "Don't say anything to the press about this," he warns. "You know how they can twist and manipulate things." I tell him I won't, not to worry about it. I leave thinking things are settled.

Next day when I arrive at the stadium I get the word from a parking-lot attendant with a crooked nose that the man wants to see me again, this time in his own office. In the corridor and the outer office they all give me the fish-eye, like my head is about to roll. Bobby Murcer, the Yankee's newest executive, scurries from the office without a word for me. First thing George says when I walk in is, "I couldn't sleep last night. I didn't like what happened yesterday in the locker room. And I don't think we're ever going to be able to resolve our differences." He accuses me of being insubordinate and challenging his authority. "How can I hold my head up in front of the players after being kicked out of my own locker room. I'm the leader," he goes on, "I'm the admiral. There are vice-admirals, but I'm the admiral. I can't have anyone thinking you own this team. You're causing dissension on the Yankees." He goes on to say that I should pick a team, any team, and he'll see if he can make a trade today, right now.

"I don't think so. I like it right here."

"I can make it hard for you." As if he hadn't already.

"What are you going to do, bench me?"

"I can do better. I can release you."

I laugh. "Oh yeah, that's a good one." I knew it was no joke, though; I wished Al or my lawyer were there to speak on my behalf, but I was in it by myself.

After that pleasant little exchange he starts back again on yesterday's confrontation. "It could have been handled a lot better," he says.

"True, but it could also have been handled a lot worse." And as I say it I realize just how much of a personal confrontation it *could* have been, how angry I was—at Steinbrenner's personal attacks in the press over the years, the insults, the way he'd treated the Foundation, the constant battling. So now in the privacy of his office I do tell him, we lay it all on the table back and forth, four years of bad feelings. It takes quite a while, with me on the offense.

"I'm hardest," George says when I'm through, "on the people I feel closest to. I try to get at the big guy on the team to motivate the others."

"Well, maybe you should stop. I don't seem to respond well to it."

But George is already looking at the larger picture and waxes philosophical. "You know, I have a football mentality," he says.

"Yeah, but this is baseball." After letting the profound truth of it sink in I ask him how he feels we should resolve the "confrontation" issue. He suggests another player meeting before the game where I tell the guys that yesterday's events did not constitute a confrontation. "Fine."

Thirty minutes later, with the team assembled in the locker room, I stand up and say that Mr. Steinbrenner and I agree on two key points. First, we both want a winner. And second, we feel there is no place for drugs on the Yankees. In closing, I assure everyone that yesterday's dialogue in the locker room between Mr. Steinbrenner and me was *not* a confrontation. Then George stands and makes a little speech. He says that we have ironed out our differences, and that he agrees that the drug-testing issue is a matter for the Players Association, but that each of you have to make your voices heard on the issue. Everyone seems to understand, but as we get up to take the field George suddenly chimes, "But keep in mind, keep in mind, there's only one admiral on this ship. There may be some vice-admirals, but only one admiral. So let's get out there and have some fun!!!" It leaves me, and everybody else, speechless.

Because of my continuing troubles with Steinbrenner, in 1986, deciding to keep as low a profile as possible, I asked Willie Randolph if he'd run for player rep, but as a family man, he was concerned about his job. I also asked Don Mattingly, but he felt it might have a negative impact on his contract arbitration. They were both probably right to beg off. Historically, the first year as a player rep for many guys has been their last with that team. In '87, though, with his contract settled, Donnie agreed to be nominated as an alternate, and was elected to that position.

LESSONS

I knew before I ever got to New York that the power of the city's media—the local press and the national magazines and television networks based there—could "create" ballplayers. They could take an average ballplayer—a Bucky Dent, for example—and make him into an all-star, while more talented players might go languishing in Houston or Atlanta. That doesn't mean, of course, that there aren't true all-stars coming from the Mets and the Yankees. It's just that there's more of a chance that a player might be overrated coming from these teams, like an inflated issue on the New York Stock Exchange.

Beyond creating players, I found that the power of the New York media could also create problems—and of a far greater magnitude than those created by the San Diego press. So, while my initial inclination was to say anything I felt to the press in New York, I soon learned to keep my guard up. Otherwise I'd slip and say something controversial, then have to spend weeks living it down. This extended to my physical appearance in public. I already knew there was no way I could go out on the streets looking raggedy because I'd immediately be recognized, written about, and dismissed by some people on that basis.

Also, where I went and whom I went with were of great concern to much of the media. Once I saw one of Tina Turner's shows, then went again and met her backstage the second night. There were some photos and the next thing I knew one of the scandal sheets had us as "traveling together with talk of marriage in the air."

Another time I was romantically linked in the tabloids with Martina Navratilova. We'd actually become pretty friendly. I'd leave her and Nancy Lieberman tickets for Yankee games, and one time she was talking to Al and me about setting up her own foundation. Before that she had talked to Al about him representing her, helping her change her image. Anyway, we were seen together a few times, and a magazine picked up on it, and soon the word was we were an item. Not that I think that's such an outrageous idea; we got along well, she's an interesting woman with an interesting past, and, of course, an extraordinary athlete. It just wasn't true. What we did do was share conditioning tips.

I couldn't have been in the city more than a month before I realized that to survive in New York I'd have to talk good, look good, have a good accountant and a good lawyer. And in New York City you don't have to be making over $1 million to know this. Everyone does.

I think every player on the Yankees sometimes feels squeezed by the press on the one side and the Yankee media machine on the other. Players come and go, but the press and team hierarchy remain, and they have to work together. So often what the "Yankees" say is pretty much what the press prints. Is Winfield a winner and a leader, or just a good athlete? Is Rickey Henderson taking it easy? Is Bobby Meacham not a smart player? A lot of what you read in the papers may not have much to do with the play on the field or the feeling in the locker room.

Then there's the problem of reporters twisting what you say. My comments have been misrepresented more than once, and after you've been burned by a reporter it's hard to respond politely to them again or with anything more than a cliché. Still, they keep coming back.

Also, there are so many reporters, some days you can't tell who they are without a scorecard. When I left San Diego, I called a final press conference. Maybe twenty reporters showed up, ten of them for the food I provided. There are that many at Yankee Stadium every game day and each one wants something special. I don't blame them. It's their job and I suppose that's what I get for playing ball and suing my boss in the media center of the world. Besides, I'm sure I've benefited more from the exposure than suffered from it.

A number of sportswriters have consistently treated me fairly, whether what they said was complimentary or critical, and I always try to give them the comments and stories they're looking for. Phil Collier in San Diego was one guy who wrote about the team pretty fairly. I also respected UPI's Milton Richmond, who passed away in 1986. He was a fair, honorable, likable man. In New York the *Times* tells it as it is, the *Post* hunts for scandal, and the *Daily News* can go either way. Jane Gross, formerly with the *Times* and one of the first women sportswriters, was consistently thoughtful and insightful and a good writer to boot. I enjoyed sitting on the bench shooting the bull with her. She's an interesting woman who loves talking, whether about baseball, world affairs, living abroad, or infighting at her job. Another writer I like is Claire Smith with the *Hartford Courant,* a real pro, a pleasure to talk to. A black woman in a predominantly white man's game, Claire has given me valuable insights into dealing with the press, minority hiring in baseball, and much more. In exchange I've revealed as much to her as I have any reporter. Still, I've never been as forthcoming as she wants. When she gets on my case for it, I tell her, "Hey, Claire, I got to save something for the book." "Yeah," she says, "I'll believe it when I see it."

I still remember the first woman sportswriter to come into a locker room where I was playing. Her name was Melissa Ludke and she worked for *Sports Illustrated.* I was on the Padres at the time and the second she walked in one of our coaches, Whitey Wietelmann, grabbed her by her coat sleeve and escorted her out saying that women didn't belong in a locker room. After being reprimanded by the league and the commissioner, Whitey wandered around for days mumbling that baseball had gone to hell.

·

SEASONS: 1986

There's a lot of uncertainty about the pitching rotation at the beginning of 1986 spring training. Tommy John and John Montefusco are brought to camp as extra roster players, without any decision about if and how to use them. Britt Burns, who'd been obtained from the Chicago White Sox in a big trade, turns out to have an arthritic hip and has to retire. Then, on our last cut day in Fort Lauderdale, Phil Niekro, a 15-game winner the year before—the same year he'd also won his 300th game—is unceremoniously dropped. Along with many others I commiserate with his brother, Joe, also on the team, about the way Phil is treated. Joe's really upset, more than Phil it seems. But the plan is to depend more on young pitchers from the farm system than on the old reliables. There's one exception: Old reliable Tommy John survives all the cuts and makes the club.

I finish spring training on a good note, hit a grand slam to destroy Toronto. As we leave Florida there's an underlying confidence about the season to come, a unity of purpose, something you usually don't find on most teams. There are no cliques, many of us had played together and played well the year before. All in all the 1986 Yankees are a good bunch; they're crazy enough, serious enough, experienced enough, hard working enough, and friendly enough. After the experimental years of '82, '83, and '84, when we were going for speed instead of power, had a platoon system and all that garbage, we'd finally discovered ourselves in '85. But that year we started slow. Rickey hurt his ankles, Donnie was coming off knee injury, and I'd been in the hospital late in the spring with a staph infection in my left elbow after a nasty spill playing the White Sox in Sarasota. In 1986 we're all healthy.

Back from Florida I'm looking forward to being a full-time ballplayer. I love the ritual of it—for a night game, I clear my head around two in the afternoon, think only of baseball, feel the adrenaline flow, drive to the stadium, hear the fans cheering me or cursing me, get to the clubhouse, Clark Kent takes off his glasses, loosens his tie, gets ragged by the clubhouse man . . . "Winfield, what are you doing? You already been down to see the mayor in that suit?" I rag him back . . . "Hey, Nick, you got a three-million-dollar complex here and a sixty-nine-cent water heater. You let hundred-and-fifty-pound guys in here early, they get into the shower, use seventy-five gallons apiece, and then when a real man gets into the shower, he's got nothing but cold water!"

Next, I check my fan mail, look into the trainer's room to see a guy on his stomach getting his butt massaged by "Joe the Rub," "riding the hump" as it's called. A full-time masseur is only part of one of the best support staffs in the majors. The Yankees have very experienced trainers, a knowledgeable strength coach, a video coordinator, and a lot more.

Time to turn up some music. It used to be who had the biggest, baddest box. Now it's the other way around, who's got the teeniest headphones. On a rocking chair atop the picnic table is Judge Guidry presiding over the Yankees' Kangaroo Court. Excessive styling at the plate? Showboating on defense? Too fancy a home-run trot? If a guy trips in the field, "a sniper got him," and he's fined for letting himself be shot. Pissing behind a dumpster outside the Long Branch, Lou's restaurant in Kansas City, two players to go unnamed were nabbed by the police—a misdemeanor in Kansas City but a felony in Kangaroo Court. Any conduct unbecoming a Yankee as perceived by your teammates and Judge Guidry slaps you with a $10 or $15 fine. Contest the charge and lose, the fine is doubled, with the kitty going toward team parties. No fines today, so I put on my uniform, pick up my bats, put on my batting glove, go out, and take batting practice. That's when the real fans show up. I anticipate the crowd, check where they're sitting. If they're in the bleachers, I know the stadium's going to be packed. If they're sitting close in, I know it's not.

I step into the batting cage, take a few cuts, look to see what ex-player or outsider is on the mound today. Tony? Vito? Johnnie the Mole? Torborg the pitching coach, who always throws me a spitter first? Ha! There's a never-ending supply of hopefuls and hopelesses eager to show their stuff pitching batting practice. One guy was so awed to be pitching BP in Yankee Stadium, he threw worse and worse, hitting a couple of batters along the way and then throwing a ball completely out of the batting cage. The harder he tried, the wilder he got, until he threw his glove and quit. Another guy, big Stanley "Steamer" Williams, six foot five, 250 pounds, was a pitching coach, but put him on the mound and he'd hit you in the head in a minute, just to let you know that you couldn't hit him.

After batting practice, I shag some flies, get loose. Back in the clubhouse the writers are foraging for material. To avoid them, I occasionally hide in the training room. Sometimes I just don't have anything to say. Next, maybe the manager calls a meeting—good chance of it if it's the beginning of a series—then finally back out on the field. The stadium's filled now. The crowd's ready for you to play ball. The guys stalk up and down the dugout, clasp hands, exhort each other. The pitcher keeps going back to the fountain for another sip of water, and each time he bends down his jacket slides off his pitching arm. Then the stadium's audio center cues us with music, the TV cameraman gives us the high sign, and we rush onto the field as the home fans cheer. Hey! Let's bump heads!

Opening day 1986, a beautiful, warm, sunny afternoon and we're playing last year's World Series champion, the Kansas City Royals, before the largest opening day crowd ever in the history of Yankee Stadium, 55,602 people. Out in right field listening to the national anthem I recall reading in *Yankee Magazine* that "Yankee Stadium ranks with the Coliseum in Rome as one of the most famous sports arenas in the world." There have been many times when I've stood in that hallowed Bronx landmark and felt like a gladiator in the center of a vast circle of lion cages with George Steinbrenner rattling the bars.

Today the fans take issue with a play in the eighth inning that sets the tone for me for the year. With a tight game in late innings, Randolph on second and Mattingly on first and no outs, the Royal defense figures I'll drive the ball. Instead, I bunt down the third-base line. A good idea, but the execution is off, the ball glances off my bat, and it's caught on the fly by Dan Quisenberry, Kansas City pitcher, who throws Randolph out at second, leaving Mattingly at first with two away. Any hope for a big inning has just gone down the tubes. Lou Piniella, our new manager, doesn't second-guess the call, but 55,602 fans do and they let me hear about it.

For the first half of the season the Yankees and I play pretty much the same way, in spurts, with long dry spells in between. Historically slow starters, our early-season record is actually better than the average for a Yankee team, but we're never able to put together the six, seven, or eight wins in a row to take us to the top of our division. Then on

June 28th we put Lou into the record books by losing eight straight at home; he curses us up and down.

By then the "fanimals" are really down on us, particularly on Bobby Meacham, who keeps making costly defensive miscues. Back on the road they take him out and play Mike Fischlin in his place. It's the start of a revolving-door roster that makes it increasingly difficult to stabilize as a team, to play in synch, to play well. The story that management gives the papers is that Meacham has lost the starting job. It's not necessarily true, but it's their way of shaking up the team and getting Meacham pissed so he'll play better the next time they put him in. The smarter move, I think, would have been to sit him down quietly, talk to him, and let him cool off. Knowing Bobby, he probably would have responded well to it. But to break him down, then try to build him back up in a new, management-approved mold wasn't going to work. He's an intelligent guy and doesn't appreciate being treated like a schoolboy.

As for the fans' treatment of the rest of the team, they're down on us all. They're vicious, brutal. They want a winner and have no tolerance for a losing streak. YOU BETTER WIN is the message they're giving. The press is on us, too. After our record-breaking eight-game home losing streak a reporter asks me, "Now that you're going on the road, what are you going to do differently?" "Leave town!" I tell him.

A lot of Yankees left town that season, but not with the team. Big, reliable Don Baylor was traded to Boston. Always a strong, pivotal guy, a good friend, lockermate, from the start of spring training the word was they weren't going to give him a chance. So when the trade came, Don welcomed it. Even more welcome, I'm sure, was the playoff and World Series money he eventually earned with the Red Sox, particularly after Steinbrenner predicted his bat would die in August. But Baylor's bat had a lot of life in it right to the end. You could sum up Don's reputation around the league: strength, class, rent-a-leader.

While the Yankees obliged Baylor with a trade, they weren't as obliging to Ken Griffey, another outfielder they'd lost use for. Grif suffered on the bench through April, May, and the first half of June with no sign of a trade. He finally decided to force the action by not showing up for a game in Yankee Stadium. Missing a practice without telling someone, much less a game, was so unlike Griffey that everyone on the team was worried by his absence. Had he been in a car crash? Was he sick? What *was* the story? Next day Grif filled us in, described how the New Jersey police and the Yankees' traveling secretary had come looking for him. When the police banged on the door, Griffey stepped out and asked, "Have I done anything wrong, officers?" They said, kind of dumbfounded, "Well, not so far as we know." So Grif said, "Thanks for stopping by," and headed straight for his car. That's when the traveling secretary showed up, under orders from the man, no doubt, to bring him back dead or alive. The picture of this little guy trying to keep Grif from stepping into his car and making his getaway had us all in stitches.

His only misgiving, he told me, was how people might interpret his missing the game. And he was right to worry. His son, Kenny, Jr., the number one pick of the Seattle Mariners, actually had high school teachers and classmates ask if his father was on drugs or had an emotional problem. Grif's only problem was scant playing time and no straight answers from management. He finally got the answer he was waiting for in July; a trade to Atlanta, a team of lesser stature at the moment, but back to the National League where he starred with Cincinnati's Big Red Machine, and the peace of mind that money couldn't buy him in New York.

I still remember Grif coming over to me in right field from center while we were changing pitchers during the seventh inning of a Sunday home game. I asked him how he was doing. He kind of smiled and said, "I'm gone, you know. This is my last game."

"What?" I said, surprised at first. But then I knew he'd finally gotten what he wanted.

All Bobby Meacham wanted was to be left alone to work through his defensive problems. I told him, "Get on base, then steal. The more runs you score, the more they leave you alone." But as the Yankees' twenty-first shortstop in the last ten years, Meacham was nervous, and rightly so. Not long after he told me that he was "anticipating something" they sent him down. The player taking his place on the roster, Ivan deJesus, arrived in the clubhouse before Meacham even knew he was out. Meacham was soon followed to the minors by his replacement at short, Mike Fischlin. And there were lots more to go after that, sent down or traded; catcher Ron Hassey, infielder Dale Berra, and a whole passel of pitchers.

Of all the trades and roster moves that season, the Hassey trade is one that sticks in my craw. Hassey had been dealt to Chicago for Ron Kittle, a big, lumbering, home-run-hitting, low-average outfielder, plus a peppery shortshop named Wayne Tolleson. Forget the pros and cons of the trade; just consider the manner in which it was presented to Hassey.

We're playing Milwaukee at home, a night game, and Hassey's called on to pinch-hit in the ninth inning, picking up a single and driving in a run. We lose anyway and, walking back to the clubhouse, Hassey's a few steps ahead of me. While I'm still on the stairs I hear what sounds like a chair being thrown at a locker, and a second later, a bat smashed against one of the dividers separating one locker stall from another. Turns out, Hassey had just been told he'd been traded during the game. It wasn't even over and he was already officially gone.

It wasn't as if Hassey was dogging it. He wasn't. He'd

made a lot of contributions. He was well liked. Anyhow, after a while a number of us gathered around him in the training room, sitting on the massage tables and on the trunks where they store the bandages and linament. We're all just talking to him to make him feel better, saying the obvious, that there's no loyalty in the game, that it's all just business, all of us wondering what it would feel like to be Hassey.

By letting Hassey go, we lost our ability to take charge of the game defensively behind the plate. Not that he was the best defensive catcher in the league, but the pitchers respected his judgment. Certainly his replacement, Butch Wynegar—the gentle guy who'd break down before the end of the season—wasn't the man to do it.

Suffering on offense with much of the rest of the team, partly from a nagging hamstring injury, I'm benched in favor of Dan Pasqua. Pasqua's an eager, youthful, strong-as-an-ox long-ball hitter who'd been promised the left-field job early in spring training, and talked like he could handle it, then had some problems at the plate and lost the job to Henry Cotto, a veteran. Now Cotto's in left, Dan's in right, and I'm on the bench, "resting." That first day Dan has a terrific game, a couple of home runs, a big catch up against the wall. Sitting in the dugout, I don't need a crystal ball to know how the media are going to react: perhaps, There it is, the man can play . . . Winfield's out . . . maybe it's time to make the switch. Back in the locker room after the game the writers are clustered around Pasqua and then they see me three lockers down. Before they can even ask I make my farewell speech: "It's been a pleasure playing for the Yankees the past five and a half years. It's been a tremendous experience. Every red-blooded American boy should have the opportunity to play for an organization like this. I would only hope that given the opportunity to perform elsewhere . . ." I know they're looking for a story, but I don't really have a story to tell them.

In the days that follow Pasqua continues to come on strong, has a number of great games, prompting a comparison to Mickey Mantle by none other than Mickey Mantle himself on TV. Pasqua's playing also pushes Phil Rizzuto's button, and he announces on TV: "He's great! The quickest hands! Have you ever seen any hands that quick? The power is fantastic!" Damn, I think, the guy just folded under pressure at spring training and now they're starting all over again. They'll build him up, he'll turn out not to be Mickey Mantle after all, then they'll do him in. I'd seen it happen before. Still, I find it an educational experience to sit in the clubhouse during a game and listen to the announcers' takes on the players. I wonder if they actually believe what they're saying, or if it's just that season's or that week's official line. Pasqua, incidentally, is dealt to the White Sox the following year. He'll play well for a team that doesn't expect him to be more than he is, a solid player with a tremendous amount of power.

As the spring progresses I develop a swelling and a pain in the back of my left leg to go along with my hamstring pull. I don't know if it's a flare-up of an old injury or something new. In professional sports you tend to fear the worst. I take some anti-inflammatory pills, get some ice treatment, some ultrasound stimulation. It cuts down the pain, takes down the swelling. Sitting on the bench watching games go by with Dan in right field, I wait and hope for a quick recovery.

I'm back in the lineup shortly. My first game back Pasqua is moved to left but continues in my cleanup spot. I'm moved down the lineup to fifth, a disappointment, and bewildering for the whole team. It's great to be back, nevertheless, but still hurting, I'm concerned I won't be effective on the base paths. Wouldn't you know it, first time up I hit one in the gap and take a double. Later in the game with a man on first I hit a bouncer to third that's a sure double play. So I run my butt off and beat it out, my leg hurting and me cussing all the way down the baseline. They appreciate the hussle, but keep me batting fifth.

Next game we play the A's in Yankee Stadium with Joaquin Andujar on the mound. By now everyone in the league knows that Dan is hitting fast balls, but they keep firing them to him, like every pitcher has to see for himself. His first at-bat he hits one out of the park. The A's homer to tie it, then I homer to give us a 2–1 lead which holds up till the sixth when Jose Canseco homers with one on to make it 3–2, where it stays until the ninth. Then *BAM!* Pasqua hits his second homer. Tie game. The crowd goes crazy. In the eleventh Pasqua is up again and the crowd roars its approval until he pops up, and has to make that dreaded right turn into the dugout. I step up to bat and an odd thing happens. The home crowd, roaring just a few seconds before, turns suddenly subdued, no cheers, like I can't possibly put the game away. That moment it feels a little like it did toward the end of the '84 season when Mattingly and I were vying for the batting title; it's as if the crowd doesn't *want* me to do as well as Pasqua.

But I put it out of my head, hit the second pitch that's thrown, and watch it roll between short and third. It's a clean single, but I want more. I know the grass will eat it up, know the left fielder is deep, know he doesn't have an arm, know the game is on the line. The first-base coach gives me the sign to hold up, everyone's yelling no, no, no, but I think yes, yes, yes, check the left fielder, take the wide turn, tag first, and am on my way. I get a double standing up. They cheer then, but I had to bust my butt to get it out of them.

Batting fifth, even sixth, the fans down on me, a popular, young turk on my tail, my leg hurting, these are tough times.

It's never easy playing through tough times. You've got to get yourself back on track before you spiral into a depression. And if you do hit bottom, you've got to storm back. Confidence is key. So is keeping things in perspective. There's no single way to deal with it. Sometimes I practice harder, sometimes practice less. Sometimes I think a lot about it. Sometimes I put it out of my mind.

Sometimes, though, no matter what you do, nothing goes right, and you're in what they label a slump. Only I rarely call it that; I call it "a period of adjustment." Sure, when a guy who can't hit anyway doesn't hit for a period of time, that's a slump. But when you know how to hit and you tail off, go a week maybe without a hit, it isn't. It's a variation from the norm, like a correction in the stock market. The year that Mattingly and I were vying for the batting crown, for example, he had a stretch where he went 10 for 54, batting .185. Was that a slump? And if it was, what do you call the time when he went, say, 30 for 54? They were both "adjustments" or variations in what in Donnie's case was a .343 year. Besides, who wants to hear "slump"—like, He's ridden with a slump. It's enough to keep you in one for the rest of the season.

Lots of times, too, the word is misused. I remember one time on the Padres, I'm back in the lineup having not quite recovered from a hand injury incurred against Tim Foli on a double play, and playing a series with Cincinnati. I'm really scalding the ball, but still go 0 for 22 or something. If you were at the game you'd say, Damn, he's really making contact! But I have nothing to show for it. Dave Conception picks off three or four sure hits and throws me out each time by half a step or less. Next day I look at the paper and see that my problems aren't my hurt hand or Conception's great fielding; I'm in a slump. I don't believe it, and I'm going to keep swinging the same way.

Forget injury or great defensive play, a batter may make great contact eight times in three days and walk away with nothing. Then again, I've seen Ralph Garr hit four quirky balls that never reached the pitcher and go 4 for 4 with two doubles. I once saw Ralph take a tremendous hack and bail out of the box. He'd hit the ball, but he had no idea where. He's looking around for it, and it caromed off the foul pole in left for a home run.

The spring of '86, to keep myself strong, fine-tuned, fitting into my clothes, and to keep from falling into a funk, I lift weights, and while I'm on the bench I study the pitchers and meditate. I develop a deep-breathing and stretching regimen, tensing individual areas of my body, stretching my calves, my legs, my chest, my biceps, then releasing all the tension. I've seen other players in my situation pace the dugout and bite their nails. My decision is not to waste adrenaline so if I'm called on to play, I won't have spent myself in anticipation.

Working with the Yankee video coordinator, Mike Barnett, I also study videotapes of my 1984 .340 season. After I analyze my form, I take some extra batting practice, start using my left arm a little more in my swing, move back a little from the plate, take a smaller stride.

Never, anyway, the kind of guy to tear up the locker room, punch friends, and break lamps like some ballplayers—though on the field it's acceptable to yell and scream and throw a tantrum when things don't go your way—I try not to take my troubles home with me. I work to maintain my sense of humor, to keep myself amused and doing things. One night after a game Dom Scala, Dave Righetti, and I stop for a bite to eat at the Border Cafe, a restaurant I own part of in Manhattan, and go down to Madison Square Garden to catch the wrestling. We're spotted by the emcee and between events we're interviewed by Gorilla Monsoon. Given the mike we're irrepressible. We do a whole macho number challenging the American League East teams in the same outrageous way wrestlers challenge each other. "We want your biggest, your baddest, your boldest, your ugliest," we rant and rave. We're joined by King Kong Bundy and Bobby "the Brain" Heenan just before we storm off the set. Steinbrenner, I'm later told, thought it undignified, but had just done an interview himself in *Sport* magazine where he'd praised wrestlers as athletes and listed his own professional wrestling favorites, including Hulk Hogan. You figure the guy out.

During the lowest of my bad times at the plate one of the coaches says it like it is. "Your hitting may be inept, but your defense is better than ever." All right! I think; I'm making a contribution and it's being noticed. Indeed, I'd caught two over the fence the day before and made a couple of dynamite plays against Toronto. That day in Baltimore I make another, charging back after a long drive, turning, always keeping the ball in sight, preparing myself for the leap and the impact against the fence. It's a timing play; I look back at the ball through the misty rain, focus on it, jump, make the catch, robbing Lee Lacy of a three-run homer and ending the inning. It's a tough play, one I'd run hell-bent for leather for, making judgments and revising them all the way.

After that catch I decide I'll change my style. Suiting up for the next game, I pull my socks way up. I look like Big Bird on "Sesame Street." Right away it draws some looks, gets some attention. I figure I'll just take batting practice like this, but I hit the ball so well, I resolve to keep them up there. A lot of guys bet me I won't, but I do. I figure that since they're talking about my playing ugly, I might as well look the part. Phil Rizzuto can't stop talking about how odd it looks. Funny thing, though, I start playing better, get a home run, do some fancy base running. A week later when we play Boston I take some kidding from Don Baylor. He says, "I know it's going to cost you some money for wearing your socks like that," referring to the Kangaroo Court he presided over the previous year. It's true, but I don't care. I want to gain back my momentum and if this is what it takes, the hell with what I look like.

Unconcerned with my socks or my momentum, Steinbrenner starts making noises in the press about my hitting. "Winfield," I read, "is a good defensive player, but he can't hit, he can't hit right-handers." Clearly, I'm through, washed up, maybe a passable DH against lesser lefties. Next thing I know I'm benched in favor of Pasqua again, and again and it's not long before I'm madder and madder. It feels like there's a storm a'brewin'.

At the eye of this maelstrom is Lou Piniella, our rookie manager. From the start when he came in to replace Billy we all liked Lou, wanted him to do well. I thought he was a natural. He knew the Yankees, knew the tradition, knew New York. The fact that he had no managerial experience only meant he wouldn't be tied to tired old ways of doing things. He was fair and open, and speaking Spanish as well as English made it possible for him to communicate easily with all his players. Also, there was no showboating and no doghouse with Lou. Starting out he seemed loose, on top of things.

But as the game went by, Lou was changing. The microscopic eye of the media and the critical eye of the man were working away at his confidence and his real strength as a players' manager. He certainly was having his ups and downs, trying to find his way through people, trying to keep a stiff upper lip and the appearance of being in charge, trying not to make too many mistakes. He probably had no choice about my sporadic benchings. If he had, because of our having been teammates, at least Lou would've let me know in advance.

In July the Yankees travel to Toronto for the nationally televised "Game of the Week"—"The Game of the World," as we call it. When I get to the park I find I'm not in the lineup; no advance notice, no warning, nothing. This time I know it's not Lou's doing, not on a day when we need to look good and win in front of the whole country. Noting my chagrin and not a great fan of Steinbrenner's, Tony Kubek, the game announcer, asks me if I'd like to give the Yankee lineup on TV. So I do, tell the TV audience that the reason I have the time to do so is because up until two minutes ago I thought I was going to be *in* the starting lineup myself. Then I do a quick little promo on everyone who's playing and close with something like, "We can't win unless we go with our best team." We lose.

During the broadcast Steinbrenner is invited into the booth and he compares our outfield unfavorably to Toronto's, though he singles out Rickey and Pasqua for praise. He then goes on to characterize himself as an innovator and a leader, not, he's quick to point out, like Eisenhower, but like Patton. "And if a player can't take that kind of leadership, he shouldn't be in New York." He closes with the observation that his favorite athletes are his racehorses because, "My horses don't talk to the press."

What George doesn't mention is that when he's not Patton, he likes to think of himself as Robert Young in "Father Knows Best," talking about his team as his "family." He's talked about this "family" a number of times, prompting Ron Guidry to say, "I never asked to be in his family. I just want to win games and pick up my check." But I don't even think that Steinbrenner is a good "family" man, running hot then cold on all of us kids all the time. Guidry loses six in a row and George is on his case; he wins a big one on TV and gets praised to the skies.

After the Toronto game I go up to Lou and ask him what the story is. "We played together. I know you and I think you know me. Why didn't I play?"

"I just wanted to give you a rest."

"Okay," I say, not sure whether to believe him, "but I

can't come to the park to find out I'm not in the lineup and have everyone see how surprised I am. That way the press makes a big deal out of it, particularly with Steinbrenner in town. If you want to sit me out for a day, fine. But, please, let me know beforehand."

Lou promises, but the benchings continue. Next stop, Texas, I ask Lou, "When am I going to play?" "Give me a couple of days," he says, wringing his hands, a gesture I'd never seen before from Lou. On July 9 I do play, hit my 2,000th hit, a pinch-hit run-scoring triple to right, to little fanfare.

One day later and again I'm not starting. I say to Lou, "I'm going to scream!" Although he didn't say it outright, his reaction told me: Do what you have to do; go to the press. See what happens; there'll be repercussions, but it may force something to change. So I do that day, knowing my next stop on the road trip is Minnesota. Once the storm breaks from what I say in Texas I'll hope for a home job, which is when the umps call a game the home team's way, from the Minnesota press. I tell the writers in the Texas clubhouse, "They're ridiculous, they're fools. They talk about winning, but as long as I'm not out there, they're not putting their best team on the field, they're not trying, they're fooling the people." Then I go out and back it up with two hits and four RBIs. Right or wrong I leave the park feeling great for the first time in weeks. It's a cathartic experience.

Following the Minnesota series I travel to Houston for my tenth consecutive All-Star Game. I'd reinjured the back of my leg in the first game with the Twins and am not sure how much playing time I'll get, but in the All-Star Game or the playoffs I'd play with my leg in a cast. I have something to prove. I know I'll probably get a crack at facing Dwight Gooden, the most heralded right-hander in the National League at the time, and I want to show my boss and my fans that I can come up against the best along with the very best of them. I have my leg wrapped and take the field, trotting, stretching, trotting. All I want is one at-bat. I get it in the second inning, give Gooden a good look, and smash a double that two-hops to the right. Moments later I score on a home run by Lou Whitaker. We win the game, 5–4.

After the All-Star break I'm back in the lineup, thinking the b.s. is over, only I'm on the bench again for a couple of one-nighters. This time when I go to talk to Lou, he won't even look me in the eye, won't talk to me about it. And then miraculously the benchings stop and my average starts to climb.

Come late summer, Harvey Greene, the Yankees' PR man, says how nice it would be if I hit my 300th home run at Yankee Stadium, and I oblige in a "Businessman's Special" afternoon game against Seattle on August 20. As I round the bases the number "300" pulses a few times on the scoreboard. Three hundred what? I think. Nothing more is said. After collecting my high-fives it's business as usual. Finally, after the inning is over and I'm grabbing my glove to take the field, the game announcer says that the home run I'd hit a few minutes before was my 300th. The announcement is met by a scattering of cheers.

Talking to the press after the game about my reputation as a talented but unreliable free-swinger, a natural athlete, I say, "You don't get two thousand hits and three hundred home runs on sheer talent." Black players hear this natural athlete stuff all the time, incidentally, just as white players are called "students of the game" or "hard working." It's like Isiah Thomas of the Detroit Pistons said during the 1987 NBA playoffs: "If Larry Bird makes a great play, the press says what a smart player he is; if Magic Johnson does the same thing, they call him a super-athlete." Contrary to popular belief, black guys do not come out of the womb turning double plays and taking jump shots.

That August I also play one game at third base—a major-league first for me—filling in for Pagliarulo, who's recovering from a bad hamstring. American League president Bobby Brown is there in his third-base box, and I see him covering a smile with his hand. What I really want, though, is a chance to pitch. There's a game where they can use me, the old college pitcher, when they've run through the pitching staff, but don't, I assume, for fear of George's reaction or an injury. Fair enough.

At the end of August I read in the *New York Post:* " 'No Takers for Overpriced Winfield,' Says Boss." George has marshaled his statistics to show that I'm not a clutch player offensively, that I can't hit when it counts. I grin and bear it, but think about showing up for a good day's work and hearing your boss say you can't do your job. A couple of days later the *New York Times* publishes a story headlined "The Worth of Winfield." In it, sportswriter Ira Berkow assembles the official American League statistics to demonstrate that I'm one of the best hitters in the majors with men on base and the game on the line, outperforming players like George Brett and Jim Rice in high-pressure situations. It's the happiest surprise I ever found in the press.

By September the team is playing loose, and Steinbrenner is for some reason off the team's case. Everybody on the team seems to be fed up with reading about Piniella's imminent firing anyway, and finally realize that the man's decisions are out of their control. Where normally in September you could cut the pressure in the Yankee clubhouse with a knife, this year is different. And suddenly we go through teams like a mower through tall grass. Donnie is running neck-and-neck with Boston's Wade Boggs for the batting title. I'm going for my fifth consecutive 100+ RBI season. A few days before the end of the season, I figure if I get two more home runs I'll definitely make it; with one I probably will, but I'll have to rely on Donnie to run the bases well for me. As for the front office, they probably don't give a damn what I do.

I'm lucky. Unlike Donnie, I only have to compete against myself. On September 29 with only a couple more games to play I get my 100th RBI of the season, moving me into fourth place on the all-time Yankee consecutive 100+ RBI seasons list, behind Lou Gehrig, Babe Ruth, and Joe Di-Maggio. A day later, following my last at-bat of the season in Yankee Stadium, the fans give me a standing ovation.

Our final series is with Boston in Fenway Park. Though Boston's already wrapped up the division, the word is if we lose this series, Lou is out. To break the tension, after the first game there's a surprise birthday party for me and a lot of guys from the team show up. It's particularly good to see Donnie there, good to know he's not off biting his nails, worrying about Boggs. Seeing the two of them battle it out for hits reminds me of my race with Mattingly two years before. Boggs is an interesting player to watch. He's a little bigger and a little stronger than Donnie, but Mattingly is deceptively powerful. Unlike Mattingly, who goes deep more often, Boggs always hits for average. He goes after those singles and doubles, using Fenway Park's Green Monster well like Donnie uses right field for home runs in New York. He doesn't deviate. It's like his diet—he eats chicken every day. So when he approaches the plate he is locked in. The thing is, in the last days of the season Boggs goes out with an injury. Now his average is on ice and no matter what Donnie does, he can't catch him.

Donnie loses the title, we win the series, and Lou keeps his job.

THE GAME

Fans, short for "fanatic," are as much part of today's game as the bat, the ball, the players, and the salaries they earn. I feel my responsibility to myself, the team, and the fans is to play hard when I'm on the field, and to work hard off the field to bring respect to the team and to the city. Off the field, too, I usually try to be polite. On the other hand, I don't feel I have to talk to a sloppy drunk or an obnoxious guy who brings his girlfriend over to my table in a restaurant and demands an autograph and a lengthy talk about the game. Inevitably, this is the guy who, when you ignore him, insists, "I pay your salary…" That's when I say, "If you paid my salary, I'd be a poor s.o.b."

Then there's the guy who wants to, who absolutely *has* to shake your hand. High flattery, but riskier business. I remember once, for example, standing at a urinal in a men's room, and the guy next to me is doing his thing, when suddenly he turns and sees me. He breaks into a big smile. "Hey, Dave Winfield!" and he lets go of his equipment and reaches his hand over the divider. "No thanks, no thanks," I tell him.

Still, I'll almost always shake a hand, give an autograph, because I feel when people ask it's usually as a measure of respect for me and my accomplishments. I'm proud and flattered, and hope I'll continue to be asked long after I'm out of the game. Sometimes, though, the requests are unreasonable. Kids—and adults, too—will hold up a line of fans and ask for six or a dozen or twenty John Hancocks on baseball cards and memorabilia. It's not so much that they care who you are, but that they need you to support their cottage industry by providing autographs for them to sell. One or two is enough.

The autograph business is transacted on a far grander scale at baseball card shows all over the country. Here professional traders set up in hotels like flea marketeers, with booths and tables for everyone to show their wares. Some of the booths may have a professional ballplayer or two signing autographs. Kids attending these shows may pay three bucks per picture and an additional five bucks to get it autographed. Eight bucks for a picture maybe worth a dollar. If a kid already has a picture and wants it signed—or a cast, or a glove, or a napkin—it's a flat five bucks. Figure hundreds of thousands of kids in dozens of cities and you get some idea of the type of money being made. The ballplayer signing names for a couple of hours doesn't do too shabbily either.

This is all separate from the bubble gum card companies that have their own industry and a contract directly with the Players Association, which then divvies the proceeds among the players. Once a year the bubble gum makers come around to take your picture for your card. They might catch you in a batting cage or while you're out in the field. You rarely ever know when it's going to happen and when you finally see the card, it's usually a surprise. There are special promotion cards, boxtop cards, ice-cream-carton cards. There must be fifty different Winfields in print.

New York fans are definitely the most rabid and fickle in the country. Every day it's What have you done for me lately, like last at-bat? It's the city that makes them that way. It's a tougher place to live than most, there's more frustration, more tension, more catastrophes and calamities, and more enthusiasm. In any event, they're the wildest fans I've ever seen, though I'll hand them this, they're also among the most knowledgeable. When they bitch and moan they usually know what they're moaning about.

Oakland fans can be pretty unruly. They used to get on me in the outfield a lot before they closed the fence in.

Chicago's also got some tough fans. So does Boston. By contrast, Seattle fans are usually nice and pleasant. Same goes for Kansas City fans, who sit up in their beautiful, immaculate stadium like they're at the theater and clap and cheer for their guys. As an opposing player you can go up there, sit in the stands, sign autographs, and no one hassles you. Minneapolis fans are very well behaved, though during the '87 playoffs and World Series they proved they could create one hell of a racket. Waving their homer hankies, they cheered like 50,000 Scandinavian James Browns, as one commentator put it. Actually, until then, the only real cheers to be heard in the Metrodome were during the Vikings' football games. But '87's rah-rah Twins reclaimed a generation of baseball fans that had been lost under Calvin Griffith's ownership.

Fan support, as demonstrated in the Twins' successful bid for the world championship, can be crucial. In football, they talk about the twelfth man, the home field advantage. Same thing happens in baseball, though you play a lot of games with much, much smaller crowds. The stadium, too, can make a difference in the fans' contribution. The older, smaller, more enclosed stadiums like Fenway Park and Wrigley Field will contain and amplify the crowd noise, while in a larger, more open stadium like the Oakland Coliseum or Toronto's Exhibition Stadium the cheering seems less intense.

Being cheered feels great, lends you confidence, makes you strut, though there are players who try to take it in stride like, Thank you, thank you very much, but it's all in a day's work. Mostly, you try not to dwell on it, just keep performing. When you're booed, however, you think a lot of things, everything from You ungrateful wretches, to Screw you! to Let's just get this inning over with so I can get a chance to redeem myself.

My first sense of just how serious professional baseball

fans are came in 1975, my third season with the Padres. I was injured, didn't suit up, and instead watched the game from the stands. We were in Cincinnati and the folks I was sitting with were really into their team winning the game—at least as serious about it as the guys on the field. At one point I made the mistake of standing up and cheering one of my guys on, and you should have seen the look on those people's faces. They didn't know who I was, but I'm sure it wouldn't have made any difference if they had. They cussed me out, told me to get the hell out of there. So I sat down. Then when I did it again a few minutes later, there was a moment when I thought they'd just converge on me and tear me to pieces. So I sat back down again and stayed cool. I told the guys on the team later, "I was cheering you in spirit, but not in the flesh."

Fans have always been serious, but the nature of fandom has changed. With salary and contract hassles followed religiously by the media, most fans today know exactly how much you make. And if you make a lot—or even *ask* for a lot—and don't perform to their expectations, they really get on you, probably more than they ever did in the old days. TV, too, has had an effect. Fans know that the cameras can catch them at any time, so they come to the stadium ready for instant stardom with freaky wigs, wild outfits, and a variety of signs and banners to share with the world.

The prospect of instant stardom sometimes results in a fan breaking the barrier between "them" and "us." That, and the courage provided by a few six-packs. In the early seventies, when it was the fad, there were quite a few streakers. There was that guy who showed his wares while Ray Kroc was on the PA system chewing his new team out. There was also a young guy in Montreal who ran naked out to second base and started making obscene gestures during a Canadian national TV game. The security guys moved right in on him, but he took off and put some great moves on them, darting and dodging. Walter Payton had nothing on this guy. Finally, he slipped on some gravel off the first-base line and they really beat the stuffing out of him. I mean, literally.

Another time we were in Seattle and I was in the on-deck circle when I saw a guy making his way across the field toward our manager, Billy Martin—with a knife, a gun, a bag of marshmallows, who knew? Instinctively, I grabbed Billy and pulled him out of the way. Then the police converged. Billy thanked me afterward, though he assured me he could have handled it.

The most cowardly, outrageous act of fandom I ever saw was in Yankee Stadium during the '81 playoffs against Milwaukee. After a questionable call by the umpire went against me at third base, a fan ran onto the field and put a picture-perfect NFL tackle on the offending ump while his back was turned. It collapsed his legs right out from under him and he went down like a sack of grain. The players rushed to the ump's rescue—no doubt a major-league first—pummeling the guy. Sounds lopsided, but one of the other umpires, Ken Kaiser, an ex-wrestler, was so livid that the fanatic was lucky only the players and security guards got to him.

No surprise, the baddest fan-on-the-rampage I ever saw was also at Yankee Stadium. I was in the outfield when I saw a guy climb over the left-field wall and hit the turf. He was about six foot one, must have weighed 260, had on a motorcycle helmet, and was clearly bombed out of his mind. I took one look at him and I started backing away. I didn't want to be within thirty yards of this guy. For a while he just stood there, arms dangling at his sides like an urban gorilla. Then he started stalking the field like, Bring on the security guards. Let me at 'em! A couple of guards hustled onto the field, but when they got close, they got cautious and called for reinforcements. When there were about six of them they surrounded him and converged on him, a big pile of bodies.

And every few seconds you could see some security guy flying off the pile. When they finally got him down with his hands behind his back the handcuffs wouldn't fit. So they hammered him real good right where he was, then dragged him by his feet face-down across the field and down the steps of the dugout.

Sometimes, rather than breaking the physical barrier between "them" and "us," a single fan crashes through the general din to break the sound barrier. One afternoon in Seattle a guy in the seats right behind the plate kept yelling, "Come on, you big gorilla, you can't hit!" each time I got up to bat against Jim Beattie. I was getting more and more pissed off, when suddenly I saw a pitch that had this guy's name written all over it. I lit into it and *POW!* It was such a devastating blow, headed straight for the Mariners' mock boat in center field, I knew it was a home run. I never even looked at the ball. I just spun and yelled at the guy, "That's for you!" And as I trotted around the bases I kept pointing at him to let everyone in the stadium know who sparked the home run that sank their Mariners.

Still other times it's the players who break the barrier between "us" and "them"; the catcher reaching into the stands to field a foul ball, the outfielder going over the top of the fence to steal a home run. Once I was going after a ball along the right-field railing when this super-fat guy jumped up in my face to keep me from making the catch. Just as he stretched his arm out for the ball, his pants fell off, right to the ground, leaving him standing in his drawers. I didn't make the catch, but the guy was so embarrassed, twenty seconds later he just shot out of the stadium never to be seen again . . . except on instant replay and by millions of TV viewers on "This Week in Baseball."

Not content to boo and cheer, some fans come to the stadium with smoke bombs, bottles, cans, all manner of weaponry. Dave Parker had batteries thrown at him. And the fans got so down on Dick Allen that he'd only take the field if he could wear a helmet. Over the years I've had fruit thrown at me, beer dumped in my face, and been hit in the back with a baseball fired from the bleachers. After the Angels' Wally Joyner was grazed by a knife thrown from the stands in Yankee Stadium, some jokesters threw rubber knives at me when we visited Anaheim. Another time in Yankee Stadium I was in the outfield, just minding my business, when suddenly *shooop!* an arrow pierced the ground right next to me. Metal tip and everything. Inches into the ground. No way it could have gotten there without a bow. A bow!? How did someone get a *bow* into Yankee Stadium?

Most serious of all are the death threats. Reggie was a notable target for these. And I'm told that when Hank Aaron was on the verge of breaking Babe Ruth's home-run record he'd get calls like "If you break that record we're going to kill you, you black s.o.b.!"

I've received death threats both as a Padre and as a Yankee. In my last year in San Diego I got a whole bunch of them. The prospect of my turning free agent after the season was my crime, and they wanted to execute me early. As a precaution, during games the police would watch my car and before I got in they'd check to see if it had been tampered with. As a Yankee during the '81 World Series with the Dodgers I got a call at 1 A.M. in my Los Angeles hotel room. A male voice said if I took the field the next day, he'd kill me. Why me? I only got one hit in the whole Series. I told the police, but there wasn't a whole lot they could do. I felt most vulnerable when I was in the outfield, but after a few innings I figured if he hadn't done it yet, he wasn't going to. So I got on with the game.

FEARS

Every now and again reality hits you right in the face, as it did the spring of 1986—not me, though, but Mike Pagliarulo, who took a glancing blow off the wrist to the nose with a pitch in Oakland. I'd been knocked down many times, but when I saw Mike actually get hit I jumped up. He'd just taken his left-handed swing at a curveball and then tried to plant himself in there, tried not to bail out of the batter's box for the next pitch. Only this one didn't break. It came right toward his chest, he put up his wrist to block it, and *bop!* it broke his nose. It looked terrible. He was okay, though. Just as he was telling his wife about it later on the phone, she saw the replay on TV. "Oh, my God!" she cried, real shocked. And that was *after* she already knew he was all right. Next day his Italian grandmother called him and said, "That s.o.b.! If he hurt you I'll put a hex on him that he should never pitch again. His arms should fall off!" Pags was laughing as he told me, his face all swollen.

It's no laughing matter. Baseball can be a dangerous game, a war, really, with teams or pitchers trying to establish position or retaliate after a loss of position. Every bit as dangerous is when there's no intent and the pitcher's just wild. The hazards are hardly limited to the batter's box. Many years ago the Texas Rangers' current manager, Bobby Valentine, once charged back to the wall to make a catch, jumped up against it, and caught his foot. Coming back down his leg bent backward and he snapped his femur, a compound fracture that ended his career. Dodger catcher Steve Yeager was hit while in the on-deck circle with the business end of a broken bat, the jagged edges lodging in his neck. Yeager fell straight to the ground, and quivered on the turf. Everyone thought he was dead, lying there with eighteen inches of the heavy bat sticking out of his neck. But he was lucky; it missed the jugular and he came back to play again that season. Spring of '86 our own catcher Butch Wynegar also got injured in the on-deck circle, bopped in the head with a foul ball.

No place and no one on the field are really safe. That's why batboys wear what look like space helmets, big double hats with triple-protected rims. It's also why most players wear helmets with single or double temple flaps, required safety equipment for players entering the leagues since the early 1980s and optional for those who entered the majors prior to that date. Still, people get hit, get hurt, and when it happens it's always a shock. Except, that is, when Don Baylor gets hit, which is often; being hit by pitchers is part of Baylor's game plan. He has the major-league record, and he can keep it.

One injury I'll never forget was one I was involved in. It's September 1986 and we're playing in Baltimore, moving up in the standings, but still a handful of games out of first place. I'm at bat, Willie Randolph is on first. I swing at a 3–1 pitch and miss as Randolph runs to second. Jumping into the batter's box to make the throw to second, Oriole catcher Johnny Stefero takes a terrific shot in the head with my backswing. Stefero's eyes roll back and he falls to the ground like deadweight. My God! I think, looking down at him, this is terrible. For a second I fear he may even be dead, but after a minute or so it seems he's okay, in pain, but still conscious. The umpire rules it unintentional and I'm still up, but Willie has to go back to first because I'd blocked the catcher's throw. Fine with me, just as long as Stefero is okay and they don't call me out.

As potentially dangerous as injuries during the course of play are the fights that stem from them. Over the years I've

seen and been involved in lots. I've seen the Pirates' big
Greg Luzinski grab Dave Roberts, our catcher on the
Padres, and drag him around the infield like a lawn mower;
or Padre catcher Derrell Thomas, who would start fights
right at home plate; or Randy Sweet, another Padre catcher,
who went at it with the Dodgers' Willie Crawford, not
exactly an even match. But Randy was a gamer, and came
out of it with only a black eye. "Gol dang it, Winnie," he
drawled to me afterward, "next time I'm just gonna keep my
mask on." Next day the papers showed Randy blocking
Willie's fist with his face.

Guys can get hurt and ruin their careers, but just about
every few days the benches will clear somewhere and all hell
will break lose. It's the tension of having to play 162 games,
it's the vendettas between players, between clubs—a shove,
a cleat, a manager's call for a brush-back pitch, an insult,
then next time you're playing, *bam!* Makes me wonder how
Ty Cobb—even if he was as tough and nasty as they say—
ever made it through his career, what with pitchers aiming
for his head, and half a dozen guys looking for him every
time the benches cleared.

KIDS

The summer of 1985 I met Bill Cosby in his dressing room
backstage at the studio in Brooklyn where his TV show is
taped. I'd come to ask him if he'd emcee a benefit concert
for the Foundation. A major talent and a big name like his
would draw top performers and a good audience. And a
successful public event would restore the Foundation's cred-

ibility after Steinbrenner's attacks in the papers and raise money for our programs. Cosby was wearing a pair of sweats and the instant we shook hands I felt at ease, which was Bill's doing—he was disarmingly straightforward.

"You've been doing stuff with kids for a long time," I said, "and we're trying to do the same. Also we want more people to know what we're doing."

"Yeah, I know what you've been up to," Cosby said. Thinking he might be referring to my publicized battles with Steinbrenner, I began to describe the Foundation's work, but he assured me he wasn't referring to any of the newspaper hullaballoo. "No, I know what your Foundation's been doing. I've been watching you for years, in San Diego and New York." And just like that one of the most sought-after guys in America signed on as our emcee. Soon after, George Benson came on board, then Chaka Khan, Nick Ashford and Valerie Simpson, Phoebe Snow, and Carl Anderson, with more to follow. Our corporate sponsors were first rate, too: *BusinessWeek*, CBS Records, Equitable Insurance, InnerCity Broadcasting, ProServe, Prudential-Bache, Schieffelin & Company, and Xerox.

On December 3, 1985, the benefit was held in front of a packed house at Manhattan Community College and netted a tidy sum for the Foundation. We were besieged by typical first-timer production problems—too many acts, some of which ran way too long, and occasional confusion with props and equipment between acts—but the spirit of the performers was wonderful and the Cos was better yet. Just by agreeing to participate he'd given the evening a special boost, and then he saved the evening by charming the audience through the delays and rough spots. I doff my cap to him.

The concert marked a turning point for the Foundation. Since opening our doors in the East in 1981 we'd kept busy taking disadvantaged kids to ball games and cultural events, funding scholarships, and organizing a community health program and a computer literacy program. By 1984, however, I sensed we were spreading ourselves too thin, and I began looking to concentrate our efforts in the solution of a single pressing problem. I found it in young people's problems with drugs.

It was a problem I knew we couldn't tackle single-handedly, so on Al Frohman's suggestion I looked for help, not locally, but in Washington, D.C. In 1985 the Foundation joined the National Partnership against Drug Abuse chaired by Nancy Reagan and funded by the federal government along with the private sector. Unfortunately, the Partnership had a hard time figuring out exactly what it wanted to do, and then a government cutback crippled the effort.

So in 1986 Al and I took another run around Washington, D.C., and met Frankie Coates, who would become like family, an intelligent, creative black woman who heads up the Drug Enforcement Administration's (DEA) Demand Reduction Section. The division's goal is to reduce the demand for drugs by educating the public, and especially young people, about the dangers of drug use. It seemed like a good fit for the Foundation, and Frankie Coates and I found out right away that we were on the same wavelength.

Not long after our visit Frankie invited me back to meet Jack Lawn, the DEA administrator. We had a nice talk, but nothing happened. I found out later that before anything could, standard procedure called for me to be checked out. They sifted through my life for days before they decided I was clean enough to take a weekend version of the DEA training program in Quantico, Virginia, complete with Uzi submachine gun practice on the firing range.

Of course, the DEA's plan wasn't to provide me with a license to kill. They wanted a spokesperson and chose me as international chairman of their Sports Drug Awareness Program. When several months later drug scandals filled the papers, a number of athletes tried to hop on the anti-drug bandwagon, but on their own terms. One pro basketball star wanted the DEA to provide a limousine and luxury hotel suite in return for his doing an anti-drug TV spot. They told him no thanks.

Still early in 1986, I collaborated with Frankie Coates and the DEA on a film that we could present to young people across the country. It was a long haul from concept to script to production, but in April we had an effective twenty-five-minute film, *Say No to Drugs—It's Your Decision*. We even did some filming at spring training and in Yankee Stadium. Assuming that Steinbrenner would frown on any of my extracurricular activities, we waited until he was out of town to do it. Don Mattingly and Roy White, then Yankee hitting coach, also appear in the film, and I'm grateful for their contribution.

During the filming some of the guys on the club were among those who had been busted for drugs a few years before. So they were pretty nervous about narcs invading the dugout. They calmed down when they realized the DEA was only going to shoot cameras, not guns, but they were still probably thinking, Winnie, this is going too far. My heart can't take it!

Also in early '86, we put together a Drug Awareness Program for the Foundation to take into schools. Since we kicked things off in New York in May of that year, we've done thirty-five Drug Awareness assemblies, and reached more than 25,000 students. I hosted several assemblies, but to keep them from turning into the "Dave Winfield Show," we recruited other athletes and entertainers including Willie Randolph, heavyweight champion Mike Tyson, Spencer Christian of "Good Morning, America," and jazz musician Chuck Mangione—successful individuals who had never had any drug problems. At each assembly the host showed the *Say No to Drugs* film, then talked to the students about achieving success and enjoying life without drugs. As I said before, I think it makes a lot more sense to put kids together with people who've never used drugs and never needed them, than with ex-users.

PEOPLE

Imagine Stevie Wonder in concert, a lone guy surrounded by electric organs, pianos, and harmonicas, playing, singing, a band in the background, filling a huge arena with sound. Suddenly he stops and every single musician stops with him, like somehow he's pulled the plug on everybody in the band. Then he starts up again and everyone plugs back in. It's awesome. And then his songs . . . right from the heart, yet deep and knowing, revealing a unique view of the world.

I meet Stevie right after one of his concerts to talk about doing some charitable work together. Not long after that we do; we work together with the jazz flutist Bobbi Humphrey on a song called "Give Me Your Love," where I do a little rap. While we're putting down the tracks I get to see Stevie in the studio where he splits his time as an improvisational genius—running off absolutely amazing riffs on his harmonica—and making calls on his portable phone. Every few minutes he puts the phone to his ear and I hear: "Yeah, I just talked to Dionne and I've got Lionel on the line." It's his lifeline to the world. Me, I could stay there forever, but the producer's impatient. "Come on, Stevie," he insists, "put your phone down and let's go."

When I first met Muhammed Ali in the late seventies he was already suffering from the early stages of Parkinson's. We were serving on the Peace Corps Advisory Board together and I'd see him nodding off in meetings and think, Damn, he's tired. Either that or he doesn't want to be here. But I'd been wrong about Ali before. Initially I thought he was just a talented loudmouth, flapping his lips in the air without thinking things out. But over the years it all started making more sense—his stand on the draft, his developing political conscience, the support he provided black causes. In retrospect, it was probably more *my* development than his that accounted for my change of feelings. By the time my tenure on the board was over we had become friendly acquaintances.

Being a high-profile athlete in New York and in the public eye because of my Foundation work, I make a lot of friendly acquaintances. Jesse Jackson has dropped by the stadium for a game a couple of times and afterward to talk in the clubhouse. Jane Fonda also came by once when her husband, California assemblyman Tom Hayden, was on the field realizing a childhood dream to suit up with the Yankees. But a presidential candidate and the world's best-known aerobicist were small potatoes as far as the batboys were concerned. What they really couldn't believe was that a nobody like Dave Winfield could know Magic Johnson, so they were speechless when Magic dropped by for a visit. They all got autographs, and I got some respect.

After the 1986 season I contracted for some TV work. I flew to California to tape a few segments of "Greatest Sports Legends," a syndicated TV sports show with a rotating-host format where I interviewed golfers Gary Player and Lee Trevino, promoter Don King, race car driver David Pearson, former Miami Dolphin Larry Csonka, former Pittsburgh Steeler Joe Greene, and others.

I was concerned what Player, a South African, and I would have to say to each other, but asked around and found that he was well respected among South African blacks, believing in the people of the country and not the system.

Player sponsors a tournament for black South African golfers so that they can win enough to get a chance to play outside South Africa. When I asked him about apartheid on the program, he was candid in his response, and after the taping gave me a "brother" handshake. We had an exceptional interview and a lot of fun as he stood on a box at the end, like Alan Ladd in the movies, to be on screen at my height.

Everyone knows Don King as the "tremendous, stupendous, self-annointed, self-elected king" of sports promoters, and as the ex-con with the outrageous "crown," his hair. Nothing in my interview with him contradicted that. He came off like he always does, the street-smart, wily guy who's made himself and others millions. One thing I didn't know was that King was a super-patriot. "Only in America," King said with a Cheshire cat smile and a deep bold laugh. "I love this country . . . I love capitalism."

The highlight of David Pearson's interview was a story he told about how race drivers talk about their shoes flying off in their final accident, the one that takes them off the oval and into the ozone. Once, Pearson said, he lost control of his car on a dirt track in Tennessee and smashed into a wall head-on, *wham!* Then everything was quiet, he couldn't hear a thing. So he looked down at his feet. His shoes were gone! They'd bounced off, landed right beside his feet. No question, he was dead. But just then he heard, "Dave? Dave? Are you all right?" They were the sweetest sounds he'd ever heard.

Larry Csonka is a big, friendly farmboy who talked mostly about what it was like to play with the Dolphins, "kinda rammin' into people and plowin' along." Joe Greene told me just how mean he used to be, then talked soberly about knowing his career as a pro was over when during a scrimmage a rookie offensive lineman held him back with one hand.

A little later in the off-season I was invited to attend a White House dinner honoring Helmut Kohl, the chancellor of West Germany. I asked Ma to be my date for the evening. A woman of many opinions, I requested that she please curb them for the dinner, to avoid any hot political issues, and by no means to mention that we both voted for the man Ronald Reagan trounced in 1984. She assured me she wouldn't. When we got there we were ushered to separate tables. There were only two other blacks among the 100 or so attendees, Melba Moore and Tony Brown. All the others were bussing tables or cooking. My mother was seated with Donald Regan and Mrs. Meese among others, and I was seated with Mrs. George Bush, who as an active supporter of Morehouse School of Medicine in Atlanta spent some time over dinner convincing me to become a member of its board of trustees, an honor I've added to serving on the boards of Hackensack Medical Center and the Black Tennis and Sports Foundation Arthur Ashe runs. As far as I know Ma didn't get either of us into any trouble.

After dinner, we were entertained by Joel Grey and I spent some time talking to Jerry Lewis about a breakthrough in muscular dystrophy research. But the high point of my evening was talking to President and Mrs. Reagan. The President remembered giving me a Youth Employment award in the Rose Garden. Mrs. Reagan seemed nice, sincere, bright, strong willed. We talked for a few minutes about the drug problem. Later, I said to the president that I didn't envy his responsibility as chief executive. "I know it's a tough job and you've got some tough decisions to make, and I sure wouldn't want to be the one to have to make them."

Reagan listened, then told me that his situation was like that of Grover Cleveland Alexander, the Hall of Fame pitcher he once portrayed in a movie who pitched his team out of a terrible jam. "You've simply just got to want it bad enough. You've got to go after what you believe in."

I suppose you could criticize the president of the United States for comparing his job to a character he played in a movie, but the man speaks to thousands of people a year, and I felt that his analogy was a very human attempt to respond to me in a language I was sure to understand.

THE ROAD

A lot of ballplayers spend so much time on the road during the season that they stick close to home the rest of the year. Not me. I love to travel, to see and learn what's happening elsewhere in the world. Usually my trips take me off the beaten path, to places where there aren't a lot of American tourists, much less black American tourists. Often when I'm abroad foreign tourists or locals will ask me if I'm a boxer, because everyone knows that boxers can be big and black and travel everywhere. Sometimes I tell them, "Yes, I'm a boxer," so that if it ever comes to anything, they'll be afraid I'll box their ears.

American tourists abroad are another story. As a member of the Yankees I find I'm recognized by Americans world-wide; as a Padre I was only recognized in San Diego. Part of it, of course, is the reach of the New York media, but also because so many of the people I run into in my travels are from New York. It seems like half of all American tourists are New Yorkers, with the rest of the country providing the other half.

The best trip I ever took I went with a woman friend to Africa. We start out in Kenya, where we go on a safari, not to hunt, but to see the sights, meet the people, and photo-

graph the animals. A small plane ferries us to a game pre-
serve, then we go by jeep to a camp area consisting of thirty
or so tents on concrete slabs, each with its own little bathroom. Pretty civilized for tent life. A giraffe checks us out
at breakfast the next morning. A family of baboons runs
shrieking through the campsite. Behind us on the banks of
the Masai Mora River hippos and crocodiles are catching
some early rays, mouths wide open. The only thing, it
seems, keeping them from rampaging through the camp is
lack of interest.

The camp is guarded by a half-dozen Masai warriors
armed not with .45s or rifles but with shields and spears.
Every now and again I try to engage one of these guys in
conversation, figuring he'd be happy to see a black face.
"Hey, how you doin'?" I say, or just, "Good morning," and
a look back says loud and clear, What are you talking about?

After breakfast that first morning we're being escorted
back to our tents when we hear a ruckus. No more than 100
yards away two lions have taken down a water buffalo and
are tearing away at his carcass. A handful of us jump into
a jeep and the driver pulls within twenty yards of the feeding lions. I note the lions eyeballing us, blood all over their
faces, interrupted while tearing their prey limb from limb.
I ask the driver if he thinks maybe we're a bit too close. He
laughs till he's red in the face.

Another time it's raining and muddy and we're in a van
when we get a flat tire. We hobble along for a bit to find an
open space to change the tire, when five elephants mosey
out of the bush and into the road, not fifty feet in front of
us. I'm already nervous when the biggest one turns in our
direction, flares his ears, raises his trunk, and trumpets. I
figure it's all over. Do you get in the van? Do you run? Here
we are on three tires and a wobbly rim in the rain and the
mud, and this bull elephant is about to ram our van, lay a
big foot down on each one of us, and rejoin his pals. Instead

of shoving the van into reverse and trying for a pathetic getaway, the driver answers the elephant's call to battle by gunning the engine in neutral, like, Okay, back at you! The elephant gives us a good, hard look, considers his options, and lumbers off after the others, already across the road and in the bush.

Later, after it's dark, one of the Masai escorts us back to our tent. Along with his shield and spear he carries a lantern. I hear a noise in the brush, see a half-dozen green eyes, some low, some high. He points the lantern to reveal three water buffalo—wild, big, heavy, stinking, snot-nosed water buffalo—not ten yards away, just getting a good fix on us as we walk by. We get into our tent, but I don't need a tent, I need a fortress. Talk about not sleeping. All night I lie in my hammock looking at the walls of the flimsy tent around us, wondering what's going to stop something from putting its horns through the canvas, bundling us up, and carrying us down to the river for its midnight snack. If I live through this, I think, I'm definitely going to have to talk about it. It's scary, but it's great.

After Kenya we fly west to the Gambia and Senegal, where my ancestors had come from. In the Gambia we decide we'll visit the village where Alex Haley found his roots. We take a small boat up the river to a town called Juferai. Except for the crew, everyone on the boat is white; we're the only non-working black faces. When we dock, a young boy picks us out of the group and asks us to follow him. Turns out he's one of Alex Haley's distant relatives. Haley had, in fact, taken the boy to America with him so he speaks a little English. He takes us on a tour of the town and finally to the hut where Haley found his kin. Haley's faded little picture is on the wall. The entire experience is wonderful and moving.

On the trip to Senegal we have another black tour guide, a guy who makes his living at it. Again, there are no other black faces among the tourists, so I ask him, "How do you feel about white tourists coming over to see where and how their forefathers enslaved your people?" He says, "This is my livelihood. Besides, it's important that people should know what went on."

Later on, after the tour is over, he shows me something not on the itinerary. He leaves me alone at a little doorway leading out of a fortress built right on the shore. There's no longer a door and all I can see through the opening is a narrow strip of shoreline where I imagine the slave ships once docked. I'm standing, I realize, on the last piece of land that hundreds of thousands of blacks stood on before they were loaded on the ships and sent west to the Americas and north to Europe, never to see their country again, never, in many cases, to be seen by their families or anybody they knew again. I look out that door for a long, long time.

Recently I traveled to Costa Rica where I went to rest, fish, do some white-water rafting. I fly to the coast from San José, the capital city, in an old DC-3, like in *Romancing the Stone*. Looking out the window I saw the rivets vibrate, the wings flap. A few days later I ran into a dozen Georgia peanut farmers in some backroads restaurant. A couple of the guys knew who I was and asked me if I wanted to go out hunting for white-winged doves with them the next day—there was an overabundance of the birds and the local farmers were encouraging hunters to trespass on their land and kill them off. I thought about it—me going out into the boonies with a bunch of certified good ol' boys who looked like your worst nightmare from *Deliverance*—but figured, what the heck. Next morning, 5:15, we were out in a decrepit, dirty school bus making our way up-country. The guys were passing out tobacco, swapping stories. I jawed some about the ol' boys I knew, Catfish and Gaylord and Mike Ivie. Finally, thirty or forty miles from nowhere, we arrived at a farm, and piled out of the bus. I bagged a handful of doves. Everybody else got about fifty. Nobody got me.

One night on that same trip I went with a group of naturalists who'd never even heard of the New York Yankees, much less Dave Winfield, to see giant, prehistoric-looking, leatherback turtles lay eggs along the beach. Twenty turtles paddled up onto the sand with their heavy fins, used their back legs to shovel out a hole for the eggs, then dropped them—90 to 100 of them, each the size of a cue ball. Out there, listening to the sounds of the huge turtles scraping away at the sand in the moonlight, gazing at the rapt expressions on the faces of the naturalists, I suddenly felt part of an enormous world I barely knew, yet I didn't feel alone. I'm not exactly sure why, but it was very reassuring. Jacques Cousteau had nothing on me.

It was this same desire to explore the unknown and the exotic that took me to Katmandu, Nepal, the farthest from home I ever traveled, exactly the other side of the world. I was tired for the moment of being Dave Winfield, the celebrity, wanted a little adventure, a little anonymity, and I figured what better place than the Himalayas. The day I arrived turned out to be a Nepalese holiday. Crowds were lining either side of the wide main boulevard three or four deep as a grand procession made its way from the Imperial Palace past where I was standing. I could see the king in his regalia in an old open Mercedes, surrounded by men on horseback, the royal guard. They were all decked out in colorful costumes, carrying lances, their horses prancing alongside the car. Except for the Mercedes, it could have been a scene from a thousand years ago. Great, I thought as I focused my camera, I'm back in time and at the far end of the earth, when suddenly, with the king and his guard almost abreast of me, from the throng surrounding me I heard, "Holy shit! It's Dave Winfield!"

SEASONS: 1987

Mikwaukee tears off an incredible string of victories to start the 1987 season, 13 in a row. The reporters keep asking, "Can you catch them, can anyone catch them?" I know we can. Turns out, the Brewers shoot their whole wad right there, and we take over where they leave off. We go into June with our best early-season record in more than a decade and we aren't even playing with a full deck. Rickey Henderson straddles the training table and rides the bench for long periods with a sore hamstring. Don Mattingly goes out for three weeks with a spinal disk injury. With these guys out I know there's a lot of slack to take up and I do my best ball of the year at the right time, error-free in the outfield, driving in runs, hitting over .300 with the big blast a grand slam to overtake Toronto in their park 15–14. Even Steinbrenner has a few nice words for me in the press. The rest of the team is also pulling its weight, and we get some good outings from our starters, from Rick Rhoden, Charles Hudson, Ron Guidry, and Tommy John. Come the All-Star break, we're in first place.

But there's trouble in paradise. A few weeks into June Willie Randolph, hitting up a storm and leading the team in runs scored and on-base percentage, and knocking in key runs, injures his knee. He's hurting. But he's so low-key, he doesn't even let on to his teammates at first. Because we're in a tough division race they play him constantly, including a fifteen-inning game with no rest the next day. Elected to the All-Star team for the fifth time in his twelve years as a pro, the Yankees insist that Willie not go. Instead, he should play right up to the All-Star Game and have the knee surgery he needs over the three-day break. Deciding to play

anyway, Willie and his family make the trip to Oakland for
the game only to find that George Steinbrenner has called
the president of the American League, Bobby Brown, to
request that Willie be taken out of the lineup. Getting no
satisfaction from Brown, the day before the game he calls
John McNamara, the American League manager, on the
practice field. Willie asks me what he should do. I tell him,
"Don't ask me. You know the answer. Play the All-Star
Game, you deserve it. Then go for the surgery. We'll hold
it together until you get back, then we'll win the division."
Willie is introduced to the nation as part of the starting
lineup, plays a few innings, then flys back to New York for
the operation. As for winning the division, well, that's another story.

The All-Star Game goes thirteen innings, ending at twi-
light, and I'm the only man who plays them all. In the
bottom of the ninth, the game still scoreless, I have a sliver
of a chance to win it. I'm on second and there's a man on
first when the Mariners' Harold Reynolds hits the ball up
the middle. I make for third, Hubie Brooks has the runner
out at second, but his throw to first sails left into the dirt.
Steve Bedrosian, the Phillies' relief pitcher, is late backing
up the first baseman and has to dive to the outfield side of
the bay for the ball. Seeing a chance to score, I barrel for
home, but Bedrosian makes a great catch, as Reynolds leaps
over him to avoid a collision, jumps up, and fires the ball
home to Ozzie Virgil of Atlanta. Ozzie's got it in his glove
in time to set himself and though I really smash into him,
he holds on to the ball. Too bad it wasn't a bang-bang play,
so they could retire the footage of Pete Rose taking out
Oakland catcher Ray Fosse a few years back. The Nationals
finally win it 2–0.

The game is the second longest in All-Star history. Later
in the season, a lot of talk spills out from the New York press
about my being the only man to play every inning, the

implication being that the game affected my second half. Heck, I love playing in exciting games and we were short of outfielders. I could have gone thirteen innings more. Still, when the Yankees travel to Boston in September, John McNamara actually apologizes for playing me the whole game. "Hey, John," I say, "I'm only sorry we lost."

Thirteen All-Star innings don't have anything to do with what happens to me or the Yankees after mid-season. We come off the break battling, but we can't seem to win. Immediately you can sense the organizational jitters. Hot on our heels, too, is the local press; the papers start yapping away about the fate of past teams in first place at the All-Star break. So we decide to relax a little, ease up on the pace, play loose, and hope for a better result. That doesn't work either.

The second series after the break turns out to be a crucial one, psychologically. We lose two of three hard-fought games to the Twins in Minnesota. Bert Blyleven's curves tear through the strike zone into the dirt, and his high fastballs send our hitters down into the dirt after them (Blyleven, incidentally, is the only pitcher in the league who still throws at me regularly). And when we do make contact, the rest of their defense throws us out on the base paths, and leaps against the Plexiglas and over the rubber band in center field to rob us. The Twins, in the meantime, get their hits and score. It's terrible!

Traveling with the team is George Steinbrenner, who shares a general belief around the league (till 1987) that the Twins are patsies, should be beatable without too much effort. After our second loss he comes down to the locker room as we eat our postgame meal. The entire time he's there he doesn't say anything, just stands at one end of the room, his arms folded across his chest, glowering, looking at us with disgust and disdain. The young guys have their faces in their plates like penitents. Later they talk about it: "Wasn't that something? Treating us like dogs, like dirt."

Occasionally someone will say to me, "The team should be used to George Steinbrenner by now. Don't you guys just use him as an excuse if you're not winning? Why can't you just ignore him?" The truth is you can't ignore George for long; his intensity goes beyond what most people can endure. You always need bigger blinders, thicker skin. Most of the veterans have learned to deal with it to survive, but some of the new guys can't even handle it for a season. Among the casualties of recent years are Ed Whitson and Steve Trout. Anyway, after Steinbrenner leaves the locker room Mark Salas, our new catcher, says, "Now I've seen it all." I tell him, "You haven't seen it all until you've seen Columbus." Two weeks later Salas boards the shuttle to Columbus.

One of the hallmarks of Steinbrenner's Yankees is impatience, and it's impatience, to a large degree, that speeds our downward spiral. If a guy doesn't produce immediately, consistently, or when he's called on, he's gone. Charles Hudson pitches to 6–2, the best record of any hurler on the team, he runs into a little trouble, and bingo, he's off to Columbus. Yankee management will pull a player, make a move, faster than any team in baseball. The reason is that George Steinbrenner reacts so quickly to losses, and because the press reacts so quickly to George Steinbrenner. It's like there are only two kinds of moves on the Yankees: the ones made because George is displeased, and the ones made because he soon will be.

Sensing this, the players begin to doubt their manager. They can't believe, any more than the press or the fans can, that any manager's moves are his own. As a Yankee manager's confidence wavers, his temper frays, and the feeling spreads down through the coaches to the team. And if a manager goes public and stops pretending that he agrees with all the strange decisions made by the "Yankees," he's

290 · ─────── WINFIELD: A PLAYER'S LIFE

gone and Billy Martin, who's been close by announcing or
scouting, is back.

The shuttle service to Columbus is even more frequent
this year than last. By August, ten of the twenty-four players
starting the season have made the flight. I hope Henry Cotto
in particular had a frequent-flyer card. You look around the
locker room and you see a shell of the team you played with
in April. Like Wayne Tolleson, who was demonstrating his
ability to be a starting shortshop and shedding the tag of
utility player, hurts his right shoulder and is unable to swing
the bat properly. His average plummets before he has to
hang 'em up for the year. Because the lineup never stabilizes,
the defense and offense suffer. You don't know that you can
depend on your teammates because you've hardly ever taken
the field with them in critical situations. You see people's
confidence slipping, and it's well-nigh impossible to recover.
One player who does benefit from the roster changes is
Bobby Meacham, with Tolleson out and Zuvella and
Velardi unable to hold the open spot. I remember his first
spring training with us, when he came over from the Cardinals in 1985. He was at short, fielded a tough grounder,
tagged the man on the way to third, then forced the runner
at second; it was aggressive, heads-up baseball. Meacham is
a smart guy with a lot of ability, but his first two seasons
with the Yankees he looks like the dumbest kid in class.
They get on him for every error, and the more they do, the
more errors he makes. By mid-1986 he's back in the minors,
where they almost break him down by playing him part
time at a new position, second base. They finally bring him
back up in '87 because they've tried everyone else in the
system. They have to put him in and stay with him, good
or bad. Just knowing he'll be in there day to day stabilizes
his performance. I can see his confidence growing. At first,
he still makes a few critical errors, but once he settles into
the lineup he plays excellent defense. And hitting only

right-handed instead of switch-hitting, he has a lot more success at the plate, hitting the ball with consistency and some pop, winding up at .270.

The pressure from the top, heavier this year than last, really takes its toll on Lou Piniella. After two years of managing he looks about as bad as Jimmy Carter did after four years as president. To his credit, for the most part Lou doesn't take his frustrations out on the team. One time in July he really rails on us in a team meeting, a sixty-two-count motherf____. But we deserve it; we're running in low gear, playing like we don't care.

Come early August, Yankee impatience extends beyond the healthy players to the lame and infirm. There's a lot of talk now about Rickey's injury, which has kept him out of the lineup for much of the season, and rumors about Lou saying that Rickey is jaking it. Around this time Mike Lupica of the *Daily News* writes a story about ownership meddling called "Butt Out." That afternoon copies of the column were plastered all over the clubhouse. Everyone wanted to know, who did it? All I can say is I didn't do it, I don't start fights. Clubhouse man Nick Priori was grilled mercilessly, since the "authorities" figured he had to know who it was.

Finally, Lou is quoted questioning the extent of Rickey's hurt. The feathers really begin to fly right after that, when Lou purportedly misses a scheduled phone call from Steinbrenner while we're in Cleveland. By the time we get to Detroit a few days later George has released a statement saying that Lou is at odds with the team, wants to trade Rickey, and so on and so forth for a page and a half. We get a copy Sunday afternoon in Tiger Stadium. When it's read aloud in the cramped clubhouse, guys shout "Burn it! Burn it!" A match is put to it while "My Way" plays on the cassette deck.

Whatever Lou and George think, those close to Rickey

know that he isn't jaking it. We see Rickey coming in every day to work out, trying to get himself ready to play. The new guys, though, don't know what to think. They don't know Rickey or Lou or George. Rickey's inability to come back during critical weeks except as an occasional DH, coupled with all the talk about it, spawns an ugly mood. The new guys wonder if Rickey really does want to play and how much he hustles when he does. And maybe they wonder how hard they should play if one of baseball's biggest names is just taking it easy.

One day we're in the training room being worked on and there's a phone call in trainer Gene Monahan's office. Gene says quietly, head down, "It's for you, Rickey. It's George." Rickey gets off the training table, goes into the back room, shuts the door behind him and gets on the horn. After a short while he emerges, totally bewildered. "He's crazy. He doesn't believe I'm hurt. He's saying he's going to dock my pay if I don't play. What's going on here?"

Impatience. The truth of it is that Rickey is hurting, tries to come back as fast as he can. And even then they have to take him out of the lineup a number of times, still hurting or reinjured. It's his first extended injury, and he doesn't know how to react.

With all the talk about Rickey, Willie foolishly comes back from his surgery and plays all-out too soon. Willie has never received his due as the glue that holds a young infield together and as the man whose consistent on-base ability always makes us a run-scoring threat. Where before he was taken for granted, now it's obvious the team misses him. Soon his knee is all right on the stationary bicycle, but not for the cuts he has to make on the field. It's downright painful just watching him run the base paths or twisting for a catch, and I grimace for him as I look on from right field. In '87 he's another case of play a few games, go back on the bench, get healed up, then get out there and play some more.

Of all the injured players, only Don Mattingly seems to take enough recovery time. Out for nearly a month, Donnie comes back to have a remarkable year, not only tying the eight-game consecutive-home-run mark, but breaking the season record for grand slams with six. He'd stopped at the break with homers four games in a row, which is good in itself. When he hit a home run in that eighth game, it was great for him and the team. The only one unhappy about the boost and RBIs Donnie gave us was George Steinbrenner. He was upset because Donnie strained some ligaments going for the streak.

Second half of August we go on a long road trip to Seattle, Oakland, and Anaheim. We know we have to regroup. We drop seven out of ten. We're trying, but by the time we hit Oakland it's individuals trying, not a synchronized team. The pitching is collapsing, people aren't getting on base, there are fewer opportunities to drive in runs. We've slipped from first to second to third place. A fourth-place finish is not out of the question. In the first half of the season I was content to take a walk, let the man behind me drive in the run if I couldn't get a good pitch to hit. But now the player behind me is always changing. A guy bats behind me for a game, two games, a week, then he's gone. Plus, they move me around in the lineup constantly, which is very disruptive for me. There's a world of difference between hitting cleanup and batting third or fifth or sixth or seventh, all of which I'm called on to do.

Trying to assume too much responsibility for our part-replacement, part-injured team, I start pressing. It's taboo, you know it, but what can you do? I swing at bad pitches. I'm frustrated and mad. I catch my own case of Yankee impatience, and a twinge from the ulcer I had in '84 flares up again and I have to go on some moderate medication to control it.

The last two weeks of the season, even with the team eliminated from contention and me 10 short of 100 RBIs, they "rest" me for two games. Then they give me back my cleanup spot, and even shift me into the RBI slot of third on the last day like they want to help me. I eke out 7 more RBIs, but still wind up 3 short. My 100+ consecutive RBI string ends at five. The 1987 season is over.

There's one small additional note. In the middle of the World Series, George Steinbrenner grabs some headlines in the face of Peter Ueberroth's request that he wait until the Series is over. Lou Piniella is "elevated" to general manager, the position responsible for personnel and trades, though George once said that Lou had the worst eye for talent on the Yankees. Our manager for 1988: Billy Martin.

COLOR

The biggest story in baseball in 1987—outside of the 150:1 Minnesota Twins—took place off the field. On opening day of the season dedicated to his memory by the commissioner, Ted Koppel devoted his "Nightline" show on ABC television to Jackie Robinson. It was the fortieth anniversary of Robinson's breaking the major leagues' color barrier with the Dodgers. One of Koppel's guests was Al Campanis of the Dodgers' front office. When Koppel asked why there were no black managers or general managers in the major leagues, Campanis said that "blacks may not have the necessities" for these jobs. Pressed further, Campanis revealed even more of his thinking: The reason black people aren't good swimmers is that they aren't buoyant.

By next morning there was a tremendous uproar across the country about Campanis's remarks, and when it didn't die down after a few days the Dodgers had no choice but to let him go after forty-odd years of service. A lot of people in baseball, black and white, were sorry to see it happen, claiming that Campanis was a good man and would never knowingly say or do anything racist. The irony of it is that in voicing the old myths about black people, Campanis may have done as much for minorities in baseball as anyone since Jackie Robinson. In just a few minutes on TV he set a public debate in motion that has already served the sport well.

One of the first to speak up was Reggie Jackson. He wrote a cover story for *Sports Illustrated* that spoke for a lot of black and Hispanic players. Reggie touched on all the white perceptions of the black athlete. He talked about how if a black isn't smiling, he's perceived as a militant; how a black player on drugs tarnishes all blacks in a way that a white player's drug problem doesn't affect other whites; how the black player is stereotyped as a natural athlete; and how a black player who is hurt is often accused of malingering.

In his article, Reggie also offered suggestions for getting minorities involved in managing and in the front office. And he named some players and ex-players he considered good candidates for these jobs, me among them—particularly flattering when you consider what a great general manager Reggie would make. He also suggested in an article in *USA Today* that he thought I should take the lead in getting active players involved in major-league minority hiring practices. Without naming anyone specifically, Claire Smith of the *Hartford Courant* wrote a column along similar lines pointing out that the Campanis controversy gave the players, minority players in particular, the opportunity for a voice in who'd be the next generation of managers and front office personnel. I thought it over and discussed it with Don Baylor, the league rep for the Players Association. With thirty years in both leagues between us, we're both men other players come to for information and advice, and to share opinions. We began to canvass players informally about their views.

Right about that time the NAACP and Jesse Jackson got involved, along with a group of black community leaders, suggesting a boycott of baseball by black players. But a boycott seemed ill advised. First of all, only 25 percent of the players in the major leagues are black, and a boycott therefore would probably not have been very effective. Second, baseball's restricted hiring practices, entrenched for decades, affect all players, not only blacks. As Sparky Anderson put it, there's no path to a non-playing job in the sport except cronyism for anyone, black or white. So the real issue was to open up the hiring process for everybody. Jesse Jackson saw our reasoning and agreed with it.

In mid-June, Peter Ueberroth hired Dr. Harry Edwards, a sociologist at the University of California at Berkeley, to work with him on minority hiring. You couldn't find two guys with more different public images: Ueberroth the white Republican who'd brought the 1984 Olympics in under budget and without controversy, and Edwards the black radical who'd been involved in the protests by black athletes at the 1968 Games in Mexico City and who'd recently called for a boycott of the NCAA over recruiting and academic violations. Their images notwithstanding, the two men are savvy pragmatists. Edwards brought things full circle when he hired Al Campanis as part of the commissioner's team.

Ueberroth also signed up Clifford Alexander, an ex-member of the Johnson and Carter administrations and now a Washington consultant, to advise baseball on hiring and government regulations on a club-by-club, state-by-state basis.

Things were moving. By late June, Ueberroth had consulted with every interest group except the active players, and we asked for a meeting to let him know that the players wanted to be involved in whatever happened, and we also wanted to find out what was really being done so that we could report back to the other men in baseball. And like everybody else, we had a few names to throw into the ring: Al Bumbry, Dave Nelson, Cito Gaston, Bobby Tolan, to begin with. The commissioner's response was encouraging. The hiring practices of all major-league teams were being investigated, and there would be discussions throughout the year to consider ways of bringing job candidates to the teams' attention.

On July 9, the commissioner invited Don Baylor and me to attend a meeting with Edwards and a number of former players in Oakland the day before the All-Star Game. Four days earlier Steinbrenner threw himself in hot water when he referred to the Yankees' chief accountant, a thirty-year-old black man, as a "young black boy" on national television. I felt bad for George. I'm sure it wasn't meant as a slur, but was merely his way of expressing himself as the father of the Yankee "family"; still, it showed what a difficult father he can be.

The meeting with Ueberroth and Edwards was an eye-opener. There were two generations of players on hand. There was Curt Flood, whose courage in calling the reserve clause the equivalent of slavery and fighting it in court ended his career but made free agency possible for those who came later. There was Larry Doby, baseball's second black manager. And there were great stars and great baseball minds like Bob Gibson, Billy Williams, Lou Brock, Joe Morgan, Tony Oliva, Bill Robinson, Manny Sanguillen, Dusty Baker, Dwight Evans, and Bill North. A similar meeting, this time players only, took place in Dallas in November, with men like Frank Robinson, Willie Stargell, and Ray Burris. Although the actual hiring by baseball teams in

1987 doesn't show it, what I saw at both meetings makes me believe the face of baseball will be changing.

One hurdle that has to be overcome is what you might call the Jackie Robinson syndrome, the notion that baseball's first enduring black manager or general manager must do no wrong, must be impeccable. We've already had strong, intelligent, successful black men in the field manager's spot in Larry Doby and Frank Robinson, and both men deserve another chance. But instead of placing so much emphasis on the one perfect individual to carry the banner for us all, we should work on putting qualified minorities into coaching and administration at all levels—and, by the way, into the Players Association office, which is now all white.

BUSINESS

The profit opportunity open to an athlete is to trade his success on the field for a voice in the business community. Often this takes the form of product endorsements, speaking engagements, becoming a corporate spokesperson or broadcaster. I've done and will continue to do all four, but I've always wanted to do more.

Back in San Diego when I was still on good terms with Ray Kroc, I asked him if he could help me obtain a McDonald's franchise. "Can't do it, can't do it," he said. I asked, "Hey, Mr. Kroc, if *you* can't, who can?"

Almost a decade later I met Gil Bland, a loan officer at Independence Bank in Chicago, through a mutual friend. We hit it off. Like a lot of folks in America, we found we were both closet restauranteurs. We both were interested in the fast-food franchise business. So we pooled our talents, combined our middle names, Tyrone and Mark, to form Tymark Enterprises, and applied for two Burger Kings in Virginia. We were awarded the franchises in 1985, and Gil moved to Virginia with his family to run them.

Franchise or not, we wanted our Burger Kings to be special. They're fresh, classy, upgraded models, and I make a number of appearances there a year to make fans and friends by giving away Yankee hats, stickers, and tote bags and by giving motivational talks to local business and civic groups. We also sponsor events for the local kids in the community. As part of that community, Gil and I want to see every kid and every business in the area do well. With the success of our first two franchises, we decided to add more, and we now own seven Burger Kings.

I've never been much of an artist, but I've always liked going to museums and galleries to see other peoples' history, culture, and art. I was interested in how they saw the world, and felt that by experiencing someone else's vision, I could broaden my own. Also, much of what I saw touched me, made me feel good. So in 1982 I decided to take part in the art world myself by representing a few artists, obtaining shows for them in galleries, hotels, and exhibition halls in the cities where the Yankees played so that I could fit the work in without its becoming a distraction. In time this evolved into opening a gallery of my own in St. Paul in partnership with one of the artists I represented, a school-mate who was a graphic artist by trade but who'd always wanted to be a fine artist. The concept behind the gallery was to sell decorative art up through expensive fine art. We also served as a channel between black artists and black consumers. We did reasonably well at it. I enjoyed taking an active role in the business, particularly going to art fairs and expos and traveling to France, Morocco, Nepal, and Egypt to buy art for the gallery. But after about two years it became clear I didn't have the time it would take to make the gallery a real success. As for my partner, he was an artist, not a businessman, and I didn't have time to be a day-to-day manager. We closed our doors at the end of 1986. Now I'm involved in art strictly as a personal collector. The works I've acquired give me a lot of pleasure. They put something into my life that it's hard to quantify.

Four winters ago in Minnesota my brother, Steve, introduced me to Steve Sagedahl, an assistant baseball coach at the university. We were in the bowels of Memorial Stadium where Sagedahl was overseeing the strangest form of batting practice I'd ever seen. Instead of free swinging at baseballs, the "hitter" was swinging a bat attached by a leather strap and a straight metal bar to a Cybex machine, which I recognized from undergoing rehabilitation for a twisted knee. There wasn't a baseball in sight. The Cybex machine is actually a flywheel with a small electric motor to provide accommodating resistance at any speed, from zero to 600 degrees per second, as preset by an operator.

I watched as the hitter took as many as forty cuts in a minute, then asked Sagedahl if I could give it a try. After all, I was a professional athlete and prided myself on the shape I was in. I couldn't believe what I experienced next. I was on the device for maybe two or three minutes and I was totally exhausted. Not just my arms, but I felt fatigue in my entire body. Clearly, I wasn't in the shape I thought I was, although it was the off-season. What was more significant was that I'd exhausted myself in performing a precise hitting motion.

Sagedahl explained that the object of the equipment was to train athletes by having them perform specific sports movements at high speed, with resistance. I thought the device—used, Sagedahl told me, primarily by hospitals as a physical rehabilitation tool—had enormous potential. Refined, I could see its appeal to athletes at all levels in every sport. Tennis players and golfers could use it to work on their stroke, pitchers to work on their motion, runners to work on their stride. All it would take would be the correct modifications and anyone, even those looking for a general body workout, could benefit from its use. I thought it could be the most significant innovation in the fitness world since Nautilus.

Sagedahl was part of a team that was developing the product. I decided to join them and provide the seed money, while Sagedahl would ride herd on the development of the equipment and attachments, now known as SST, or Specific Sports Training, system. The market is definitely there. Individuals are looking for effective conditioning. Teams from high school to professional want an edge in preparing athletes for competition. Professional and world-class athletes want to maximize their ability and increase their longevity. Regular workouts on the SST system can provide them precisely what they're looking for.

As for my own future in business, I intend to stay in New York, though California and the Midwest are possibilities. I've been asked to run for public office—most often in Minnesota—but would rather remain behind the scenes, conferring with those in power, perhaps, rather than being a candidate. I've considered representing a few athletes, friends I'd like to see do well. I've considered acting, though I definitely don't see myself as one of those jocks turned full-time actor. Whichever direction I turn, I'd like to remain active, not just sit around and watch my money earn money. That may result in my sticking with SST. Whatever I do, I've always loved to compete, and when baseball no longer provides me with that arena, business will.

KIDS

The Foundation's Drug Awareness assemblies in schools and in towns like Bridgeport, Connecticut, and Wilkes-Barre, Pennsylvania, were a big success. I could tell from people's reactions that we were really reaching them with our message. But I began to wonder if by themselves they weren't just half a measure. It felt like spitting in the wind. Sure, we could convince individual kids to say no to drugs, but for how long? When we moved on we left the kids on their own to fight the appeal that drugs have in our society and the peer pressure to use them. I felt it was important to do something that would provide continuing support to those who said no and a continuing message to those who were still on the fence or still using drugs.

That realization set me thinking about ways to mobilize a school, a neighborhood, a whole community or town to fight drugs together. Reducing drug abuse would alleviate problems throughout the community, and help achieve what should be the main goal, improving the entire community's quality of life.

I decided it should be an effort centering on young people, but enlisting parents, teachers, business people, clergy, local government, and the media in a partnership against drugs. My own family—Ma, Steve, and the Allisons—had shown me how a group of people can affect everybody in it for the good. The folks in my neighborhood also played a part; they had gathered together when I was a kid to transform a vacant lot into a baseball diamond, and then into a real community center complete with playgrounds and ballfields and activities every day. Without those resources to turn to, Steve and I might have fallen into serious trouble even back in the safe fifties, and raising us would sure have been a lot tougher on Ma.

My thought then for the Foundation was to bring the same community partnership strategy into today's communities around the country, with a focus on drug abuse. To make it happen, we saw we would need to tie together education, law enforcement, and rehabilitation. And it would take the following elements: a task force of community representatives committed to helping young people stay off or quit drugs, and improving the quality of life in the community; effective tactics for reaching students; a calendar of activities throughout the year that would highlight the drug problem and reward young people who say no to drugs and help others to do the same; and an organization to act as a catalyst and consultant by offering the community a plan and expertise. The Foundation, I decided, would be that catalyst and consultant, and would in the months and years to come focus most of its energies and monies to that end.

By late 1986, we had refined these ideas and developed a program for the Foundation's future, but not a name to go with it. Then it occurred to me: The number of users is rising, we should turn it around; schools are declining, we should turn it around; communities are crumbling, we should turn it around. In college sports when a new coach comes in to take over a losing team he promises to turn the team around. That's the situation the entire country is confronting with drugs today. We've got to turn a losing situation into a winning one. So I dubbed the program "Turn It Around! There's No Room Here for Drugs."

Now that we had a concept the next step was a pilot campaign. After talking to community leaders around the country, we decided on Norfolk, Virginia. Norfolk made particular sense to me as a starter site because that's where Gil Bland and I bought our first Burger Kings. We had profited from that community, and it was time to reinvest something in it. More important, Norfolk was aware of its drug problem, committed to change, small enough to work together, and not afraid to be the first Turn It Around Community Partnership. On February 25, 1987, "Turn It Around! There's No Room Here for Drugs" started for real in Norfolk.

That spring I put the ideas behind the program into a paperback book, *Turn It Around! There's No Room Here for Drugs*. The book was written with Eric Swenson, and it was aimed at schoolchildren and teachers as well as the general public. I took the book with me and as I traveled around the country with the Yankees that summer, I talked about it and the Turn It Around! campaign in Detroit, Kansas City, Seattle, Dallas, Minneapolis, Milwaukee, Cleveland, and New Jersey.

The response has been very encouraging. On January 15, 1988, Martin Luther King, Jr.'s birthday, the city of Washington, DC, and the Justice Department proclaimed Dave Winfield Day and invited me to introduce the Turn It Around/ Community Partnerships approach to the Washington area. I'm confident that when other communities and towns see Norfolk's success in fighting drug abuse, we'll have Turn It Around Community Partnerships all across the country. Ultimately, I see Turn It Around as a campaign for America and Community Partnerships as the grass roots initiative to fulfill the campaign. That's my dream. It's a lofty one, but I've always thought big. It's said, though, that thinking small is a sign of maturity. If that's the case, I suppose I'll be a kid all my life.

WOMEN

By the fall of 1986, Sandra Renfro and her big-time Texas lawyer were angling for a big settlement, a really BIG settlement. We had a child together—I accepted that and the responsibility that goes with it—but now they claimed that Sandra and I were married by common law. If that were true I'd owe her a bundle of money, half of what I'd earned since 1982—millions. My guess was that it was a grandstand play they hoped would win Sandra the $100,000 a year she had asked me for earlier. Millions now or $100,000 a year, either way it's a lot of money, and I suppose it might be justified if Sandra and I had ever lived together as husband and wife. But we never did, and it's sure too much to pay for one week in Rio.

The whole situation is very unfortunate. For one thing, I've always liked Sandra and hate to have to fight her in court. For another, I've always provided for Lauren and always will. I helped Sandra out when she needed it. I bought a condominium for them to live in when Lauren was born, sent plenty of money for child support, helped Sandra out with cash when her car broke down, when she needed to go to the dentist, when her son got his teeth knocked out playing sports. If there's a court-ordered settlement, though, my inclination will be to live by it, but no extras. I'm afraid that the rigidness built into that kind of settlement could cause a lot of unhappiness on both sides, with Lauren caught in the middle. That's fine in theory, but in fact I'd never let that happen. If that kid ever needed anything, I'd give her the shirt off my back.

Like any absentee-father relationship, Lauren's and my times together have been somewhat frustrating for us both.

Last year, a few days before her birthday, I went to visit her at her Montessori school in Houston. I brought her some birthday gifts. When I walked into the classroom she looked more surprised than enthusiastic. My stomach sank. Then I realized—how else *could* she react? She doesn't see me that often; what should she do, jump for joy? I stayed with her maybe fifteen minutes, then left the classroom because I thought she was too uncomfortable. Later, after school, I went back to see her. She was waiting with a few other kids whose parents wouldn't be by for another hour. She was playing with some hats. I went over and bent the hats funny and put them on and made her laugh. Then I got some crayons and paper and drew a picture for her, copying the cover of a Doctor Seuss book. It was pretty good, and when one of the other kids asked Lauren if I'd traced it she said, "No, my daddy drew it." Later, she pulled out a jigsaw puzzle of the United States. I asked her if she knew all the states. She knew New York, Minnesota, New Jersey, and Texas. Trying to do the puzzle she got frustrated and said, "I can't do this." I told her, "Never say 'can't,' " and helped her finish it. I wished then that I could be around more, help more, be a stronger influence. My mother and father had separated when I was a little boy, Sandra herself was brought up by foster parents, and now here we are repeating the pattern.

Always important to my personal life are my mother and family. I really get a kick out of doing things for Ma, fulfilling a few of her dreams, taking her to the White House or Hawaii, sending her and her best friend, Angie, on a vacation trip to Alaska. But she's hard to give things to. One time in New York I gave her $300 to go shopping and she brought me back $298 in change. I tried to get her to move from the old house where I grew up to a place that was a little nicer and easier to take care of, but for years she wanted to stay right where she was, on Carroll Street. She wanted to stay close to family and work, and she always felt she had enough—enough, that is, of what was important to her. Now that she's living in a new condo she says, "I never knew things would work out like this, but I'm very comfortable living this kind of life. I have my friends and I walk with my head high." The one thing that upsets her is that my differences with Sandra make it hard for her to see her only grandchild.

Her own mother, Grandma Allison, was extremely important to her. She died in 1986, the first time that death hit my immediate family. We all took it hard, Ma especially. Just a few months later, she was diagnosed as having cancer and had to undergo surgery and chemotherapy. The doctors are optimistic about her recovery. Ma has a lot of spirit, she's one indomitable lady, and if anyone can rally from the passing of her own mother and beat cancer in a single year, she's the one.

I couldn't finish this book without mentioning someone else. From the time I first met her during the World Series in Los Angeles in 1981, I knew we had a chance to make it as a couple. I kept a certain distance, and didn't make any promises. I didn't ask her a lot of questions, didn't want her to ask me a lot. Because in those years our lives were just too far apart. I'm glad we put up with each other. We're going to spend our lives and build a family together. My friends never believed I'd do it, 'cause I'm the last of the Mohicans, but on February 18, 1988, Tanya Turner and I were married in the French Quarter in New Orleans.

5

Extra Innings

SEASONS: 1988

About spring training, Yogi said it best: "You only got a certain amount," so my thought before this spring is to work into it gradually. If it's true that everyone has a quota like Yogi suggests, I don't want to spend it in Florida. There are guys who bat .450 in the pre-season, but come July they're gone; you never hear from them again.

A few years back when there were constant legal battles with Steinbrenner the press asked, "How do you get ready for spring training?" I said, "I get my lawyers ready, my accountant ready, and my agent ready because that's what I need to play Yankee baseball." It would be nice if it were only a matter of getting the car sent down, the apartment in order, and the phone hooked up.

Still, every spring training there's pressure from management to arrive early, less I think because they want to build a better team than because they want to start generating income and hyping the season. However, the Players Association agreement with the clubs stipulates a March 1 report date, and ten days in camp before you are required to play in a game—although you're allowed to show up early and/or play early, at your option. Typically, the Yankees will announce that spring training starts on February 21 or 22, a week before you're actually required to show. I arrive on the 27th, they tell the press I'm late. Late! Hell, I'm early.

But right on time for my first media roller-coaster ride of the season.

First day back is always good. It's great to see the guys come in healthy and eager; a real contrast from the end of the season—particularly the end of last season, when guys started to grate on one another and I was tired of hearing about their girlfriends or their troubles and they were tired of hearing about mine. Anyhow, first day back you go through the locker room: "Hey man, what's up!" "Shake!" "Give me five!" "What's going on?" "What's happening?" Even on the field during the first full team workout everyone's talking and joking, getting on one another.

It's always interesting to see the young rookies come to camp for the first time, as wide-eyed as kids, hoping for a chance, glad to be in camp, a little uptight, sometimes very uptight, because they're playing with guys they've read about for years. Like kids, too, many of them will come up to, say, Ron Guidry or Rickey Henderson and ask for autographs.

In addition to the rookies on the forty-man roster, there are always some non-roster players who've got an even slimmer chance of making the team or breaking into the lineup. Every now and again, though, one of these guys will surprise you, someone like Tommy John in 1986, for example, who comes to camp as a non-roster player and ends up a starter. Every spring I follow the rookies' and non-roster players' progress through camp, and sympathize with their frustrations when they're sent down. For some it's a relief; in the minors they can play their game, regain their confidence. If I like the guy, think he's a gamer, I'll often give him a pair of cleats, a glove, a T-shirt, or some advice if he wants it.

By the second day the talking and joking die down as everyone—rookies and veterans alike—gets down to the business and the pressure of making the team. Still, throughout spring training there's considerably more lightness in the air than during the season. Guys will stand around b.s.ing about what they did the night before, the week before, or on their winter vacation. There's also a lot more socializing together because everyone's away from home and sometimes family. During the season players get more protective of their time, have business of one kind or another to attend to. Spring training is like summer camp for a bunch of kids with an average age of twenty-eight. For most everybody, though, it's a serious business from the start. If you're from the Dominican Republic and you mess up in spring training, cutting sugarcane may be your only option.

I work hard physically the first few weeks, but always arrive in good shape anyway. Facing a 162-game season, though, I don't put an excessive amount of mental energy into spring training and early exhibition games. A lot of veterans who are reasonably assured of their jobs will do the same, particularly when it comes to hitting. They just take their time, get themselves ready for the real games. It's different for pitchers, whose arms are their sole livelihood and who work out a lot during the winter to keep their arms loose. As it is, these guys come in two weeks or so before the everyday players, so generally they're well ahead of the hitters and can embarrass them early on.

I make sure I'm not embarrassed for long. As the spring progresses and the challenge of the season nears, I get mentally tougher and meaner and nastier. So do the others. Every man starts thinking the team can win—not because we're entitled to, or because we're the New York Yankees, but because we have a good bunch of guys looking to play better together than ever before. As for me, I always intend to perform better than I did the previous year, more of everything—steal more bases, hit more home runs, get more RBIs, score more runs. And zero errors, though I know a few will crop up. Still, maybe this year . . .

Maybe this year, maybe this year. Listen, baseball is what I do the best, what I enjoy the most. Though sometimes I've hated it all, I love being a Yankee, I love playing in New York. I also want to be the best ballplayer I can be; I want to be good at it because it's important to my life and my own sense of self-worth and satisfaction. The uncertainty of the outcome, season after season, satisfies my creative needs more than any of my other endeavors. The fact is, if someone handed me the 1988 world championship today on a silver platter, I'd reach for it, hold back, and choose to play through it, experience it, all the disappointments, all the highs, play a major role. Only then will I have what I want: the continuing respect of the fans, and yes, even the begrudging respect of George Steinbrenner. I want it today for my accomplishments on the field, and down the line for what I accomplish afterward. And I intend to accomplish a lot.